Intercultural Philosophy and Environmental Justice between Generations

This anthology combines an intercultural approach with intergenerational ethics to address critical environmental challenges. Written by scholars from all over the world, including Canada, the US, New Zealand, Nigeria, Ethiopia, Japan, the UK, China, and Spain, this book offers new perspectives on how to foster sustainable societal practises that draw on the past and are fair to future generations. It introduces the Māori idea that views all things and human generations in layered relations; Indigenous accounts of spiraling time and reciprocities among ancestors and descendants; the philosophical dimensions of Chinese conceptions of ancestor spirits and future ghosts; and African accounts of anamnestic solidarity among generations. These ideas influence proposals for how to confront ending worlds and address the environmental future of humanity, making this book a valuable resource for scholars and students of environmental law and policy, environmental humanities, political science, and intercultural and comparative philosophy, as well as policymakers.

HIROSHI ABE is Professor of Philosophy at Kyoto University, Japan. He received the Philipp Franz von Siebold Prize in 2017. He has published extensively on the topics of ontology, environmental philosophy, and Japanese philosophy. He coedited *Environmental Philosophy and East Asia: Nature, Time, Responsibility* (2022) with Matthias Fritsch and Mario Wenning.

MATTHIAS FRITSCH is Professor of Philosophy at Concordia University, Canada. His previous publications include *The Promise of Memory* (2005) and *Taking Turns with the Earth* (2018), as well as the edited volumes *Environmental Philosophy and East Asia: Nature, Time, Responsibility* (2022), *Eco-Deconstruction* (2018), and *Reason and Emancipation* (2007).

MARIO WENNING is Professor of Philosophy at Loyola University, Spain. Recent publications include the coedited volumes *The Right to Resist: Philosophies of Dissent* (2023) and *Environmental Philosophy and East Asia: Nature, Time, Responsibility* (2022). He has been a Humboldt Research Fellow at the University of Frankfurt and is a recipient of the Dao Annual Best Essay Award (2019).

Intercultural Philosophy and Environmental Justice between Generations

Indigenous, African, Asian, and Western Perspectives

Edited by

HIROSHI ABE
Kyoto University

MATTHIAS FRITSCH
Concordia University

MARIO WENNING
Loyola University

CAMBRIDGE
UNIVERSITY PRESS

CAMBRIDGE
UNIVERSITY PRESS

Shaftesbury Road, Cambridge CB2 8EA, United Kingdom

One Liberty Plaza, 20th Floor, New York, NY 10006, USA

477 Williamstown Road, Port Melbourne, VIC 3207, Australia

314–321, 3rd Floor, Plot 3, Splendor Forum, Jasola District Centre,
New Delhi – 110025, India

103 Penang Road, #05–06/07, Visioncrest Commercial, Singapore 238467

Cambridge University Press is part of Cambridge University Press & Assessment, a department of the University of Cambridge.

We share the University's mission to contribute to society through the pursuit of education, learning and research at the highest international levels of excellence.

www.cambridge.org
Information on this title: www.cambridge.org/9781009343749

DOI: 10.1017/9781009343756

First published 2024

A catalogue record for this publication is available from the British Library

A Cataloging-in-Publication data record for this book is available from the Library of Congress

ISBN 978-1-009-34374-9 Hardback

Contents

Contributors

Hiroshi Abe Kyoto University

Joseph C. A. Agbakoba University of Nigeria

Matthias Fritsch Concordia University

Stephen M. Gardiner University of Washington

Marion Hourdequin Colorado College

Jing Iris Hu Concordia University

Workineh Kelbessa Addis Ababa University

Yat-hung Leung East China Normal University

James Miller Duke Kunshan University

Tim Mulgan University of St Andrews and University of Auckland

Krushil Watene University of Auckland

Mario Wenning Loyola University

Acknowledgments

The chapters collected in this volume were, for the most part, first presented at a hybrid conference organized under the auspices of the research network Nature-Time-Responsibility (NTR) in October 2021. The event (we call it NTR 6) took place on unceded Indigenous lands at Concordia University in Tiohtià:ke/Montréal. Accordingly, the conference organizers and volume editors would like to recognize the Kanien'kehá:ka Nation as the custodians of the lands and waters on which the in-person participants gathered, and which continues to serve as host to some contributors. We wholeheartedly agree with the words of the Indigenous Directions team at Concordia: "Tiohtià:ke/Montréal is historically known as a gathering place for many First Nations. Today, it is home to a diverse population of Indigenous and other peoples. We respect the continued connections with the past, present and future in our ongoing relationships with Indigenous and other peoples within the Montréal community." In this context, we also wish to express our deepest gratitude to Mona Polacca, who generously opened the conference with her teachings as a member of the International Council of Thirteen Indigenous Grandmothers, and as a member of the Secretariat of the Indigenous World Forum on Water and Peace.

We would like to add some reflections upon the special significance the territorial acknowledgment holds for the conference and for this volume. As the major sponsor of both, the research network NTR understands itself as a forum for the intercultural exchange of ideas around the intersection of the themes of nature, time, and responsibility. This exchange of ideas, including Indigenous ideas, needs to avoid a self-interested extractivism of knowledge vis-à-vis Indigenous teachings. There is the worry that, initially, land is taken from Indigenous peoples; when careless use of that land destabilizes it, the dispossessors then try to mine Indigenous knowledge with which to fix it and learn how to live more sustainably. Further, we should not assume that the space for the exchange of ideas is neutral, when in fact, of course, access to such space is not the same for all. In addition, embodied minds need land upon which to live and breathe: land that has a history, which, in this case, is one of colonial dispossession and ongoing marginalization. This history needs to be acknowledged, including the limitations this may pose for access to the exchange of ideas. Another reason for the special significance of the territorial acknowledgment is the great significance of land and the environment to intergenerational justice, which is the theme of both this volume and the conference from which it has emerged. Many of the benefits and harms the current generation will leave for future people, in particular those affecting the long term, pass by way of the land. Future people, whatever they will be, will be *of* us as well as *of* the land, and *of* the earth. Like us, they will not only have to confront the legacy of climate and land destabilization, but their links with the history of colonialism.

Given the contributions of the conference to the volume, the coeditors wish to thank all those whose funding or support made the hybrid event possible: the Social Sciences and Humanities Research Council of Canada, with special thanks to Professor Jing Iris Hu for serving as Principal Investigator and Professor Matthias Fritsch as Coapplicant; the Alexander-von-Humboldt Foundation, Germany, which has been supportive of our activities over the years and indirectly helped fund the conference and this publication by giving NTR the Award for Innovative Networking Initiative; the Consulate General of the Federal Republic of Germany, Montréal, for hosting a wonderful reception; the Workgroup Representations of and Rights for the Environment of Earth Systems Governance (with special thanks to Sandy Lamalle); the Canadian Commission for the United Nations Educational, Scientific and Cultural Organization; and, at Concordia University, the Department of Philosophy, the Centre for Interdisciplinary Studies in Society and Culture; the Social Justice Centre, 4th Space (with special thanks to Anna Waclawek and Doug Moffat), and the Next-Generation Cities Institute (thank you, Ursula Eicker). We also thank all the conference participants and graduate student organizers, including Rebecca van der Post and Joëlle Dubé.

As with the previous NTR volume (*Environmental Philosophy and East Asia: Nature, Time, Responsibility*, edited by Hiroshi Abe, Matthias Fritsch, and Mario Wenning; Routledge, 2022), Rebecca van der Post has been a superb copy-editor and collaborator, whose keen eyes detected many faults the reader would otherwise have encountered. Doctoral student Tobias Bartneck, at Kyoto University, has created the index for the volume, and we are most grateful for his work. Last but not least, we express our special gratitude to the contributors to this volume, while looking back and forward in thanks to previous and future NTR conferences.

A previous version of Krushil Watene's chapter in this volume was first published as part of *Reimagining the Human–Environment Relationship: Indigenous Philosophy and Intergenerational Justice* (United Nations University, 2022), which appeared at this website: https://unu.edu/cpr/project/reimagining-human-environment-relationship. We, and Professor Watene, greatly appreciate the permission to include this revised version.

Introduction

Why Approach Intergenerational Justice from Intercultural Philosophy?

Hiroshi Abe, Matthias Fritsch, and Mario Wenning

This anthology is published under the auspices of the award-winning research network "Nature, Time, Responsibility" (NTR), which began its operations in 2011 and is led by Hiroshi Abe (Kyoto University, Japan), Matthias Fritsch (Concordia University, Montreal, Canada), and Mario Wenning (Loyola University, Spain). NTR promotes sustained intercultural dialogue on the topic of moral, legal, and political responsibilities to future generations and to nature across time.

The primary objective of this anthology is to make intergenerational justice an issue for intercultural philosophy, and, conversely, to allow the latter to enrich the former. In times of large-scale environmental destabilization, fairness between generations is an urgent issue of justice across time, but it is also a global issue of justice across geographical and nation-state borders. This means that the future generations envisioned by the currently living also cross these borders. Thus, different philosophical cultures and traditions of thought should converse to reflect on what is fair to future people. In the remainder of this introduction, we will detail these claims and give an overview of the volume's chapters.

Intergenerational Justice

In recent years, the global public has become increasingly aware that the actions of the current generation, in particular via global heating and environmental degradation, will have adverse effects on future generations. As a result, policymakers and citizens struggle to formulate and enact policies that enshrine sustainable societal practices that are fair to future generations. Several theories of intergenerational fairness have been put forward since the 1970s. In English at least, the large majority of extant theories have been drawn from the Western moral and political tradition (for edited anthologies that provide good overviews, see Laslett and Fishkin 1992; Dobson 1999; Tremmel 2009; Gosseries and Meyer 2009; Meyer 2016; Gonzalez-Ricoy and Gosseries 2017; Gardiner 2021).

Justice between generations can serve as a key issue in uniting the global public. We might not have to decide what "nature" is and whether it holds intrinsic moral value to argue that sustaining it is morally demanded for the sake of future generations (Gardiner 2011). Some scholars argue that sustainability should be understood as an issue of intergenerational justice (Holland 1997, 1999; Habib 2013). Famously, the Brundtland Commission defines sustainable development as meeting "the needs of the present without compromising the ability of future generations to meet their own needs" (WCED 1987, p. 53). Arguably, however, discussions of sustainability fail to be sufficiently informed by moral-philosophical accounts of justice between generations (Gosseries 2008, p. 62), despite the promise such accounts may hold in highlighting the stark injustices to future people while also motivating different cultures and value orientations around concern for descendants.

To address these issues, however, the accounts of justice between generations should not be based on a single tradition or culture of morality, however diverse that tradition may be internally. Scholars have suggested that many Western accounts suffer from so-called "ontological problems" and motivational weaknesses (the failure to adequately explain our motivation to be responsible for future generations; for critical overviews, see Page 2006; Callicott 2013, esp. chapter 10; Fritsch 2018, chapter 1). The main traditions of "Western ethics" in the intergenerational context rest on moral ontologies that are rather individualistic and assume dichotomies between the generations, as well as between the self and others or humans and nature. In contrast, many non-Western traditions promise to offer insights comparatively free from such assumptions because they conceive of humans as members of communities across generations and within a shared cosmos (Hu 2018a, 2018b). Thus, it is worthwhile to seek out novel solutions from heretofore neglected traditions of thought, in particular in view of the long-standing approaches to intergenerational ethics in, for example, Chinese Confucianism (Ames 2011) and Daoism (Girardot et al. 2015), African thought (Behrens 2012), and Indigenous traditions (Jojola 2013; Watene and Yap 2015; Whyte 2018; Watene, Chapter 1).

Another reason to put Western ethics in dialogue with non-Western traditions is based on the nature of the problem itself. Of course, we live in a time in which most human beings are interconnected economically, technologically, and politically. But also, many of the problems faced by theories of sustainability and intergenerational ethics, especially climate change and the environmental crisis more broadly, are intrinsically global problems that call for global solutions: that is, solutions to be supported by different moral cultures and political traditions from around the world. Addressing the massive environmental challenges demands collaborative initiatives from global civil society. These initiatives must emerge in dialogue among and across the many cultures that make up the currently living generations. Such dialogue, we contend, should also concern the very normative framework on which it is based. Possible attempts at mitigation, adaptation, and compensation when it comes to climate change and environmental destabilization are best borne by a truly intercultural and dialogically achieved consensus. Agreements motivated exclusively by self-interest tend to come apart more quickly and may not persuade members of different cultures. Ongoing support for the actions required, including changes in quotidian spheres, ought to be embedded in different life-worlds with their own histories, languages, norms, and cultural experiences without, thereby, denying some shared moral dimensions.

Agreements on these measures, then, or at least an overlapping consensus around global governance, should result from intercultural dialogue on normative frameworks in justice between generations. As recent international climate change negotiations show, we need global understanding and agreement on how to inherit as well as pass on humanity's shared environment. Global cooperation, especially if it demands support for large-scale societal changes, ought to be embedded in different life-worlds with their own self-understanding in view of nature and relations with ancestors and descendants. We need intergenerational justice not just within nations, but also at the global level.

This intersection of the spatial and the temporal, the intra-generational and the inter-generational, may also remind us, in what we may call a scale critique (Woods 2014) of cultures, that the separateness of traditions, languages, nations and cultures looks different from longer cross-generational perspectives (see also Gardiner, Chapter 10). Over longer timelines, the unique characteristics of different cultures and "nations" emerge and consolidate themselves in exchange with others. Going sufficiently far backwards and forwards in time, we witness peoples and cultures become transformed by these exchanges. Through migration, commerce, cultural exchange, biological reproduction, warfare and other forms of contact, peoples and cultures merge with and divide from one another. We should keep this scale critique in mind in particular in a time of environmental destabilization, which itself suggests that the time and space we inhabit is indeed scaled: sustained and upset by long-term, distant effects usually – in day-to-day lives that often live off fossil-fuel infrastructure – shielded from view, but now coming to haunt taken-for-granted life-worlds and inherited self-conceptions. In this sense, both climate change and the intergenerational perspective it demands render dubious all forms of xenophobic particularism, nationalism, and narrow-mindedness. For example – and given the call for intercultural philosophy in this book, this is not a random example – we should take seriously current research that shows how the idea of philosophy as essentially Western, allegedly born in ancient Greece, is a post-Kantian construction allied to European colonialism and imperialism (see, e.g., Park 2014; Elberfeld 2017; Ambrogio 2020).[1] Scale critique informed by both the long-term view of intergenerational justice and intercultural philosophy rejects such Eurocentrism, which conveniently forgets the North-African, Asian, and other non-European sources of ancient Greek philosophy itself (Yoyotte 1969; Rutherford 2016), as well as the existence of modern philosophy outside of "the West," also, thereby, making it easier to neglect different forms of philosophizing the world over (Van Norden 2017).

For these reasons, this volume stages intercultural philosophical dialogue between various Indigenous, African, Asian, and Western traditions, in view of formulating adequate frameworks, instruments, and approaches in policy and governance for justice between generations. We add a few more thoughts on conducting philosophy interculturally.

Intercultural Philosophy

Comparing cultural traditions has become an increasingly accepted mode of inquiry in the humanities. The term "comparative philosophy" has been commonly used in the English-speaking world. We decided to adopt the term "intercultural philosophy" instead, which has been more common in the German-speaking tradition since it emphasizes a normative dimension and the task of thinking in-between and beyond cultural traditions (Mall 2000). Comparing different cultural, linguistic, and philosophical traditions entails a moral commitment to dialogue. According to the Vienna-based journal polylog, intercultural philosophy is defined as the "endeavour to give expression to the many and often marginalized voices of philosophy in their respective cultural contexts and thereby to generate a shared, fruitful discussion granting equal rights to all, particularly including Asian, African, and Latin American perspectives" (Polylog, 2023).[2]

[1] See also the massive work undertaken by Rolf Elberfeld and the Koselleck-Project "Histories of Philosophy in a Global Perspective" www.uni-hildesheim.de/en/histories-of-philosophy/

[2] Unfortunately, due to various limitations, the inclusion of Latin American voices has not yet been possible here, but took place at NTR7 at Loyola University in Sevilla 2022, and is planned for future NTR publications.

Dialogical engagement across cultural, linguistic, and philosophical traditions is intended to correct ethnocentric biases and embraces the plurality of visions of what it means to be a human being in a shared world. Intercultural philosophy, thus understood, requires respect, openness, and interest in learning from other cultural traditions. The focus of intercultural philosophy is not on eradicating cultural otherness, but on taking the other seriously and thereby opening up "a liminal landscape which simultaneously connects and separates" (Waldenfels 2011, 71). While comparative approaches have gained traction in recent decades, those engaged in cross- and transcultural theorizing are often situated at the margins of academic discourse. Before the recent growth of comparative or intercultural philosophy, mainstream philosophy in the West was frequently equated with the study of Western sources and conducted in Western languages, such as Greek, English, French, or German. Conversely, the systematic study of non-Western realities was relegated to area studies programs. One drawback of having situated the study of non-Western traditions in, for example, Sinology, Japanology, Indology, or African studies departments was a tendency to treat complex traditions as homogeneous entities. Certain essential identity traits were attributed, often unreflectively, to entire cultures that were regarded as static monolithic entities without internal dynamics and external relationships. As indicated, modern European philosophers, beginning with Kant and Hegel, contributed to a systematic exclusion of Africa, Asia and precolonial American traditions from what they considered serious philosophy. While there were exceptions to the trend, and some philosophers emphasized cosmopolitanism and had an avid interest in world history, mainstream philosophy was normatively biased. It was common to conceive of Western modernity as the measure and endpoint of historical evolution processes.

The systematic exclusion of Africa and Asia, as well as Indigenous traditions, from hegemonic philosophical discourse did not remain uncontested. It gave rise to a tendency to either idealize or dismiss the cultural other. From a normative perspective, viewing the cultural other has been used to either embrace or reject potential contributions to civilization processes. The Enlightenment philosopher Voltaire, for example, praised Chinese culture for its civility while Montesquieu highlighted the existence of oriental despotism. The binary dichotomy between "Sinophilia" and "Sinophobia" made a nuanced cross-cultural dialogue difficult.

While the early modern philosophical engagement with non-Western traditions was based on exotic orientalizing fantasies and the high-modern engagement served to differentiate the allegedly superior West from an inferior other, current approaches in post- and decolonial philosophy turn to formerly marginalized belief and knowledge systems to critically work through the legacy of ethnocentrism and Eurocentrism. Contemporary scholars have started to reengage with perspectives from Asia and the Global South in an attempt to contribute to a broadening and deepening of transcultural perspectives. In part, the motivation to correct conceptual blind spots in mainstream Western philosophizing has contributed to a change in attitude. Rather than epistemic assertiveness and arrogance, there is a growing sense of humility and a willingness to learn from previously marginalized conceptions by formerly colonized peoples. The goal of advancing the project of global epistemic justice and contributing to the continuing task of decolonizing hegemonic knowledge systems (Chimakonam 2017; Mignolo & Walsh 2018) can be seen as a continuation and extension of comparative and intercultural philosophy.

The two most significant methodological challenges that have been identified by comparative approaches consist, first, in the question of relativity versus universality in cross-cultural comparison and, second, in the challenge of interpretation and translation across cultural and linguistic boundaries (Ma and van Brakel 2016). It is not realistic to adequately compare cultural traditions in their entirety to settle the question of whether they are to be seen as largely different or the same. From where would such a comparison take place? It is impossible to completely step out of determinate cultural contexts to compare cultures as if they were planets. Which values should intercultural comparison rely on? The attempt of comparing an entire culture A and a culture B has given rise to overgeneralizations. These lack sufficient detailed engagement with differences within cultures and commonalities between them. Often, intracultural difference is more significant than intercultural diversity. The movement from apparent universality to diversity or the reverse movement from apparent diversity to universality, in addition to being overly schematic, hardly does justice to the complexity of cultural practices and beliefs and the entanglement between cultures. As the chapters in Part I and Part II of this volume demonstrate, there are significant differences as well as overlaps in distinctive Indigenous and East Asian perspectives on intergenerational and environmental justice.

In addition to the issue of conceiving of different cultures from the perspective of either cultural particularism that overlooks commonality or a universalism that is blind towards cultural difference, the second central methodological challenge faced by comparative or inter-cultural approaches consists in the difficulty of translation. The challenge of the translation and interpretation of concepts across diverse traditions arises at the level of everyday concepts such as soft and hard, abstract concepts such as cosmos and nature, and at the level of core ideas such as equity, sustainability, or harmony between generations. Philosophers of language have not only pointed out that the conceptual register of a language influences perception, reflection, and communication. They have also revealed the problem of possible incommensurability arising from conceptual diversity (Wong 1989). While we do not deny the extent of conceptual diversity and the importance of cultural context for cross-cultural encounter, we believe that such encounter is, while often difficult, indispensable in a highly interconnected world that is facing severe ecological threats.

We do not pretend that a world civilization with a shared sense of future-oriented environmental responsibility will come about, yet we consider the task of practicing intercultural philosophy to be a crucial, and perhaps necessary, precondition for the future survival of humanity and its habitat on earth. The present volume also does not pretend to be a handbook that would offer an exhaustive overview of intercultural as well as intergenerational justice. Rather, the chapters are interventions that seek to offer diagnostic and potentially therapeutic contributions to the environmental crisis that we identify as being both a reason for as well as an effect of a crisis of intergenerational relations. As stated, we believe that a transcultural approach provides promising resources to tackle the entanglement of environmental and intergenerational crises.

The unique selling proposition of the book is the combination of an intercultural approach to the topic of intergenerational ethics. In English there are a number of books and edited collections on non-Western environmental philosophy (Ames and Callicott 1989; Parkes 1991; Tucker and Berthrong 1998; Callicott and McRae 2015; Chang 2019; Abe, Fritsch and Wenning 2022). However, despite an obvious need, to our knowledge there are to date no edited volumes or monographs addressing intergenerational ethics and politics from an intercultural perspective. We have reason to hope, then, that the chapters in this volume will be of interest in beginning to address this gap.

Overview of the Chapters

Part I: Indigenous Philosophies on Justice Between Generations

The volume begins with "Indigenous Philosophy and Intergenerational Justice" by Krushil Watene. While the importance of Indigenous socio-ecological values to our search for answers to environmental problems cannot be overstated, it is also important to inquire into what we may learn from them in concrete terms, as, for example, in respect to the relationship between the past, the present, and the future. In this first chapter, Watene instructs us in Indigenous philosophies pertaining directly to this concern. Focusing on the notion of Māori philosophy whakapapa (or "to place in layers"), for instance, Watene contends that Māori people apprehend all things within an all-encompassing spatiotemporal network of relationships. Based on this relationalist view of the world, Māori philosophy teaches us how different narratives can make us aware of a variety of intergenerational connections and help us not only to protect, but also to recreate and reinforce them.

The second chapter, "Climate Ethics and Intergenerational Reciprocity in Indigenous Philosophies" by Matthias Fritsch, also takes off from Indigenous concepts, especially the Māori idea of intergenerational time as a double spiral connecting past and future as well as time and space or lived time and the land. The concept of spiraling time has been used by some Indigenous scholars to criticize mainstream views that locate the dangers of climate change entirely in the future, thereby severing environmental degradation and the exploitation of the land from the history of colonialism. Motivating care for future generations merely by projecting impending climate horror scenarios, even if these are said to have already begun, tends to betray a privileged, often settler-colonial perspective. On the basis of this critique, Fritsch then argues for a view of intergenerational relations according to which present generations owe to descendants in part because they received a gift from ancestors. Indigenous views of generational relations, such as some interpretations of the well-known Haudenosaunee seven-generation model, are, thus, more suitable for the twofold task of assuring a sustainable future for the generations who follow our own, while taking into account the past history of colonization. Fritsch proposes a social ontology of "asymmetrical reciprocity," thereby advancing a model for decolonizing the future by promoting the differentiation of the past as the condition for the present.

The third chapter, "Intergenerational Justice and the Environment in Africa," also revisits Indigenous philosophies of intergenerational relations, this time with a focus on Africa. In his chapter, Workineh Kelbessa maintains that in many African worldviews, contemporary people have an obligation to respect their ancestors that, in turn, obliges them to ensure the continuing health and viability of the environment for the sake of future generations. Thus, the "anamnestic solidarity" of the living with the generations to come has its original roots in the memory of their ancestors. To put it another way, African moral values do not require the current generation to reward its forbears directly for all that they did for the sake of their offspring and the generations to follow; rather, the current generation rewards its ancestors indirectly by fulfilling its obligations to its own successors. In the special emphasis they place upon the importance of returning favours to people of the past by passing them forward to future generations, African concepts of intergenerational justice remind us of Fritsch's notion of asymmetrical reciprocity. In light of Kelbessa's account, we might add that it is characteristic of African philosophies to place a significant emphasis on comprehensive considerations that encompass not only the continued survival of humans, but also the well-being of non-human generations and of Mother Earth.

Following Kelbessa's chapter, the fourth chapter "Reasonabilism, Homeostasis and Intergenerational Justice in African Thought" also thematizes African Indigenous thought, bringing it directly to another question of central relevance to this section of the volume: What ought to be the principle of governance if there is to be justice between generations? Focusing on the Igbo philosophical tradition, Joseph C. A. Agbakoba's chapter contends that the principle governing the relationship between things in the universe, as well as between human generations, should be that of dynamic harmony or homeostasis. According to this idea, the various roles that each of us plays in society are indeed different from, but should be complementary to, each other, and must be both supple and just in their responses to the changing situations and contexts of the complex web of interpersonal and intergenerational relations in which human beings find themselves. Agbakoba, thus, argues that justice based on dynamic harmony, or harmonious justice between generations, consists in complementarity between the living (or the present generation), the living-dead (or ancestors), and the yet-to-be-born (or future people).

Part II: Intergenerational Ethics in Dialogue with Confucianism and Daoism

As we all know, turning policies and institutions of environmental justice between generations into reality requires global cooperation. It is no exaggeration to say that one can hardly enter into serious deliberations regarding international negotiation and conflict resolution in these areas while excluding China from the conversation. Thus, we should ask how people who are members of or significantly influenced by Chinese civilization tend to see intergenerational justice from the perspective of their own rich and unique traditions. In order to address this question, Part II of the volume provides four chapters dedicated to classical Chinese ethics across generations.

The first chapter, "Ghosts and Intergenerational Justice: A Confucian Perspective" addresses Confucianism, which has held a position of centrality in the establishment and maintenance of core Chinese values. The authors of the chapter, Yat-hung Leung and Mario Wenning, explore a unique feature of the Confucian view of ancestor ghosts and spirits. According to their reading, it is characteristic of Confucius to think of ghosts and spirits neither as fully existent (in the same way as the living are existent) nor as non-existent, but as "subjunctive" beings that are, so to speak, "as if (ru 如)" present when we participate sincerely in ritual exercises, commemorating and thereby expressing our gratitude, piety, care and respect toward the dead. According to Leung and Wenning, this conception of an "as if" attitude toward the spirit world is also significant for intergenerational justice, because it teaches us that, as the current generation, we live within a web of interdependence that laces us together with our ancestors and with future people "as if" they were present; and that we thereby incur an obligation to keep in mind the consequences of our own actions for both past and future people.

In the second chapter of this section, "Intergenerational Ethics and Sustainability: A Confucian Relational Perspective," Marion Hourdequin provides a new model of intergenerational ethics inspired by early Confucianism. Her model contrasts sharply with the dominant rights-based philosophies of sustainability, focusing on the following three points instead of discussing distributive justice and trade-offs between generations: first, it offers not an individualistic, but a relational conception of the person; second, rather than postulating a conflict of desires and needs between different generations, it emphasizes a gratitude for the care one has received, which (reminiscent of Kelbessa's and Fritsch's indirect reciprocities) can weave people into communities extending backward and forward in time; and third, it does not require trade-offs between present and future well-being but, instead, a shared commitment to a sustained and flourishing community across generations.

The third chapter, "Moral Motivation for Future Generations, Naturally: A Mencian Proposal," advances an alternate, Confucian-inspired approach to intergenerational ethics that could be read as a challenge to Hourdequin's account in a specific respect. Generally speaking, ethics across generations is confronted by the vexed question of how to build bridges between people at great distance from one another, given the various generational differences and the spatial, temporal, social, and cultural gaps between them. The author of the chapter, Jing Iris Hu, answers this question by arguing that Confucian moral naturalism can motivate us to care about others across time, space, and culture because it focuses on emotions and normative sensibilities shared by people in the past, present, and future – no matter whether such normativity is rooted in basic, human, psychological characteristics, as Mencius proposes, or whether it is something to be cultivated through socialization, as Xunzi maintains.

The fourth chapter in this section turns our attention away from Confucianism and towards an alternative philosophy of ancient China, which also laid many important foundations of Chinese culture: Daoism. In this chapter, titled "Transience, Responsible Transformation, and Deep Time in Daoist

Thought," James Miller questions the ability of Confucian intergenerational ethics to motivate us to take long-term responsibility toward future people. Rather, in his view, Confucianism primarily emphasizes the obligations of descendants to take care of their ancestors, including ancestors from the distant past (see also Abe, Chapter 9). In this regard, Miller sees Daoism as a complement to Confucianism, especially in reference to the Daoist commitment to transience. Transience is here taken as the very condition of possibility for the perpetual processes of transformation that characterize all life and differentiate the living from the dead or inanimate. In this sense, transience helps us to realize that cosmic "deep" time not only inscribes itself in human history, but also indwells our own "porous" bodies, in whose exposedness or openness the barriers between present and future people are dissolved.

Part III: Humanity Facing the Near Environmental Future

The third and final part of the volume turns to the question of what we should do now in order to be able to cope with the environmental challenges confronting us and those that follow in the near future.

With the themes and discussions of the preceding chapters in mind, the opening chapter "Double Intergenerational Responsibility: From a Western-Eastern view," by Hiroshi Abe, emphasizes that, for the purpose of taking seriously our responsibility toward the future, we, as the currently living, must also bear a responsibility that is oriented toward the past. Drawing upon the work of Hans Jonas and the Japanese philosopher Tetsuro Watsuji, Abe seeks to show that our responsibility toward the future, which he formulates as a "foreseeing-care-prevention" type of responsibility, comprises an obligation to the past: a type of responsibility guided by the historical wholeness of human beings, and that therefore renders us accountable to the authority of our ancestors. At the same time, this past-oriented, historical vector of responsibility, which Abe calls a "letting-the-dead-be" type of responsibility, also presupposes the "foreseeing-care-prevention" type, since it would not be possible for our ancestors to be kept "present" in the future unless we, the people of today, are held, and hold ourselves, responsible for the existence of generations to come. In this reference to ancestors as key to the relation to future generations, we once more hear references to Watene, Kelbessa, Fritsch, Hourdequin, Leung, and Wenning.

Looking back on the history of global politics over the last few decades, however, one must reluctantly admit that the effects of its policies have been too small to achieve substantial improvements in mitigating climate change. As is often said, in theory there is no difference between theory and practice, while in practice there is. How, then, can we effectively put ideas of intergenerational environmental justice into practice? Stephen M. Gardiner's chapter "Guidelines for a Global Constitutional Convention for Future Generations" maintains that the massive policy failures have resulted from a lack of institutions that are in a position to effectively implement intergenerational concerns, and a deep denial of this lack. Building upon his previous work, in which he diagnoses a major "tyranny of the contemporary" – to which modern institutions have succumbed and that they therefore perpetuate – Gardiner proposes a set of ten initial guidelines for how to go about constituting a global constitutional convention whose overall aim would be to develop new institutions to protect future generations and further their interests. This proposal can, thus, be understood as implementing the intercultural dialogue on intergenerational justice that this volume calls for, while at the same time opening the question of cultural difference for the convention.

The final chapter, titled "Philosophy for an Ending World" can be read as addressing "future ethics" in a double sense: an ethics which factors future generations into our current moral decision-making and an ethics that future people themselves will hold. In this chapter, Tim Mulgan shows that thought experiments help us to concretize future ethics in the first sense, for these imagined experiments enable us to ask how future people might evaluate our moral legacy and, thereby, to regard the interests of future people as in competition with, rather than subordinate to, our own present interests. Taking as its object the notion of an unavoidable and imminent – but not immediate – extinction of humanity, Mulgan's own thought experiment raises questions that are germane to future ethics in the second sense: What ethical values might ensure that the people of the last generation, at humanity's end, could enjoy morally worthwhile, meaningful lives? What would or should be an ideal ending for humanity?

In drawing our introduction to a close, the editors of this volume hope that the diverse cultural perspectives from which the chapters consider the central theme of justice across generations will invite as many readers as possible from many a different background to engage with the important and urgent challenge of finding solutions to the problems that the volume has tackled.

Bibliography

Abe, Hiroshi, Matthias Fritsch, and Mario Wenning (eds.) 2022. *Environmental Philosophy and East Asia: Nature Time Responsibility*. London: Routledge.

Ambrogio, Selusi. 2020. *Chinese and Indian Ways of Thinking in Early Modern European Philosophy: The Reception and the Exclusion*. London: Bloomsbury.

Ames, Roger. 2011. *Confucian Role Ethics: A Vocabulary*. Hong Kong: Chinese University Press.

Ames, Roger and J. Baird Callicott (eds.) 1989. *Nature in Asian Traditions of Thought: Essays in Environmental Philosophy*. Albany, NY: State University of New York Press.

Behrens, Kevin Gary. 2012. "Moral Obligations Towards Future Generations in African Thought." *Journal of Global Ethics* 8, no. 2–3: 179–191.

Callicott, Baird James. 2013. *Thinking Like a Planet. The Land Ethic and the Earth Ethic*. Oxford: Oxford University Press.

Callicott, Baird James, and James McRae (eds.) 2015. *Environmental Philosophy in Asian Traditions of Thought*. Albany, NY: SUNY Press.

Chang, Chia-ju (ed.) 2019. *Chinese Environmental Humanities: Practices of Environing atthe Margins*. Cham: Palgrave Macmilllan.

Chimakonam, Jonathan O. 2017. "African Philosophy and Global Epistemic Justice." *Journal of Global Ethics*, no. 13-2: 1–19.

Dobson, Andrew (ed.) 1999. *Fairness and Futurity. Essays on Environmental Sustainability and Social Justice*. Oxford: Oxford University Press.

Elberfeld, Rolf. 2017. *Philosophiegeschichtsschreibung in globaler Perspektive*. Hamburg: Meiner-Verlag.

Fritsch, Matthias. 2018. *Taking Turns with the Earth: Phenomenology, Deconstruction, and Intergenerational Justice*. Stanford, CA: Stanford University Press.

Gardiner, Stephen. 2011. *A Perfect Moral Storm. The Ethical Tragedy of Climate Change*. Oxford: Oxford University Press.

Gardiner, Stephen. (ed.) 2021. *The Oxford Handbook of Intergenerational Ethics*. Oxford: Oxford University Press.

Girardot, Norman J., James Miller, and Liu Xiaogan (eds.) 2015. *Daoism and Ecology*. Cambridge, MA: Harvard University Press.

Gonzalez-Ricoy, Inigo and Axel Gosseries (eds.) 2017. *Institutions for Future Generations*, Oxford: Oxford University Press.

Gosseries, Axel. 2008. "Theories of Intergenerational Justice: A Synopsis." *Sapiens* 1, no. 1: 61–71.

Gosseries, Axel, and Lukas H. Meyer (eds.) 2009. *Intergenerational Justice*. Oxford: Oxford University Press.

Habib, Allen. 2013. "Sharing the Earth: Sustainability and the Currency of Inter-Generational Environmental Justice." *Environmental Values* 22: 751–764.

Holland, Alan. 1997. "Substitutability: Or Why Strong Sustainability Is Weak and Absurdly Strong Sustainability Is Not Absurd." In *Valuing Nature?*, edited by John Foster, 119–134. London: Routledge.

Holland, Alan. 1999. "Sustainable Development: Should We Start from Here?" In *Fairness and Futurity*, edited by Andrew Dobson, 46–68. Oxford: Oxford University Press.

Hu, Jing. 2018a. "Empathy for Non-kin, the Faraway, the Unfamiliar, and the Abstract – an Interdisciplinary Study on Moral Cultivation and a Response to Prinz." *Dao: A Journal of Comparative Philosophy* 17, no. 3: 349–362.

Hu, Jing. 2018b. "Between Nature and Person: What the Neo-Confucianist Wang Fuzhi Can Teach us about Ecological Humanism." *Comparative and Continental Philosophy* 10, no. 3: 1–12.

Jojola, Ted S. 2013. "Indigenous Planning: Towards a Seven Generation Model." In *Reclaiming Indigenous Planning*, edited by Ryan Walker, et al., 457–472. Montreal: McGill-Queens University Press.

Laslett, Peter and James S. Fishkin (eds.) 1992. *Justice Between Age Groups and Generations*. New Haven, CT: Yale University Press.

Ma, Lin and Jaap Van Brakel. 2016. *Fundamentals of Comparative and Intercultural Philosophy*. Albany, NY: SUNY Press.

Mall, Ram Adhar. 2000. *Intercultural Philosophy*. Lanham, MD: Rowman & Littlefield.

Meyer, Lukas H. (ed.) 2016. *Intergenerational Justice*. London: Routledge.

Mignolo, Walter D. and Catherine E. Walsh. 2018. *On Decoloniality: Concepts, Analytics, Praxis*. Durham, NC: Duke University Press.

Page, Edward A. 2006. *Climate Change, Justice, and Future Generations*. Cheltenham: Edward Elgar.

Park, Peter K. J. 2014. *Africa, Asia, and the History of Philosophy*. Albany, NY: SUNY Press.

Parkes, Graham. 1991. *Nietzsche and Asian Thought*. Chicago, IL: University of Chicago Press.

Polylog 2023. Forum for Intercultural Philosophy e.V. Website. https://ev.polylog.org/.

Rutherford, Ian. (ed) 2016. *Greco-Egyptian Interactions. Literature, Translation, and Culture, 500 BC – AD 300*. Oxford: Oxford University Press.

Tremmel, Jörg (ed.) 2009. *Handbook of Intergenerational Justice*. Cheltenham: Edward Elgar.

Tucker, Mary Evelyn and John Berthrong (eds.) 1998. *Confucianism and Ecology: The Intersection of Heaven, Earth, and Humans*. Cambridge, MA: Harvard University Press.

Van Norden, Bryan W. 2017. *Taking Back Philosophy. A Multicultural Manifesto*. New York, NY: Columbia University Press.

Waldenfels, Bernhard. 2011. *Phenomenology of the Alien: Basic Concepts*, transl. Alexander Kozin and Tanja Stähler. Evanston, IL: Northwestern University Press.

Watene, Krushil and Yap, Mandy. 2015. "Culture and Sustainable Development: Indigenous Contributions." *Journal of Global Ethics* 11, no. 1: 51–55.

WCED. 1987. *World Commission on the Environment and Development: Our Common Future*. Oxford: Oxford University Press.

Whyte, Kyle. 2018. "Indigenous Science (fiction) for the Anthropocene: Ancestral Dystopias and Fantasies of Climate Change Crises." *Environment and Planning* 1, no. 1–2: 224–242.

Wong, David. 1989. "Three Kinds of Incommensurability." In: *Relativism, Interpretation and Confrontation*, edited by Michael Krausz, 140–159. Notre Dame, IN: Notre Dame University Press.

Woods, Derek. 2014. "Scale Critique for the Anthropocene." *Minnesota Review* 83: 133–142.

Yoyotte, Jean. 1969. "La Pansée préphilosophique en Égypte." In: *Histoire de la Philosophie 1. Orient-Antiquité-Moyen Âge*, edited by Brice Parain, 1–23. Paris: Gallimard.

PART I

Indigenous Philosophies on Justice between Generations

1

Indigenous Philosophy and Intergenerational Justice

Krushil Watene

> Whakapapa became a series of never-ending beginnings.
>
> Moana Jackson, "Where to Next? Decolonisation and the Stories of the Land"

> We re-member hundreds of thousands of relationships – to wind, to flora, to fauna, to humans, to the dead, the star world, sky world, sea world. Everything from the humble snow flea on a glacier to the glacial age is re-membered for today and for tomorrow. There is no time differentiation in the conjuring of memory. Future is a remembered thing the very moment I give voice inside my mind to my imagined participation in tomorrow.
>
> Lee Maracle, "Memory Serves: Oratories"

1 Introduction

This chapter details several insights for the pursuit and realization of intergenerational justice that Indigenous philosophies contain. Following an explanation of some key Māori concepts in particular, the chapter outlines an intergenerational orientation that situates these concepts in ways that chart pathways through complex intergenerational challenges. In this manner, the chapter describes how Indigenous philosophies enhance relationships through regenerative practices, invest in relational repair, and enable the ongoing transformation of concepts and ideas toward new imaginaries. This chapter ends

I would like to acknowledge David Passarelli and the United Nations University-Centre for Policy Research team for their guidance, and for organising helpful commentaries from Daniel Perrel, Jasmina Byrne, and Poonam Ghimire. I also wish to acknowledge Okusitino Māhina, Vincent van Uitregt, Tim Mulgan, Andrew Moore, and Marco Grix for their comments and suggestions. As always, my heartfelt thanks to the communities to which I belong.

by articulating several practical implications that follow on from these philosophical insights. The chapter highlights how Indigenous philosophies support empowering local communities, rethinking responsibilities, and enabling innovation. In so doing, it notes some of the ways that policies and processes can function to realize intergenerational justice and ground an enduring sense of responsibility to its pursuit and realization.

2 Indigenous Philosophy

Māori philosophy situates all things within a complex system of relationships reaching as far back as the origins of the universe and as far forward as can be imagined (Royal 2003). On such a widely inclusive view, relationships, too, are highly inclusive. Relational constituents (relatives) include all human beings, non-human animals, flora and fauna, and natural entities such as land and waterways, as well as such things as knowledge and practices. Similarly, relational combinations (relations) stretch across diverse and multiple constituents in both linear and lateral directions – extending backwards and forwards in time, as well as outward to include all things in the present (Kawharu 2000; Watene 2022).

The Māori term used to capture this complex relational system is whakapapa (literally, to place in layers).[1] Whakapapa layers and records numerous relationships, interacting across vast distances in time and space. These relationships are recorded as connections and separations – the meeting places and the spaces in between those meeting places. By recognizing both, whakapapa can help to explain the importance of similarities and differences, and can help to unpack the ways in which distance is navigated and associations are forged. In so doing, whakapapa can begin to elucidate the normative significance of relationships by providing a framework to explore further the extent to which relationships can be enhanced and/or diminished – and thus provide a range of insights for relating well. In Māori philosophy, well-being, development, and justice are, consequently, understood primarily in relational terms, bound up with a set of associated normative values and reciprocal responsibilities for relating well embedded in them.

For many (if not all) Indigenous peoples, navigating our complex (multiple and multidimensional) relationships is vital to intergenerational well-being

[1] In Aotearoa New Zealand, Te Reo Māori (The Māori language) is an official language. Māori and other Indigenous terms throughout this chapter are translated or explained when first used rather than italicized. This is in recognition of the importance of language for understanding Indigenous concepts, and to contribute to decolonising the discipline of philosophy.

and justice. In southern Africa, for example, the notion of ubuntu encompasses the idea that a person's humanity is inextricably bound up with a life lived in relation to and within human and non-human communities (see Tutu 1999; Metz 2007; Okeja and Watene 2020). Similarly, thriving relationships with other people and the natural environment play a central role in mabu liyan, or the notion of well-being held by the Yawuru in Broome, north-western Australia (Yap and Yu 2019). In North America, relationships as well as the need for cooperation and justice between all beings ground the Anishinaabe good-living concept of minobimaatisiiwin (McGregor 2009; Reo and Ogden 2018). In Latin America, the Quechua good-living notion of allin kawsay takes reciprocity in human interactions with nature as fundamental (Huambachano 2023). Across the broader expanse of the Pacific, too, such as in the ethical framework of teu le va (Anae 2010) and the ontological theory of Tā, Vā (Māhina 2010), navigating complex relationships play a primary role. For these and many other Indigenous communities, well-being and justice begins at the intersections of widely inclusive relationships – not least where our relationships with each other and the natural environment meet. By taking relationships as basic, these philosophies recognize that all things stand in relation, and that flourishing is a joint and collective endeavor.

3 Kaitiakitanga

For philosophies that place such a high emphasis on relationships, regenerating relationships is vital. Whakapapa is, thus, not merely a conceptual framework in which to situate various combinations of relational constituents, but something that informs processes and practices to reinforce and remake relationships, too. The Māori word whenua, for example, means both land and placenta, recognizing and honouring intimate human–nature relationships in language. In addition, Māori botanical naming practices contain records of how plants function within a particular ecological system – such that the same plant species can have distinctive names across (often radically) different ecological contexts (Wehi, Brownstein and Morgan-Richards 2020). More generally, as Robin Kimmerer details, the word used for plants in some Indigenous North American languages literally means "those who take care of us" (2015, 228). These relational sentiments are further exemplified in rituals of encounter in which Indigenous individuals will situate their identities in relation to stars, rivers, mountains, ancestral lands, and generations of people – detailing their places within a wider socioecological network. And this is all transmitted and remade in various artforms, too, that embed and extend these relationships through narratives in a range of customary and contemporary forms – storytelling, weaving, carving, music, and dance.

Kaitiakitanga (often translated as stewardship or guardianship) is another important way in which Māori philosophy captures, protects, and reinforces socioenvironmental relationships. As detailed elsewhere, one way to think about kaitiakitanga is in terms of whakapapa: situated at the intersection of human–nature relationships, constituted by a diverse set of socioenvironmental practices, and relying on deep local knowledge, relevant practical experience, and structures enabling the transfer of both (see Grix and Watene 2022; Watene 2022). In such a way, kaitiakitanga can be understood as a collection of responsibilities enacted by Māori communities to reinforce and enable flourishing socioenvironmental relationships (Watene 2022).

The Māori concept of rāhui, for instance, places temporary constraints on human activities to ensure immediate responses to threats of serious harms. A key component of Māori customary fishing, for example, is harvesting limits based on securing flourishing in the long run. Temporary closures of marine areas or restrictions on harvesting would be used whenever species monitoring indicated that recovery was required (Scott 2010). Similarly, to prevent the spread of kauri dieback disease (*phytophthora agathicida*) and thereby prevent further kauri tree deaths, the Māori tribal community Te Kawera ā Maki restricted human access to the Waitākere forest to enable environmental regeneration.[2] Legislative developments in environmental law such as the granting of legal rights to natural entities similarly provide insights for relational restoration in more permanent forms (Ruru 2014). The Te Urewera Act of 2014, for instance, gives legal rights to the forested area Te Urewera to "strengthen and maintain the connection between Tūhoe [the Māori tribal community of the area] and Te Urewera [the forested area]" (Te Urewera Act 2014). These and other Indigenous restorative processes draw attention to the ways that communities recognize, and take responsibility for protecting, socioenvironmental relationships – even when (as in the case of rāhui) doing so is (temporarily) costly to them in one way or another. These restorative practices reflect the importance of innovation and responsiveness. For many Indigenous communities, protecting relationships and relating well has often meant adapting to different environments to maintain both individual and communal flourishing. The Polynesians travelled across the Pacific and then through Aotearoa New Zealand, bringing knowledge with them, building on some of this existing knowledge, and developing new knowledge and practical innovations in radically different environments (Smith et al. 2016). Kaitiakitanga is, then, an

[2] See waitakererahui.org.nz/kauridieback

overarching concept that describes a rich and evolving tradition, inclusive of the cumulative socioenvironmental knowledge and practice of ancestors, and that continues to respond to the (ongoing) experiences of communities now and in the future.

4 Insights for Intergenerational Justice

Ideas such as whakapapa and kaitiakitanga help to demonstrate the way that Māori and other Indigenous philosophies begin at the intersections of our intergenerational responsibilities. By contrast, in mainstream Western philosophy intergenerational justice is still an emerging field. For much of its history, mainstream Western philosophy ignored the future – in large part due to the privileging of technology and economic growth found in the philosophical perspectives that prevailed (see Mulgan 2006). As I (and others) have argued elsewhere, recognition of Indigenous and other marginalized philosophical traditions is an issue of justice (Watene and Palmer 2020; Okeja and Watene 2020; Watene 2018; Watene and Merino 2018; Watene and Yap 2015).[16] Here, however, I also focus on the way that Indigenous perspectives provide opportunities for vital insights and novel possibilities. As discussed further later, Indigenous philosophies can help to find enriching ways forward. Indigenous philosophies do this not merely by shining light on the limits of mainstream views, but by giving rise to different questions and methods for thinking through challenges that we (past, present, and future generations) collectively face.

A well-known Pacific adage is that we "walk forwards into the past and backwards into the future." This metaphor is embedded in many of the languages in the region, where words denoting the past translate as "in front" or "before," and the future as "behind" or "after" (see: Kame'eleihiwa 1992; Hau'ofa 2008; Māhina 2008). Among other things, the adage animates an important epistemic fact about intergenerational uncertainty: one walks forwards into the past because the past is (compared to the future) clear to us, and backwards into the future because the future is (compared to the past) unclear to us. This contextualizes why Pacific and other Indigenous communities look to the past, and the collection of epistemic resources found therein, to help navigate present and future challenges.

The chapter looks, however, to unpack a suite of values crystalized by the temporal orientation entrenched in this act of intergenerational "facing." In particular, the chapter draws out the following three insights. First, that this "face-to-face" encounter with ancestors symbolizes an intimate connection and mutual recognition of inter- and multigenerational purpose and accountability

(Mulgan 2006). That such recognition, secondly, leads present generations to turn their attention to, and thereby "face," each other in order to learn collectively from past generations – their struggles, feats, failures, and intentions. And that this act of facing ancestors and contemporaries, thirdly, forces a responsibility: to reimagine and recreate the world with and for future generations, too. The adage, thus, situates each generation as both a custodian of the collective memories and aspirations of previous generations and an agent of change and transformation responsible for, and to, the flourishing of those in the future.

5 Facing Our Ancestors

To embed the idea that present generations "face" the past, Indigenous philosophy needs to bridge vast distances by building intimacy between them. One of the ways that Indigenous philosophies do this is through social practices that animate these connections – thereby embedding ancestors in our everyday lives. According to Olúfẹ́mi O. Táíwò (2022), age plays a powerful organizing role in Yoruba culture, such that when one addresses an older person the appropriate pronoun is the same plural pronoun used to address a group of people. For Táíwò one way to make sense of this linguistic practice is to say "that to speak to someone older is to speak to history, and all its attendant accumulations" (2022, 201). In such a way, or so one might add, someone older animates, embodies, and bridges history, and thereby brings ancestors metaphorically closer. A similar occurrence can be found in the Māori language. When one asks another who they are – which is customarily the first thing uttered upon meeting – the question asked can literally translate to "who are your waters?" The practice of communicating who one is, therefore, often involves communicating the network of socioenvironmental and intergenerational relationships in which one is situated. In addition, this network includes both social and ecological communities to which one connects in Aotearoa New Zealand, as well as the distances travelled by Polynesian ancestors across the Pacific Ocean. For our purposes, both examples illustrate the way in which languages embed narratives of connection that continually place the past in front of us.

Broader traditions of storying and storytelling help present generations imagine and connect with people, places, and events across vast distances in time and space too. Polynesian ocean-voyaging narratives tell of navigators who mapped journeys by stars in the night sky that metaphorically lifted land from sea, or imagined islands moving toward a stationary vessel (Howe 2007; Lewis 1972). These narratives trace descent lines across the expanses of the Pacific Ocean, the largest body of water on earth and, according to some narratives, draw connections to the Southern Ocean and Antarctica (Wehi et al. 2021a, 2021b). Land-based narratives story ancestral migrations that weave networks of tribal communities into the land and waterways – embedding connections and responsibilities across multiple generations through to today (Watene 2022). In this way, narratives provide conceptual and cognitive tools that bring us "face-to-face" with distant people and places. In so doing, ancestral narratives force us to situate ourselves as part of an intergenerational community – inspiring us to recognize and imagine relationships far beyond our own temporally and spatially bound lives.

6 Facing Each Other

When present generations face the past, they face all the interwoven histories that shape their collective lives and the world they have inherited. In these moments, present generations come face-to-face with each other. At least two things come to bear on this face-to-face engagement: first, recognition of the structural injustices (past and present) that shape our harmful interactions; second, our shared connections and potential to create new beginnings.

As pointed out to some extent already, Indigenous philosophies understand the importance of relational repair as part of living well. Recent events faced by Indigenous communities and pervasive global inequalities are a testament to the urgent need for relational repair across and within communities and generations today. For Indigenous (and many other) communities around the world, processes and practices of recognition that enable self-determination lie at the heart of this healing. As whakapapa helps to highlight, tracing the origins of these damaged relationships and mapping their continuing harm is vital for healing, too. Of significance is the way unequal power relations are distributed, clustered, and advanced. In addition, un-telling the narratives that enable and reinforce these degenerative relationships is significant, as is the retelling of stories that bring us face-to-face with each other's truth (Watene and Palmer 2020).

Reversing our continued destruction of our natural environment is central to this healing as well. As Indigenous communities and scholars have long held, relational repair is not something to be applied exclusively to relationships among people but, rather, to "other dimensions of human experience – our relationship with the earth and all living beings" (Mi'kmaq Elder Augustine as quoted in McGregor 2020, 101). Our continued unwillingness to restore relationships with nature exemplifies a failing of the present generation to uphold our side of a healthy relationship, which McGregor, drawing on Anishinaabe philosophy, refers to as madjiijwe baziwin (2020, 101). These sentiments are echoed by Robin Kimmerer:

> We need acts of restoration, not only for polluted waters and degraded lands, but also for our relationship to the world. We need to restore honor to the way we live, so that when we walk through the world, we don't have to avert our eyes with shame, so that we can hold our heads up high and receive the respectful acknowledgment of the rest of the earth's beings. (Kimmerer 2015, 194)

Facing all our relatives is vital to bridging the growing distance between us. And as Kimmerer helps us to recognize, being able to face each other without shame is vital to well-being and justice. When we face our ancestors, we unpack the historical threads that locate our complex connections. These complex connections force us to turn our attention to each other – our histories, places in the world, and our collective responsibility for reimaging it anew.

7 Facing Descendants

Sometimes discussions of intergenerational justice build from the powerlessness of our descendants – beholden as they are to our decisions and actions. Indigenous philosophy, however, places them in a position of power as well. This is because "facing" our ancestors forces us to acknowledge the way we each embody collective memories, hopes, and aspirations for the future. Just as our ancestors did, we too hope for a world that we know we will never live to see ourselves. And we know that these hopes and aspirations, and indeed the way we will be remembered, depends on our descendants who will embody them. In this sense, we stand in a position of powerlessness with respect to our descendants. That our descendants will one day face us, and all that we have collectively storied (into them, lands and waterways, and the natural world) is a powerful reminder of our responsibility to work together to enact change: not least, to write a different story.

Epeli Hau'ofa (2008) is insightful here. Detailing how narratives come to frame our way of thinking in (sometimes) harmful ways, he explains that when the South Pacific is framed as "islands in a sea," opportunities and challenges are constrained by separate land masses that take (social, economic, historical, geographical) differences between them as the focus. A more constructive framing, he contends, is to understand the South Pacific as a "sea of islands," thereby turning attention to the ocean as something that makes connections and shared purpose the focus instead: "If we listened attentively to stories of ocean passage to new lands, and of the voyages of yore, our minds would open up to much that is profound in our histories, to much of what we are and what we have in common" (Hau'ofa 1998, 57).

Global narratives, driven by a view of the world as a collection of bounded entities separated by geography, culture, and gross domestic product, have much in common with this "islands in a sea" framing. Indigenous philosophies, in line with Hau'ofa's insights, understand that our narratives are critical to our connections and identities – shaping not just who we are but what we believe we can do and be: "Just as the sea is an open and ever-flowing reality, so should our ocean identity transcend all forms of insularity, to become one that is openly searching, inventive, and welcoming. In a metaphorical sense the ocean that has been our waterway to each other should also be our route to the rest of the world" (Hau'ofa 1998, 57).

The narratives we use to frame our generation will come to define our places in this world. Facing our descendants, therefore, prompts us to draw inspiration from our connections – integrating narratives woven across skies, oceans, and entire continents – and to explore and renew pathways to each other. Indigenous philosophies, thus, recognize that flourishing is not limited to our own lifetimes. By facing our descendants, we are prompted to cultivate the courage to undertake innovation and action in pursuit of collective well-being and justice.

8 Some Implications

Motivating and enabling responsibility-taking is the lifeblood of kaitiakitanga and wider Indigenous notions of socioenvironmental guardianship. As such, and to contribute to existing and further conversations, several implications can be garnered from these philosophical insights. In particular, this chapter focuses on the following three: (1) the importance of empowering and learning from local communities for charting change; (2) centring socioenvironmental responsibilities in policy and legal solutions; and (3) enabling flexibility and innovation in our processes and practices.

9 Empowering Local Communities

Indigenous philosophies and their revitalization are embedded in movements and on-the-ground initiatives enacted by Indigenous communities worldwide. These struggles have called attention to social and environmental injustices in their multiple forms, led to local, regional, and/or global statements for environmental protection, and enacted commitments to protect a range of natural entities. Legal reforms around the world, too, such as Te Urewera Act of 2014, have themselves been the outcome of decades-long struggles (Ruru 2014). Indigenous and other local communities worldwide continue to organize and enact these social movements and struggles, many of which remain vital to broad transformative change.

There is much to learn from Indigenous and other local communities about how to enact change in even the harshest contexts and under conditions of intergenerational oppression. At least for our purposes, two lessons are particularly useful. The first concerns the role of Indigenous and other local communities in our conceptualizations of well-being, development, and justice. As argued more fully elsewhere, Indigenous and other local communities have tended to be treated as passive recipients of social and environmental policy and reform, rather than as active agents capable of responding locally and contributing to agenda- and policy-setting globally (Grix and Watene 2022; Watene and Merino 2018; Watene and Yap 2015; Watene 2016). Transforming how policies and processes are designed and implemented so that they prioritize the contributions of activists and on-the-ground practitioners for reform is an important starting point for realizing just development pathways.

A related insight is that capabilities must be a core focus of such things as well-being, development, and justice, and thus an important aspect of enabling intergenerational relationships (Robeyns 2017; Sen 1999; Nussbaum 2006; Deneulin 2009; Comim, Qizilbash and Alkire 2008). A focus on what people (as individuals and communities) are able to do requires us all to adopt the intimate intergenerational "facing" that underpins Māori and other Indigenous philosophies, and acquire the (social and global) practices required to responsibly enact them (Grix 2019). Such a capabilities-based approach, however, also requires that we work together – not least in genuinely equitable partnerships and for all our relatives – creating opportunities to work across cultures, age cohorts, and territorial boundaries. Here too, we can look to the way communities have been forging new ways of working together in multi-jurisdictional contexts (van Uitregt et al. 2022), as well as to the various ways that local communities are being empowered and remade around the world (Matheson et al. 2020). Investment in and learning from these initiatives is vital.

10 Rethinking Responsibilities

Just as global narratives have much in common with the "islands in a sea" view, our ideas about intergenerational responsibilities and decision-making often take this view also. For a long time, we treated past, present, and future generations as separate entities, sometimes requiring our attention, and often causing no conflicts at all (Mulgan 2006). Whatever was good for present generations, or so it was thought, would be good for future generations. This assumption no longer holds, if indeed it ever did. We know that there is a good chance that future generations will inherit a world which threatens their survival.

For Māori and other Indigenous communities, the natural environment provides the metaphorical ocean that connects us across the world and through time. We see these connections in nature in multiple forms. Just as humans have voyaged across land and sea, birds too migrate across the globe, undertaking perilous journeys guided by the moon and stars as they travel across the night sky. The Arctic tern, for example, travels thousands of miles from the Arctic to breeding areas in the Antarctic. Whales and sea turtles too range across the world's oceans during their natural life spans, sometimes taking years to cross entire oceans to warmer feeding grounds.

For Indigenous philosophies, responsibilities principally concern our relationships with the natural world. We see this emphasis in various Indigenous (and non-Indigenous) documents from global statements (UNDRIP 2007; Rights of Mother Earth 2010; Kari-Oca 2 Declaration 2012; IPBES 2019; UNDP 2020, 2021/22; IPBES and IPCC 2021), to national policy papers (O'Connell et al. 2018; Hughes 2021; Matike Mai Aotearoa 2016), through to local tribal community strategic planning documents (Ngāti Whātua Ōrākei 2018). By centring our responsibilities so as principally to restore human–nature relationships and to enable human–nature flourishing, Indigenous philosophies provide a profoundly different starting point. Such a starting point is likely to require temporary global restrictions (such as rāhui) on various practices to protect the natural environment. It would similarly require widespread legislative protections for several natural entities. In addition, it would require restrictions on consumption and production practices and the various (corporate and political) systems that underpin them. Central too would be the pursuit of just transitions with and for local communities – in some cases requiring constitutional transformation (Matike Mai Aotearoa 2016). In collaboration with local communities, combining provisional restrictions with enduring legislative protections will help to meet the urgent need for action now, inclusive of the urgent need for long-term thinking and change.

11 Enabling Innovation

To meet the challenge of intergenerational justice in the ways suggested, we must be willing to transform our theories and practices in profound ways.

We need policies and processes that nurture and cultivate good relationships. In addition, we need policies and processes that enable rather than constrain these relationships. Our theories and practices of intergenerational justice must provide guidance at both deeply intimate and extremely remote levels for how we foster justice and solidarity within present generations and in ways that cultivate a concern for future generations (Watene 2022).

A fundamental challenge, however, is to find the courage to look beyond our immediate shores. As we have argued elsewhere, the uptake of Indigenous insights are often constrained by existing (local and global) policy and agenda-setting systems (Waldmüller, Yap and Watene 2022; Watene and Merino 2018). We need to find the courage to undertake the complete transformation and remaking of development infrastructures and policymaking. To this end, flexibility in our systems is vital. Policies and processes, in line with ideas such as kaitiakitanga, should not merely be stable and secure over the long term, but should allow responsiveness and adaptation as well. This is likely to require a richer set of policymaking tools, diverse methods, and systems that encourage collaboration. Importantly, while long-term thinking is important, innovation is not to be found by adopting only a forward-looking orientation. Flexibility is likely to involve looking to the past for guidance – to find value in understanding how opportunities and challenges were navigated previously, to reframe and grow existing solutions in different ways, and to retrace our steps in search of opportunities for change. By doing this, the global community will be better positioned not only to support and enable the adaptive social practices so vital to Indigenous and other local communities (Grix 2019; Grix and Watene 2022), but also to realize the transformative philosophies that underpin them and on which our collective socioenvironmental flourishing depends.

12 Conclusion

Indigenous philosophies bring to life the idea that we are all part of an intergenerational journey. Each generation (to borrow from Moana Jackson) is part of a never-ending series of new beginnings – each born in the imaginations of generations past, with the responsibility to set the course for the journeys that follow. To embed this idea, Indigenous philosophies emphasize the importance of nourishing relationships – embedding the importance of cultivating intimate connections to a past that we were not part of and a future we will not live to realize ourselves. To this end, rich and diverse social practices facilitate our remembering (to borrow from Lee Maracle) of hundreds of thousands of relationships across vast distances in time and space. Such an intergenerational orientation reminds us that, together, we walk backwards into the future – facing our ancestors, each other, and ultimately our descendants' flourishing. Perhaps most urgently, it reminds us that we need to find the courage to change our story profoundly, to be bold enough to set a new course, and to inspire the will to hold the course toward a just future.

Bibliography

Anae, Melani. 2010. "Teu Le Va: Toward a Native Anthropology." *Pacific Studies* 33, no. 2–3: 222–240.

Comim, Flavio, Mozaffar Qizilbash, and Sabina Alkire. 2008. *The Capability Approach: Concepts, Measures and Applications*. Cambridge: Cambridge University Press.

Deneulin, Séverine (ed.). 2009. *The Human Development and Capabilities Approach*. London: Earthscan.

Grix, Marco. 2019. "The Ethics and Politics of Consumption." Auckland: University of Auckland, PhD thesis. http://hdl.handle.Net/2292/49071.

Grix, Marco, and Krushil Watene. 2022. "Communities and Climate Change: Why Practices and Practitioners Matter." *Ethics and International Affairs* 36, no. 2: 215–230.

Hau'ofa, Epeli. 1998. "The Ocean in Us." *The Contemporary Pacific* 10, no. 2: 392–410.

2008. *We Are the Ocean: Selected Works*. Honolulu, HI: University of Hawaii Press.

2020. "Epilogue Pasts to Remember." In *Remembrance of Pacific Pasts: An Invitation to Remake History*, edited by Robert Borofsky, 453–471. Honolulu, HI: University of Hawaii Press.

Howe, Kerry. 2007. *Vaka Moana, Voyages of the Ancestors: The Discovery and Settlement of the Pacific*. Honolulu, HI: University of Hawaii Press.

Huambachano, Mariaelena. 2023. "Indigenous Development: The Role of Indigenous Values and Traditions for Restoring Indigenous Food Sovereignty." In *The Routledge Handbook of Indigenous Development*, edited by Katharina Ruckstuhl, Irma A. Velásquez Nimatuj, John-Andrew McNeish, and Nancy Postero, 325–331. Abingdon: Routledge.

Hughes, Tim. 2021. *Towards a Living Standards Framework for All Aotearoa: Culture, Children and Wellbeing*. New Zealand Treasury Discussion Paper 21/01.

Intergovernmental Panel on Biodiversity and Ecosystem Services (IPBES). 2019. Summary for Policymakers of the Global Assessment Report on Biodiversity and Ecosystem Services. Bonn.

Intergovernmental Panel on Biodiversity and Ecosystem Services (IPBES) and Intergovernmental Panel on Climate Change (IPCC). 2021. *Co-sponsored Workshop Report on Biodiversity and Climate Change*. Bonn: IPBES and IPCC.

Jackson, Moana. 2020. "Where to Next? Decolonisation and the Stories in the Land." In *Imagining Decolonisation*, edited by Rebecca Kiddle, 96–112. Wellington: Bridget Williams Books.

Kame'eleihiwa, Lilikalā. 1992. *Native Land and Foreign Desires: Pehea Lā E Pono Ai?* Honolulu, HI: Bishop Museum Press.

Kari-Oca 2 Declaration. 2012. Indigenous People's Rio +20 Earth Summit, Rio de Janeiro, June 17, 2012.

Kawharu, Merata. 2000. "Kaitiakitanga: A Maori Anthropological Perspective of the Maori Socioenvironmental Ethic of Resource Management." *Journal of the Polynesian Society* 110, no. 4: 349–370.

Kimmerer, Robin Wall. 2015. *Braiding Sweetgrass: Indigenous Wisdom, Scientific Knowledge and the Teachings of Plants.* Minneapolis, MN: Milkweed Editions.

Lewis, David. 1972. *We, the Navigators: The Ancient Art of Landfinding in the Pacific.* Honolulu, HI: University of Hawaii Press.

Māhina, Hūfanga Okusitino. 2008. "From Vale (Ignorance) to 'ILO (Knowledge) to Poto (Skill) the Tongan Theory of Ako (Education): Theorizing Old Problems Anew." *AlterNative: An International Journal of Indigenous Scholarship* 4, no. 1: 67–96.

2010. "Tā, Vā, and Moana: Temporality, Spatiality and Indigeneity." *Pacific Studies* 33, no. 2–3: 168–202.

Maracle, Lee. 2015. *Memory Serves: Oratories.* Edmonton: NeWest Press.

Matheson, Anna, Krushil Watene, Grace Vujnovich, and Turei Mackey. 2020. "Collective Impact: Shining the Light on Community Post Covid-19." The Spinoff, August 20, 2020.

Matike Mai Aotearoa. 2016. "He Whakaaro Here Whakaumu Mō Aotearoa: The Report of Matike Mai Aotearoai." In *The Independent Working Group on Constitutional Transformation.* Auckland: Matike Mai Aotearoa.

McGregor, Deborah. 2009. "Honouring Our Relations: An Anishnaabe Perspective." In *Speaking for Ourselves: Environmental Justice in Canada*, edited by Julian Agyeman, Peter Cole, Randolph Haluza-DeLay, and Pat O'Riley, 27–41. Vancouver: University of British Columbia Press.

2020. "Reconciliation and Environmental Justice." In *Reconciliation, Transitional, and Indigenous Justice*, edited by Krushil Watene and Eric Palmer, 100–117. New York, NY: Routledge.

Metz, Thaddeus. 2007. "Towards an African Moral Theory." *Journal of Political Philosophy* 15, no. 3: 321–341.

Mulgan, Tim. 2006. *Future People: A Moderate Consequentialist Account of our Obligations to Future Generations.* Oxford: Oxford University Press.

Ngāti Whātua Ōrākei. 2018. *Te Pou o Kāhu Pōkere: Iwi Management Plan for Ngāti Whātua Ōrākei.* Auckland: Ngāti Whātua Ōrākei.

Nussbaum, Martha. 2006. *Frontiers of Justice: Disability, Nationality, Species Membership.* Cambridge, MA: Harvard University Press.

O'Connell, Emily, Tia Greenaway, Trevor Moeke, and Sacha McMeeking. 2018. *He Ara Waiora: A Pathway Towards Wellbeing.* New Zealand Treasury Discussion Paper 18/11.

Okeja, Uchenna, and Krushil Watene. 2020. "Introduction: Reimagining Justice, Preliminary Remarks." *Ethical Perspectives: Options in African Philosophy* 27, no. 1: 1–8.

Reo, Nicholas, and Laura Ogden. 2018. "Anishnaabe Aki: An Indigenous Perspective on the Global Threat of Invasive Species." *Sustainability Science* 13, 1443–1452.

Robeyns, Ingrid. 2017. *Wellbeing, Freedom and Social Justice: The Capability Approach Re-Examined.* Cambridge: Open Book Publishers.

Royal, Charles, ed. 2003. *The Woven Universe: Selected Writings of Rev. Maori Marsden*. Otaki: Estate of Rev. Maori Marsden.

Ruru, Jacinta. 2014. "Tūhoe-Crown Settlement – Te Urewera Act 2014." *Māori Law Review*, http://maorilawreview.co.nz/2014/10/tuhoe-crown-settlement-te-urewera-act-2014/.

Scott, Nigel. 2010. *Does the Commercial Fishing of Antarctic Toothfish Have a Future? A Critical Assessment from a Ngāi Tahu Tikanga Perspective*. Postgraduate Certificate in Antarctic Studies, University of Canterbury, Winchester.

Sen, Amartya. 1999. *Development as Freedom*. New York, NY: Random House.

Smith, Linda Tuhiwai, Te Kahautu Maxwell, Hupai Puke, and Temara Pou. (2016). "Indigenous Knowledge, Methodology and Mayhem: What Is the Role of Methodology in Producing Indigenous Insights? A Discussion from Mātauranga Māori." *Knowledge Cultures* 4, no. 3: 131–156.

Táíwò, Olúfẹ́mi O. 2022. *Reconsidering Reparations*. New York, NY: Oxford University Press.

Te Urewera Act. 2014, Wellington, July 27, 2014, No 51. Te Awa Tupua (Whanganui River Claims Settlement) Act 2017 (Parliamentary Counsel Office, New Zealand Legislation, last accessed September 16, 2020).

Tutu, Desmond. 1999. *No Future without Forgiveness*. New York, NY: Image/Doubleday.

United Nations Declaration on the Rights of Indigenous Peoples (UNDRIP). 2007. United Nations, September 13, 2007, A/RES/61/295.

United Nations Development Programme (UNDP). 2020. *The Next Frontier: Human Development and the Anthropocene*. New York, NY: UNDP.

United Nations Development Programme (UNDP). 2021/22. *Uncertain Times, Unsettled Lives: Shaping Our Future in a Transforming World*. New York, NY: United Nations Development Programme.

Universal Declaration of the Rights of Mother Earth (Rights of Mother Earth). 2010. World People's Conference on Climate Change and the Rights of Mother Earth. Cochabamba, April 22, 2010.

van Uitregt, Vincent, Isabella Sullivan, Krushil Watene, and Priscilla Wehi. 2022. "Negotiating Greater Māori Participation in Antarctic and Southern Ocean Research, Policy, and Governance." *The Polar Journal* 12, no. 1: 42–61. DOI: 10.1080/2154896X.2022.2058222

Waldmüller, Johannes, Mandy Yap, and Krushil Watene. 2022. "Remaking the Sustainable Development Goals: Relational Indigenous Epistemologies." *Policy and Society* 41, no. 4: 471–485.

Watene, Krushil. 2016. "Valuing Nature: Māori Philosophy and the Capability Approach." *Oxford Development Studies* 44, no. 3: 287–296.

Watene, Krushil. 2018. "Transforming Global Justice Theorising: Indigenous Philosophies." In *The Oxford Handbook of Global Justice*, edited by Thom Brooks. Oxford: Oxford University Press (online edition).

2022. "Kaitiakitanga: Toward and Intergenerational Philosophy." In *The Oxford Handbook of Intergenerational Ethics*, edited by Stephen M. Gardiner. Oxford: Oxford University Press https://doi.org/10.1093/oxfordhb/9780190881931.001.0001.

Watene, Krushil, and Roger Merino. 2018. "Indigenous Peoples: Self-Determination, Decolonisation, and Indigenous Philosophies." In *Routledge Handbook of Development Ethics*, edited by Jay Drydyk and Lori Keleher, 134–147. New York, NY: Routledge.

Watene, Krushil, and Eric Palmer. 2020. *Reconciliation, Transitional, and Indigenous Justice*. Meadville, PA: Routledge.

Watene, Krushil, and Mandy Yap. 2015. "Culture and Sustainable Development: Indigenous Contributions." *Journal of Global Ethics* 11, no. 1: 51–55.

Wehi, Priscilla M., Gretchen Brownstein, and Mary Morgan-Richards. 2020. "Indigenous Plant Naming and Experimentation Reveal a Plant-Insect Relationship in New Zealand Forests." *Conservation Science and Practice* 2, no. 10: e282.

Wehi, Priscilla M., Nigel J. Scott, Jacinta Beckwith, Rata Pryor Rodgers, Tasman Gillies, Vincent van Uitregt, and Krushil Watene. 2021a. "A Short Scan of Māori Journeys to Antarctica." *Journal of the Royal Society of New Zealand*. doi:10.1080/03036758.2021.1917633.

2021b. "Transforming Antarctic Management and Policy with an Indigenous Māori Lens." *Nature Ecology and Evolution* 5: 1055–1059. doi:10.1038/s41559-021-01466-4

Yap, Mandy, and Eunice Yu. 2019. "Mabu Liyan: The Yawuru Way." In *Routledge Handbook of Indigenous Wellbeing*, edited by Christopher Fleming and Matthew Manning, 261–280. Manning. London: Routledge.

2

Climate Ethics and Intergenerational Reciprocity in Indigenous Philosophies

Matthias Fritsch

1 Introduction

Today, we frequently hear the phrase "climate justice," a battle cry for some on the streets, but also a term of relevance to global climate negotiations. Like "justice in sustainability" or "just transition," climate justice is used in recognition of the dual task of achieving sustainable living for future generations while taking into account massive, often history-based injustices in the present. These injustices carry the threat of a transition made at the expense of the most vulnerable, such as developing nations, in particular those in the Global South, Indigenous peoples, and workers, especially within the fossil fuel infrastructure.

Though every party will be adversely affected by the ongoing failure to curb emissions, an injustice exacerbated by climate change is the fact that the emissions, as well as the worst outcomes, are very unevenly distributed. The major emitters (largely in the Global North) tend to be less affected than those most vulnerable to climate change (especially in the Global South), such as Small Island Developing States, Least Developed Countries, and Indigenous peoples. This stark inequality has to do with fossil-fueled industrialization and its historical links with colonialism, the slave trade, and the dispossession of Indigenous populations.

This chapter's focus on Indigenous peoples is motivated by three important truths. First, Indigenous peoples make up less than 5 percent of the global population; but, despite the legacy of colonial land dispossession, they "manage" or hold tenure over 25 percent of the world's land surface and support about 80 percent of global biodiversity (National Geographic Society 2018). Second, given Indigenous knowledge of land and intergenerational teachings, Indigenous peoples are central to protecting nature and fighting climate change – which also highlights the importance of respect for their rights in the face of global mining firms and agribusiness. Third, Indigenous peoples, in line with the first two truths, are frequently at the forefront of resistance to new fossil fuel extraction.

As the Canadian Indigenous Climate Change Action Network recently declared in rather bold terms, "Colonialism caused climate change. Indigenous Rights are the Solution" (Indigenous Climate Action 2021). For these reasons – Indigenous land tenure, Indigenous teachings, and unequal vulnerabilities – respecting Indigenous and human rights in the requisite transitioning away from fossil fuels is key to any fair and efficacious action on climate change, beyond the mere lip service that we find, for example, at the recent United Nations (UN) negotiations (the so-called COP meetings). For instance, the final COP26 agreement (Glasgow 2021) does reference respect for Indigenous rights, but the deal's overarching focus on "net zero" and a regulated global carbon trading market threatens to do the very opposite.[1] A carbon market allows countries to meet their emission targets in part by carbon offsetting: buying credits that embody reduced emissions by others. The goal is not zero emissions, but "net zero" – meaning that offsetting emissions could provide a way to keep on investing in fossil fuels.

Carbon offsetting involves re- and afforestation, hydroelectric dams, and other projects that, as is well known in Canada, frequently take place on Indigenous lands. Investors in such offsetting projects often demand collateral in the form of land titles. In addition, carbon credit schemes tend to work by sequestering land, forests, and rivers needed by Indigenous and local communities for food, water, medicine, and spiritual traditions. That is why Indigenous voices at COP26 argued that "net zero" will lead to decreasing Indigenous land tenure; these voices fear what we might call carbon colonialism. The Indigenous Environmental Network, for one, worries that so-called "nature-based solutions," so widely touted in Glasgow (2021) and Sharm-El Sheikh (2022), are "a new form of corporate land grabbing" (Indigenous Environmental Network 2021).[2]

The centrality of Indigenous teachings for combating climate change was recognized by the UN, for instance in the founding of the Local Communities and Indigenous Peoples Platform at the COP in 2015. And yet, many Indigenous communities are excluded and feel angered by the inclusion of more fossil-fuel industry lobbyists than Indigenous participants, including by Canada. "Indigenous nations were not part of the negotiations [at COP26]

[1] For more details, see my *Hill Times* article (Fritsch, 2021).

[2] See also the more detailed reports by the Indigenous Environmental Network (2022) and by Indigenous Climate Action (2021).

despite the fact that 80 percent of the planet's biodiversity survives in our territories," said Andrea Xieu, a spokesperson for the Mexican collective Futuros Indígenas (Lakhani 2021).

These concerns were reiterated at COP27 in Egypt. In early November 2022, Nourene Ahmet Yaya offered the opening statement on behalf of Indigenous peoples organizations by stating that "climate change is a matter of life and death" for Indigenous peoples: "We have the right to full and direct participation, including our youth, women, persons with disabilities and knowledge holders, in all UNFCCC bodies and processes." Given the lack of independent statehood or sovereign status – a result of colonialism – participation has most often been denied to Indigenous peoples, no matter what colonial state they reside in. Nourene continued to highlight that, "Carbon markets and offsets, geo-engineering, Net Zero frameworks, Nature-based solutions, ecosystem services do not cut emissions and are new forms of colonization" (Climate Action Network International 2022).

The historical and, typically, ongoing links between colonialism and environmental destabilization explain in part the feeling among many Indigenous people that locating the climate emergency only in the future betrays a privileged perspective that not all can afford. Indigenous communities in particular have suffered the trauma of a colonialism whose effects are similar to the outcomes now feared by non-Indigenous peoples as a result of global heating, such as forced dispossession and migration, degradation of land, and loss of self-governance: sufficient reason, then, to inquire into the ways in which some Indigenous scholars consider the dual task of a fair and urgent transition in view of justice for generations to come. Given the links between present, past, and future, how should we think about time in a way that does not avoid the linkages between colonial history and climate change? How do Indigenous intergenerational teachings suggest we think about the dangers and realities of climate change, and how can we construe a politics of justice in response?

While it is not possible to address all of these issues here, this chapter seeks to propose a concept of justice for future people that is mindful of Indigenous critiques of climate eschatologies, eschatologies that locate the issue merely in the future, dropping or sidelining the context of colonialism. I write as a non-Indigenous beneficiary of settler colonialism who can, at best, consider himself a humble student of some Indigenous authors whose written work was accessible to me. I consider my response here an offer of dialogue, and apologize for my limited knowledge.

The second section (this introduction being the first) will review these critiques of the "Anthropocene" and the associated eschatologies. Some of these suggest that motivating pro-futural care by the dread of an impending climate crisis tends to betray a privileged, often settler-colonial perspective. For many Indigenous peoples, what is feared the most in such apocalyptic narratives has already happened to colonized peoples the world over (Dillon 2012, 2016; Scott 2016; Whyte 2018). Thus, a more appropriate relation to the future calls for a differentiated grasp of the past, including an understanding of what one owes to one's ancestors. While the third section will address the Indigenous notion of spiraling time suggested by this coimplication of future, past and present, the fourth section will discuss the relation between intergenerational dialogue and Indigenous gift practices. Potawatomi scholar-activist Kyle Whyte, for one, suggests in response to problematic notions of the Anthropocene that Indigenous approaches to climate change are often motivated through dialogic narratives with descendants and ancestors (Whyte 2018). If we all placed ourselves in our historical lineage – if we all engaged in intergenerational dialogue with our ancestors – we would see that some of our contemporaries today live the dream of their ancestors and others, a nightmare. The beneficiaries of colonialism now have the dubious "luxury" of viewing the environmental crisis – long-term environmental destabilization might be more apt – as one that lies wholly in the future, even if that future starts here, while Indigenous communities have been living with such a crisis, such destabilization and destruction of people and land, for a very long time.

In the wake of this dialogue with past and future, the fifth section will introduce the idea of asymmetrical gift-reciprocity. It will briefly review various Indigenous accounts of intergenerational ethics, from the seven-generation model of the Haudenosaunee Constitution to Māori gift practices. Here, I will propose that a fundamental and common family-resemblance idea in the accounts I have selected – making no claims to unity or universality – seems to centrally include the view that present generations owe to the future in part because they received from their past. The present is not viewed, here, as a distinct moment on a linear timeline – as per the dominant Western view that arguably privileges the present. Rather, the present moment is seen as the overlap of past and future. Accordingly, the currently living are understood, first and foremost, as the descendants of their ancestors, and the ancestors of their descendants. Drawing on some intergenerational economics, where owing to the future as a result of having received from the past is discussed as "indirect reciprocity," I will seek to model and defend this view, as I see it, and its social ontology.

The sixth and final section addresses how asymmetrical reciprocity can aid in the task of demarginalizing the future, that is, can help avoid the impression that there is one future for all humanity (e.g., the future of climate horror). Narratives about the future are, more often than not, centered on European concepts of technological or economic progress – or decline, as the case may be – and sideline representations of the future stemming from marginalized political actors or social groups. To demarginalize and decolonize the future, then, means to take into account the margins, to differentiate futures and imaginations. As I will argue, the social ontology of asymmetrical reciprocity entails the insight that the relation to the future is inseparable, both ontologically and normatively, from relations with the past. This universal historicity thus implies that to decolonize the future means differentiating the view of the past. Instead of "one history, one humanity," as in accounts of the Anthropocene, the resulting view addresses people like me – neither architects of colonial institutions nor members of Indigenous nations – as beneficiaries of an inherited world that is thoroughly structured by the history of colonialism, and asks them to take responsibility for past and ongoing colonial violence.

2 Indigenous Critiques of the Anthropocene and Climate Horror Scenarios

In this section, I will examine Indigenous critiques of the notion of the Anthropocene. For many Indigenous authors, problems with standard Anthropocene narratives include:

(i) The assumption that Indigenous communities have been gradually deteriorating to the point that today's climate and environmental crises of the Anthropocene threaten to kill them off permanently.
(ii) The enclosing of Indigeneity in the Holocene epoch, without consent, which thereby denies the adaptability and historical change of Indigenous peoples.
(iii) The assumption that Indigenous peoples are pure and untouched by colonialism.
(iv) The failure to recognize that, for many Indigenous peoples, the apocalypse has already happened in the past and continues in the present.

The last of these assumptions conflicts with the frequent refrain in climate change literature that the challenge facing "*us*" "*now*" is unprecedented (e.g., Singer 2002, 9 and 19ff; Gardiner 2011, 7; Jamieson 2014, 8). While these claims are understandable in their context – much about current environmental destabilization is novel – they typically assume a unified humanity. Here, examples include the idea that the challenge is new for a "young humanity," as Jamieson puts it (2014, 8), or Singer's titular "one humanity" (2002), and the frequent assumption that humanity already exists as "one": a claim Adorno saw as the hallmark error of Enlightenment views of history (Adorno 2005). In addition, these claims suggest, without further ado, a novelty that is divorced from the history of colonialism, slavery, and industrializing capitalism. Even if the latter is recognized as having started greenhouse gas emissions on a massive scale, this view suggests that the victims are largely to be found in the future and, perhaps, increasingly in the present.

By contrast, Indigenous authors contest the description of our time as being haunted by an unprecedented dystopian or apocalyptic future of climate disaster, often on the basis that it forgets or sidelines the past and present while utilizing a linear conception of time that has the primary effect of permitting the divorce of the present from putatively non-present times (past, future). The linear view is contested as a form of presentism that, parading as an objective view of time, privileges some peoples and perspectives at the expense of others. Whyte calls this a "presentist crisis epistemology": "That a narrative is presentist means that time is put together (arranged) to favor a certain conception of the present as a means of achieving power or protecting privilege" (Whyte 2021, 54). Linear time permits the focus on novelty and, in assuming its objectivity and independence from historical events, masks the unequal power relations that direct the view to the future alone. Documenting Indigenous refusal of the colonial state and the "settler colonial present" (Veracini 2015), Audra Simpson writes:

> Indigenous peoples are reminders, sometimes indecipherable *announcements* of other orders, other authorities, and an earlier time that has not fully passed. "Settler time" is revealed as the fiction of the presumed neutrality of time itself, demonstrating the dominance of the present by some over others, and the unequal power to define what matters, who matters, what pasts are alive and when they die. (Simpson 2017, 22)

Understanding the climate crisis as an entirely novel, unprecedented challenge for humankind, as is very common in much of the literature, avoids the question of the social origins of this very perspective and the power relation embedded in the use of the "one humanity" – the unassuming "we" – that *now* faces the Anthropocene and climate change.

Common narratives of climate disasters, then, tend to marginalize or erase the experience of some populations, particularly of Indigenous people, who have already been subjected to violent transformations of their way of life through colonial violence. As indicated, for Indigenous populations, the consequences of colonialism are, in some ways, similar to the much feared, "apocalyptic" consequences of the Anthropocene, which include forced displacement from the land, loss of meaningful reciprocities with animals, plants and land, as well as a loss of agency and self-determination (Whyte 2017, 2018). Rather than a disaster looming on the horizon, these consequences articulate the actuality of the colonial past and present for Indigenous populations. Thus, Indigenous perspectives on climate change situate the present time as already dystopian. As Conrad Scott writes: "Indigenous dystopian fiction presents not only the crisis of the future, but the ongoing crisis of the present time, and that which is still resonant from the past" (Scott 2016, 73).

Fear for the future of humanity at large, as the very notion of the Anthropocene would suggest, tends to forget the violence of the past and the present, and, thereby, betrays an illegitimate marginalization of the Indigenous experience. Developing a theory of intergenerational justice for future people that is not mindful of violent histories betrays a limited perspective unconcerned with marginalized peoples and Indigenous populations. The "we" to be protected turns out to be an exclusionary group of the most privileged and *their* progeny: "While it might not be too late for some privileged people to continue to live out their dreams and aspirations for future generations – even if they do so in a bubble – I do not see how it cannot be anything but too late for some indigenous peoples to avert further injustice" (Whyte 2020, 5).

In its anthropic universality, the notion of the Anthropocene equally fails to connect the violence of colonialism to the present ecological crises. In recent years, authors such as Ian Baucom (2020), Olúfẹ́mi O. Táíwò (2022), and Kathryn Yusoff have related the climate crisis to the history of slavery as well as the history of colonialism. As Yusoff puts it in *A Billion Black Anthropocenes or None*,

> If the Anthropocene proclaims a sudden concern with the exposures of environmental harm to white liberal communities, it does so in the wake of histories in which these harms have been knowingly exported to black and brown communities under the rubric of civilization, progress, modernization, and capitalism. The Anthropocene might seem to offer a dystopic future that laments the end of the world, but imperialism and ongoing (settler) colonialisms have been ending worlds for as long as they have been in existence. The Anthropocene as a politically infused geology and scientific/popular discourse is just now noticing the extinction it has chosen to continually overlook in the making of its modernity and freedom. (2018, 3)

For this reason, climate change is inseparable from the breaking of "kin" relations of reciprocity, trust, accountability, and consent among populations that are affected differently by colonial history and, in the present, by ongoing marginalization and environmental change. Indigenous peoples have often understood themselves as responding to environmental changes with renewed and transformative kin relations. Thus, for Whyte, we should not only speak of climate tipping points but also "relational tipping points" that settler-colonial states have been unwilling or unable to address:

> The indigenous climate justice movement has been seeking to articulate indigenous cultural orientations on climate change. In some, if not many, of these orientations, the very fabric of the complex phenomena of climate change has to do with kin relationships or their violation … This indigenous orientation … explains why some of us have pointed out that colonialism is itself a form of anthropogenic climate change. (Whyte 2020, 4–5)

In addition, as I noted at the outset, Indigenous peoples often fear that the idea of an urgent response to the climate crisis will be used to sideline or harm them once more, as "the needed relational qualities for coordinated response are missing" (Whyte 2020, 5).

3 Spiraling Time

In contrast to the erasure of colonial and Indigenous histories, Indigenous approaches to climate change are often motivated by dialogical narratives between descendants and ancestors. Reviewing various Indigenous accounts and following discussions with several Indigenous scholars and elders, Whyte suggests that such dialogue relies upon what he calls "spiraling time" (Whyte 2018, 228ff.; Stewart-Harawira 2016, 74ff.; Harjo 2019).[3] He refers to the work of Māori scholar Makere Stewart-Harawira:

[3] See also James Maffie on the spiral and other linked motifs (e.g., the Janus-face, looking backward and forward in time at the same time). In Aztec art, the spiral and similar motifs "depict simultaneous inward-and-outward, coming-and-going, and back-and-forth reciprocal motion and hence the ambiguous motion of agonistic inamic unity… Spiral motifs function the same way. They are ambiguous since they simultaneously exhibit inward and outward motion. Like the xicalcoliuhqui, they express the mutual spinning together and hence unifying of white and black agonistic inamic partners" (Maffie 2014, 161–2). The nonlinearity of the time of generational relations also appears in Indigenous science fiction. Regarding the latter, Grace Dillon describes a genre of speculative fiction entitled "native slipstream" as follows:

> Native slipstream, a species of speculative fiction within the sf realm, infuses stories with time travel, alternate realities and multiverses, and alternative histories. As its name implies. Native slipstream views time as pasts, presents, and futures that flow together like currents in a navigable stream. It thus replicates nonlinear thinking about space-time. (Dillon 2012, 3)

As we can see, native slipstream narratives do not work with linear time, in that they permit time travel to visit the past in the future, the future in the past, and so on.

> Within Maori ontological and cosmological paradigms, it is impossible to conceive of the present and the future as separate and distinct from the past, for the past is constitutive of the present and, as such, is inherently reconstituted within the future. (Stewart-Harawira 2005, 42)

For Stewart-Harawira, the notion of spiraling time (which also includes the non-separation of time and space, of history and land), is not an ahistorical account of time, but is much-needed today to situate ourselves in this ecological crisis:

> As a hermeneutic and traditional symbol, it [the Māori double spiral] also represents the cusp on which we find ourselves at this critical juncture in time, the cusp of our own great Turning, towards an urgent reconsideration of the fundamentals of our socio/politico/economic ontologies of being. (2016, 74)

Centrally, spiraling time – which for Stewart-Harawira is also inspired by Heidegger and Gadamer's hermeneutic circle – connects the present in its opening of the future both to past generations *and* to the land:

> I have taken the notion of a hermeneutic "circle of understanding" and reformulated it as a "spiral of understanding". Here the metaphor of the spiral signifies the turning back … to the sacred teachings of the ancestors, to the source of "the primal energy of potential being" and the returning of these to the forefront in a dynamic process of re-creation and transformation. (2005, 24)

I comment briefly on the spiral of understanding before noting some caution about the idea of "primal energy." The hermeneutic "circle" of understanding, which in Heidegger emerges with the "circular" being of human existence, both individual and collective (Heidegger 2008, §32, 63; Caputo 1988, 61ff.), is motivated first of all by the reading – neither linear nor literally circular – of any text or any phenomenon: to grasp individual elements, we need the whole, but the whole is made of singular aspects. As any careful reader of texts knows, no understanding can circumvent this spiraling forth in a way that is, in principle, endless, and that, thereby, retracts the notion of the whole just referenced provisionally. Such is this spiraling that, ontologically, our understanding of anything whatsoever entails finding ourselves already situated in the world along with that which is to be understood. Being situated in the world is, thus, presupposed by every act of understanding or acting, including the attempt to grasp this very situatedness. And, while the metaphor of the spiral still suggests a line, past and future are not opposed here as different locations on a bar, string, or thread. Understanding can move forward to a more comprehensive understanding only by "turning back" to aspects and elements already traversed or inherited with language and from ancestors. The future is anticipated on the basis of past understanding, and the past is reopened for new possibilities by ongoing futural discoveries. More generally, the possibilities for understanding and acting, of individuals or communities, open up futures that are informed by a past they also reshape. While this back-and-forth movement, this fore- and backgrounding traversal, already suggests that dialogue with others is needed for understanding – as Gadamer's philosophical hermeneutics has insisted in the wake of Heidegger (Gadamer 1989; Warnke 2011) – we can perhaps already intimate the tight link between intergenerational dialogue and spiraling time that we find in the work of the Indigenous scholars discussed here.

We find what I take to be a similar understanding of spiraling time in Muskoke scholar Laura Harjo's recent work, *Spiral to the Stars*. Re-reading traditional Muskoke stories, Harjo seeks to return to the past to activate unrealized possibilities. It is this process that Harjo calls "spiraling through space and time," where "[t]hese iterative spirals of praxis are also a practice of futurity" (Harjo 2019, 14). In turn, futurity names

> the enactment of theories and practices that activate our ancestors' unrealized possibilities, the act of living out the futures we wish for in a contemporary moment, and the creation of the conditions for these futures. This is futurity: it operates in service to our ancestors, contemporary relatives, and future relatives. (Harjo 2019, 5)

Just as in Stewart-Harawira's account – which speaks of the double implication of times (past and future in the present) and of space (space in time and time in space) as best represented by the Māori "double spiral" (2005, 34) – time, here, is not separated from space:

> Since the tools of futurity are processes of relationality, they are carried out in a location, or are connections to a spatial imaginary in which meaning, memories, and desires are shared among community. For this reason, spatialities are a common thread throughout *Spiral to the Stars*. Indigenous spatialities are needed because Western spatial imaginaries are not complex enough to imagine and carry out Indigenous futurities. (Harjo 2019, 41)

More could be said here about this complex notion of time-space, and, indeed, I would like to learn more about spiraling time. For now, let me stress that the spiral denotes neither cyclical nor linear time.[4] The opposition

[4] Referring to an oral presentation to which I did not have access, Whyte notes "[Joanne] Rappaport gave an insightful commentary that engaged differences between time as a cycle or as a spiral" (Whyte 2018, 239n4).

between these two has often been used in the West to assert its superiority, the Eurocentric and logocentric vision of a people of linear history, relegating others to mere mythos in a cyclical return of the ever same (see Arendt 1961; Eliade 1963, 1971). The spiral ontology offers the chance to avoid both cyclical foundationalism (and its Rousseauist schemata) and historical teleology (Fritsch 2018, 123f.). Despite its constitutive role and its "primal energy," nature need not be understood here as the bedrock foundation, the ultimate donor of the gift, from which all turns and to which all returns. Nor is the time of history independent of the space of nature and land. As we heard Stewart-Harawira say, the spiral signifies a "dynamic process of re-creation and transformation" (2005, 24).

Nonetheless, there remains the worry that giving forward to future generations is ultimately understood as proceeding from a nature conceived as the single and unified source of all things in which nothing would be lost. Overcoming modern "alienation" from nature, including what Marx called primitive accumulation (Marx 1992, Part 8) and the so-called "metabolic rift" (Foster, Clark, and York 2010), to which Stewart-Harawira refers (2016, 77–79), would then be an archeoteleological return to nature as primal energy: "the spiral also symbolizes the ongoing evolution of humankind as spiritual beings whose ultimate destiny has been described as 'to become one with the source of all things'" (Stewart-Harawira 2016, 84). By contrast, as we will see, asymmetrical reciprocity insists on withdrawal and disunity in space-time that puts generations in relation with each other and with the land and its multiple beings. The withdrawal, or excess of time, which I already hinted at by retracting the notion of the "whole," will not permit a return to the *arche* nor a reunification with nature in the *telos*.

If spiraling time is not linear, the Indigenous response to the Anthropocene is not just a question of moving its start date further back in time, say, from industrialization to early modern colonialism, from 1750 to 1492. (In this vein, some scholars have suggested that we ought to consider the beginning of industrialization as in the mid-eighteenth century, or perhaps as beginning in the "long sixteenth-century" or 1450, with the developments of colonialism.) Rather, to my understanding, spiraling time means, in essence, that the presently living are first and foremost the descendants of ancestors and the ancestors of descendants (thus undoing the Western privileging of the present, which, since Heidegger and Derrida, has come to be known as the "metaphysics of presence").

4 The Gift in Intergenerational Dialogue

For this reason, the intergenerational dialogue with ancestors and descendants, while counterfactual, is not "imaginary" in the sense of a binary contrast with what is "real."[5] The dialogue is not between an actual (real) present and the non-actual past and future. Rather, dialogue with ancestors and progeny is seen as social-ontological, as constituting the present in the first place. As I understand it, this teaching regarding relations between generations views the present as constituted by the dialogue with the past and the future. The notion of generational time as spiraling dialogue is exemplified by some interpretations of the well-known "seven-generations" model of some North American Indigenous peoples. While some view this model as projecting seven generations into the future,[6] others emphasize more strongly the role of ancestors as well as of descendants. As Ted Jojola, the renowned Indigenous planner at the University of New Mexico (and enrolled member of the Pueblo of Isleta), writes:

> Within an individual's lifetime, it is not unusual [for Indigenous peoples] that an extended family consists not only of oneself, but those that are three generations before and three generations after. This is the intergenerational family – great-grandparents, grandparents, parents, "you", children, grandchildren, and great-grandchildren. Fundamentally, the middle generation – you – represents the centre point of a bridge that spans the past and the future. The knowledge of the past informs the present and, together, it builds a vision towards the future. This is known as the seven generations model. (Jojola 2013, 457)

We should recall here that there cannot be a bridge without that which it bridges on either side; thus, here too the present is not self-standing, but dependent on the past and the future. Thus understood, the seven generations model determines the present in its reference to three generations in the past and three in the future. It is this strong determination of the present as a bridge, resting on the past and the future, which accounts for a renewed sense of intergenerational dialogue. As a bridge supported by a spiral – forgive the mixing of imagery – this dialogue is, as we have said, not simply imaginary as opposed to real, but, in fact, concerns the very constitution of the present.

But what can we say about the content of this dialogue? That is, what will be talked about? The conception of intergenerational dialogue leads Whyte to pose two key – and interrelated – questions:

[5] Similarly, in Whyte (2018) science and fiction are not simply opposed. And storytelling is, for many of the authors under consideration here, not merely fictitious.

[6] See, for example, Clarkson et al. 1992 and Oren Lyons, as cited here: www.pbs.org/warrior/content/timeline/opendoor/roleOfChief.html

> First, in the words of Robin Wall Kimmerer, how do we return the gifts from our ancestors? [Kimmerer, 2013] In having received gifts from the past, what do we owe? And second, how are we to become good ancestors ourselves? (Whyte 2018, 229)

Note that these two formulations do not divorce the issue of relations with the past from relations with future people. Having received gifts from our ancestors, the question, then, is how we can be good ancestors ourselves in returning the favor by passing it forward.

In asking these questions, it becomes clear that (for Whyte and others) the notion of dialogue among generations is inseparable from intergenerational obligations revolving around the notion of the gift. The presently living are asked, at the same time, to look forward and backward in time and, thus, to see themselves as receiving a gift, however modified, that will and should be passed on to future generations. In Section 5, I will seek to capture this normative inseparability of past and future by proposing the notion of asymmetrical reciprocity among generations.

Before doing that, however, I would like to address a concern about the usage of the terminology of the "gift" in the context of colonialism, for, after all, the historical violence of colonialism could hardly be described as a positive gift to Indigenous peoples in the present. Of course, we have to disaggregate the meaning of the gift for Indigenous peoples and for settlers, even if this cannot be done in a simple binary way. Indigenous peoples speak of gifts from the land and from ancestors, with the latter referring to teachings, practices, and lifeways that help them to resist colonial violence. *Grosso modo*, settlers receive from their ancestors the material and social benefits of colonial violence that our ancestors either committed directly or complied with and tolerated indirectly. But, despite this necessary distinction, we should not overlook the overall claim that the nature of the gift, in its link with spiraling time and intergenerational dialogue, is ontologically constitutive of the present, for both settlers and Indigenous peoples. For many of the Indigenous authors from whom I am trying to learn here, the present generation would not *be* without the gift of the past and of the future, of the ancestors and of the land. So while we need to retain the ability to distinguish, despite the conceptual and empirical difficulties, between benefits and harms in relation to what a people has inherited, the notion of the gift also speaks to the general dependency of the present on the past and the future. In doing so, it demonstrates the persistence of the violence of colonialism, as the past given to the present generation. We cannot sever ourselves from what has already occurred, nor deny our responsibility for it, as it comes toward us as our past, and, thus, as, already, our future.

With this in mind, I now turn more directly to the notion of the gift of the ancestors and the gift of the future. As the Potawatomi scholar Robin Kimmerer writes,

> For much of human time on the planet, before the great illusion, we lived in cultures that understood the covenant of reciprocity, that for the earth to stay in balance, for the gifts to continue to flow, we must give back in equal measure for what we take. (Kimmerer 2013a)

Thus, under the heading of reciprocity, we see that gifts and responsibilities are two sides of the same coin (see also Kimmerer 2013b, esp. 380ff.). The reception of a gift is coupled with a duty to use it for the benefit of all. This way of thinking about reciprocity, particularly reciprocity with the earth, is similarly found in Glen Sean Coulthard's *Red Skin, White Masks*, in which he proposes a "grounded normativity" in contrast to the "politics of recognition" that defines the Canadian settler-colonial state. This notion of grounded normativity, or "place-based ethics," contests the drive for accumulation and capitalist expansion that has determined the history of Canadian–Indigenous relations. To motivate this further, Coulthard draws on the Dene elder Philip Blake, who is cited as saying:

> We have lived with the land, not tried to conquer or control it or rub off its riches. We have not tried to get more and more riches and power. We have not tried to conquer new frontier or make sure that every year we are richer than the year before. We have been satisfied to see our wealth as ourselves and the land we live with. We did not try to improve the land and we did not try to destroy it. This is not our way. It is our greatest wish to be able to pass on this land to succeeding generations in the same condition that our fathers have given it to us. I believe your nation might wish to see us not as relics from the past, but as a way of life, a system of values by which you may survive in the future. This we are willing to share. (Philip Blake, in Coulthard 2014, 63)

In these teachings from Kimmerer and Blake, then, we can identify a dual conception of reciprocity, both with the land or earth, as well as with ancestors and descendants. Similarly, James Tully reports on the centrality of the idea of "gift-gratitude-reciprocity" or "gift-reciprocity" for the First Nations on the Northwest Coast of what is now called Canada, where reciprocity refers simultaneously to the gift relations between people–people and people–earth (Tully 2020). The gift of land is seen as constitutive of the humans living on and from it. As Coulthard says, land here is identity, an "identity that locates us as an inseparable part of an expansive system of interdependent relations covering the land and animals, past and future generations, as well as other people and communities" (Coulthard 201, 63). It is this Indigenous identity that serves as the basis from which capitalist expansion and colonial sovereignty are rejected. While non-Indigenous people cannot simply claim this identity for themselves, and so need to find different and additional resources for resisting racial and colonial capitalism, there is often, nonetheless, a suggestion that the understanding of the human condition (here, grounded normativity and land-based intergenerational reciprocity) is either universal or an offer of dialogue: as Blake says, "this [system of values] we are willing to share."[7] Below, I will discuss asymmetrical reciprocity as a differentiating universal.

5 Asymmetrical Reciprocity

I would now like to develop the notion of intergenerational, land-based reciprocity further. I believe the notion of reciprocity in question can be productively linked, in the spirit of dialogue that I mentioned at the outset, to what I have sought to develop elsewhere as asymmetrical reciprocity (Fritsch 2017, 2018, chapter 3; 2020a). I propose this concept as a contribution to accounts of intergenerational justice. The development of this concept draws on contemporary literature on intergenerational economic transfer and, centrally, on the anthropologist Marcel Mauss, whose celebrated 1921 *Essay sur le don* attempts to synthesize Indigenous gift practices.

Let me begin by seeking to explain what I mean by "asymmetry." First, I mean the power asymmetry between the present and past as well as future generations. Despite the constitutive nature of the past and the future in relation to the present, and despite the reciprocity obligations I will discuss in a moment, a present generation can seriously short-change future generations. Furthermore, as we can learn from the Indigenous discussion of presentist power and settler time, the present can – or in fact always does – selectively remember events and ancestors, effectively imposing a second death on some individuals and populations while giving itself an undeserved good conscience.

Second, asymmetry implies an *indirect* relation of reciprocity. Contrary to the common definition of reciprocity, which indicates a two-way relation of giving in which A gives to B, and then B returns the gift to A (thus making of it an exchange), indirect reciprocity implies a three-way relation: A gives something to B, and B returns it to C. Despite her emphasis on circularity, Kimmerer, commenting on the difference between an economy based on

[7] Kimmerer, in fact, encourages everyone to affirm themselves as Indigenous to place and as inheritors of the gifts of Indigenous teachings (Kimmerer 2013b, 207). According to this view, to become Indigenous means to situate oneself, essentially, in a land-based intergenerational reciprocity: "For all of us, becoming indigenous to a place means living as if your children's future mattered, to take care of the land as if our lives, both material and spiritual, depended on it" (2013b, 9). Whyte and others claim, by contrast, that Indigenous teachings are not for all humanity (Whyte, Caldwell, and Schaefer 2018). I suspect that this latter view is in part motivated by the fact that, today, the word "Indigenous" carries a political meaning that, informed by the brutal history of colonialism, cannot be claimed by all.

property and exchange and the Indigenous understanding of a gift economy, writes that "Many of our ancient teachings counsel that whatever we have been given is supposed to be given away again" (Kimmerer 2013b, 28).

In addition to the power imbalance and the indirectness of giving, asymmetry implies two other key aspects. Asymmetry attempts to capture the *constitutive* nature of the gift. In this sense, the gift stands in a relation of dissymmetry to recipients. It is not seen as a mere object that the recipient may or may not accept. Rather, as we have seen above with the Indigenous grasp of land received from ancestors, the gift received from A is co-constitutive of B in B's very being. The land (we could add languages and traditions to this) is "identity-forming" in a cultural sense that is inseparable from the material dependency on natural systems. To the extent that this dependency on nature, as well as on previous generations, applies to all cultures, one may wish to speak, here, of "earth" or indeed "nature" in contradistinction to land. Even the settler understanding of land as chiefly property – stolen property, we should say, anachronistically (see Nichols 2020) – does not escape this constitutive nature of the gift. Fantasize as we might about space travel and the "colonization" of other planets, settlers remain earthlings (Fritsch 2018, chapter 5). And, as this determines intergenerational relations, it implies that all contemporaries in the present are co-constituted by the reception of the gift from the past. They would not be what they are without the gifts in question.

And this constitutive nature brings us to the fourth and final aspect of asymmetry: namely, the fact that the gift cannot be appropriated completely, no more than reading a text or understanding in general can come around full circle. Spiraling time, as I have sought to understand it here, is infinite, though neither in the sense of a never-ending line nor as an endless cycle. In addition to the co-constitution of the past by the present, the asymmetry of the gift – tied as it is to the spiral – also implies an excessive quality in that the totality of the gift received from the past is essentially inappropriable. In this sense, Kimmerer's account of Indigenous gift-giving may be seen to flow from a universal insight: "Wealth among traditional people is measured by having enough to give away. Hoarding the gift, we become constipated with wealth, bloated with possessions, too heavy to join the dance" (Kimmerer 2013b, 381). Land, languages, traditions, customs, and so on, cannot be appropriated in the way consumables are imagined to be – though they, too, leave a remainder – but will always remain in excess of the recipient. This inappropriable excess is the condition of the appropriation of the past by the present, as well as the opening and linkage of the appropriators toward the future.

For if the gift was entirely appropriated by the present, entirely consumed without an outstanding remainder, there would be nothing left, even for the present itself, to read, to eat, to temporalize, to spiral. However much expansionist fantasies and instrumental rationality tend to equate the capitalist drive for more and more with life itself, total appropriation amounts to death. The excessive nature of the gift, then, indicates that the present receives something beyond itself, and is responsible for the passage of this beyond in such a way as to give beyond itself as the condition of its "own" future – a future already slipping away into the other's. As such, the gift calls us back to the past and the future in their indirect reciprocity, as the co-constitutive condition of the present that, we have seen, can be grasped as the bridge between the past and the future. Speaking of asymmetry in intergenerational reciprocity is meant to capture this ultimate impossibility of clearly assigning the source of intergenerational obligation to either the past or the future. In spiraling time, the gift of the past always calls to us from the future, and, in this way, obliges us to pass on the gift.

With the help of Mauss's account of Indigenous gift practices, I would like to show briefly how the gift gives rise to the obligation of reciprocity and return. The basic argument is based on the asymmetrical excess of the gift, which implies that the gift does not just come from the donor – the individual or group who gives – but, rather, is dependent on a much larger field of traditions, ancestors, and the land or earth, which Mauss terms the "native soil" (Mauss 2002, 16). So, when the recipient accepts the gift, what is received is always more than just the thing given, and this excess implies the obligation to return. For the acceptance of the gift affirms that which remains inassimilable, so that it cannot but be passed on to others, and to nature. Thus, the giving of the gift articulates a field of dependency and relationality, in which the possibility of giving, receiving, and passing on a gift necessitates both ancestors and descendants and the land or earth, as well as the aid of contemporary others who enable the recipient-donor to maintain the gift in its middle-voice passage. Kimmerer calls this larger field of dependency "a landscape of gifts peopled by nonhuman relatives, the sovereign beings who sustain us, including the plants" (Kimmerer 2018, 27). This landscape of gifts is constitutive of every gift and also of every article of exchange, and, as such, remains inappropriable and irreducible to mere property, exchange, and consumption.[8]

[8] I have presented this reading of Mauss on the sources of normativity in greater detail in Fritsch 2018, Chapter 3 (see also Fritsch 2020b). There (Fritsch 2018, 137ff.), I have also sought to show that asymmetrical reciprocity does not entail an underhanded linearity of time, as the talk of gifts passing via the present from the past to the future might suggest. In fact, the gift – as I would say, now and here, with the invaluable insistence of Indigenous authors discussed here – "spirals" from past to future as much as from future to past, from past to further past, from future to further future, and so on.

6 Demarginalizing the Future

In this final section, I would like to address the question of how the notion of asymmetrical reciprocity can aid in the task of demarginalizing the future. But before that, permit me to address a worry about cultural extractivism, which concerns whether asymmetrical reciprocity ought to be proposed for a global humanity. Not being an Indigenous scholar myself, there is a legitimate worry that the appropriation of ideas from Indigenous culture operates under the same logic of extraction that dispossessed native peoples of their ancestral lands. Perhaps cultural extractivism follows on the heels of resource extractivism.

As we heard, the very relation between Indigenous peoples and non-Indigenous populations may be so fraught that a common approach to climate change proves very difficult, if not too late. In this context, Kyle Whyte recently wrote that, "It may be too late to achieve environmental justice for some indigenous peoples, and other groups...," for climate change coordination would call for qualities that today are still sorely lacking:

> The required qualities include, among others, consent, trust, accountability, and reciprocity. Indigenous traditions of [responding to] climate change view the very topic of climate change as connected to these qualities, which are sometimes referred to as kin relationships. The entwinement of colonialism, capitalism, and industrialization failed to affirm or establish these qualities or kinship relationships across societies. (Whyte 2020, 1).

In response to these worries about extractivism and a lack of trust and reciprocity (among Indigenous and non-Indigenous peoples), I would like to begin by noting, in humility, that not all accounts of indirect reciprocity are drawn from Indigenous sources in the strict sense. For example, Mauss draws on early Germanic as well as Roman traditions. Indirect intergenerational reciprocity has been proposed by Western philosophers as well (Gosseries 2009; Kolm 2006), though some appropriately refer to Mauss's work on Indigenous gift practices (Arrondel and Masson 2006). And second, as cited above in the case of the Dene elder, some Indigenous scholars themselves universalize this point. For it is intergenerational and land-based reciprocity that Philip Blake proposes as a future system of values for our world. Similarly, Stewart-Harawira hopes that,

> far from being irrelevant in the modern world, traditional indigenous social, political and cosmological ontologies are profoundly important to the development of transformative alternative frameworks for global order. (Stewart-Harawira 2005, 24)

I agree. Further, I think the third and fourth sense of asymmetry discussed above – the constitutive and inappropriable nature of the gift, including cultural inheritance – advise against overly strict delimitations of culture, inheritance, and tradition, without thereby licensing a free-for-all attitude that would, once more, benefit the more powerful. But above all, I want to stress a related point: The notion of asymmetrical reciprocity avoids constraining the sense of the future to a future that would be the "same for all." Asymmetrical reciprocity forestalls the view that "humanity" is sufficiently one, or non-problematically unified, so that we could simply speak of it facing a common future. Rather, this notion of intergenerational reciprocity differentiates relations to the ancestral past.

If this is right, then asymmetrical reciprocity provides a model for demarginalizing the future by taking into account the differentiation of the past as a condition for the present. For example, in the Indigenous context, the past (and ongoing) violence of colonialism shapes the possibilities of Indigeneity in the future. Conversely, and without wishing to equate harms here, the history of colonialism, while bestowing many benefits upon its beneficiaries, can also be seen to impoverish possibilities for settlers and settler descendants, for instance by encouraging an understanding of co-constitutive earth as property and relations with others as the economic transactions of an atomistic self. Thus, we must remember the past, but remember it in multiple forms, in order to make sense of differentiated horizons of possibility.

Furthermore, I think the social ontology of asymmetrical reciprocity deepens the point that the relation to the future is inseparable, both ontologically and normatively, from relations with the past. The overall idea then, is that because the very definition of "Indigenous peoples" – for example by various UN declarations, but also those put forward by Whyte and others (Whyte, Caldwell, and Schaefer 2018) – includes references to colonial dispossession, the possibility of respectfully learning from Indigenous people demands, especially of settlers like me, grasping the processes that robbed them of their lands and aiding in the struggle for their self-determination and the return of stolen lands in the future. In this sense, the conditions under which non-Indigenous peoples could inherit the gifts of Indigenous teachings include resistance to ongoing colonialism – partly because of the inherent wrong of colonial violence and land theft, and partly because intergenerational reciprocity and the associated liabilities demand this resistance more on this below. Such resistance includes the need to build the capacity to receive these gifts, which is not just a cognitive effort, but is part of alternative world-building more broadly.[9] And this contemporary resistance would, in another form of the spiral, do well to recall anticolonial resistance in history, thereby repotentializing the present

[9] I thank Lisa Guenther for helping me to grasp these points.

for a different future, in the way Walter Benjamin famously recommended in different circumstances (Benjamin 2003; Fritsch 2005). Crucially, it is precisely in the recognition of the strong connection between the future and the differentiated past that the notion of asymmetrical reciprocity can, indeed, become a common reference point, and so recommend itself to us all.

There are, then, four ways in which asymmetrical reciprocity helps to differentiate the past and demarginalize the future. The first, which we just discussed, constitutively links the future to the past, and so calls for vigilance regarding inherited wrongs and their associated prejudices. So, one advantage of asymmetrical reciprocity is that this complex account of relations between the generations (and with the land, with nature, or the earth) necessarily and always takes the past into consideration: There could be no relation to the future (apocalyptic or hopeful) that, in its very grasping of what time is in general, would not take account of the specificities of the past and the specific histories of oppression, dispossession, and colonization. According to this view, in seeking to demarginalize futures, we not only *should* consider the past, but *must* do so, as asymmetrical reciprocity and the gift are constitutive of being and identity in the present. Further, as we saw Mauss argue, asymmetrical reciprocity implies that the very source of the normative lies, in part, in intergenerational relations. As moral agents, we are necessarily born as mortals: born of previous generations and dying to leave the world to others after us.

A second advantage of asymmetrical reciprocity is that, against a sort of presentist phantasm that pretends we are self-standing, self-birthing individuals, and against a merely forward-looking account based on linear time, it calls attention to the fact that we are always passing on an inherited life-world, along with taken-for-granted background assumptions, traditions and languages, socio-economic structures, and so on. (For example, simply by communicating in English here, we are contributing to its global hegemony, which owes itself to a colonial history). The historical process of transmission and inheritance includes the danger of passing on oppressive life-worlds and associated prejudices. This might be held against models of asymmetrical reciprocity. So, where one objection might urge us not to look to the contested past but the shared future and its (environmental) dangers for all of "us" (a universal humanity), asymmetrical reciprocity responds by pointing to, and making us aware of, the ontologically constitutive role of historical reciprocities and the power of inheritance, such that asymmetrical reciprocity at least has the advantage of calling for vigilance on the part of heirs to avoid, as much as possible, passing on inherited wrongs. Even if we cannot survey and master inheritance *in toto* – for reasons having to do with what I earlier called the inappropriable – asymmetrical reciprocity calls on us to more consciously filter the inheritance that we cannot avoid passing on to the future. In other words, asymmetrical reciprocity demands that we be more self-critical about "our" world, which may not be everyone's, and which may harbor deep-seated forms of oppression that formed the inheritance in question (classism, colonialism, racism, sexism, ableism, and, today, also presentism).

Third, as discussed above, one might think that the gift is only ever a benefit, at least on balance, and not a harm, and, thus, it would be wrong or even perverse to utilize this notion in the context of colonialism, that is, to speak of inherited gifts with deep historical harm. In other words, the mere application of the "gift" to this legacy would only privilege the victors of history, to borrow a phrase from Walter Benjamin. However, one may find that the notion of intergenerationality implied by the gift is useful for undermining the denial of the inherited past. For example, Whyte discusses how non-Indigenous would-be allies of Indigenous peoples tend to believe that they are innocent, free of any culpability that would stem from their own ancestors.[10] By forgetting their "ancestral fantasies" – the hopes for the future of their settler-ancestors, for example – these allies tend to deny the violent gifts they have received from their ancestors, who colonized, oppressed, displaced, and murdered Indigenous peoples.

> Many of the ancestors of today's allies designed the worlds we live in today to fulfill their fantasies of the future. Today's worlds, such as those of US settler colonialism in North America, were constructed to provide privileges to their descendants. They were gifts of a troubling sort … Perhaps it is all part of allies' ancestral fantasies that their descendants would have the privilege of unlimited individual and collective agency to exploit Indigenous peoples and the privilege of claiming moral high ground as saviors. Detaching one's self from one's ancestral fantasies is a problematic activity because we cease to acknowledge the counterfactual space of unfolding dialogue with our ancestors and descendants from particular generations. (Whyte 2018, 237–8)

The troubling gifts include the wide-spread absence of Indigenous control of land, sovereignty and self-determination in legal systems, and so on – but also the very capacity of non-Indigenous people to believe themselves innocent, and, thus, imagine themselves as potential saviors of threatened Indigenous peoples. In response, then, the beneficiaries of this history of colonialism should themselves take the notion of intergenerational gifting and spiraling time seriously, so as to engage in a dialogue with *their own* ancestors – what Alexis Shotwell has called "claiming bad kin" (Shotwell 2019) – and to understand the costs of the troubling gifts they received. As the dialogue is counterfactual, moreover, it could suggest alternative possibilities in the past for the future.

[10] On settler moves to innocence, see also Tuck and Yang 2012.

This allows us to transition to my fourth and final point, which is how asymmetrical reciprocity supports the argument for the "liability for compensation." Reciprocity duties are often given in the form of equivalence. We found this, for example, in Philip Blake, and the notion of passing the land on in "the same" or, we might add, as good a condition as it was received from the ancestors. Now, one may rightly wonder, if that is the normative content of the notion of reciprocity, what if the inheritance is received in a degraded state? In response to this, it is important to differentiate the cause of the degradation, so that one can see how a present generation could come under an obligation to improve the inheritance. To illustrate, an example: If a previous user damages a bicycle by overusing it for, say, delivering newspapers, and passes on both the damaged bike and the profits from the delivery, then, all other things being equal, the subsequent user, we might say, should use the inherited profits to fix the damage for the sake of the third user. This kind of argument is transferable to the role of improving environments when it comes to climate change. Arguably, this is indeed the situation in which the current generation of the developed world – the Global North, shaped by the history of colonization – finds itself: Having inherited the benefits of industrialization and colonization, the beneficiaries, above all, must now compensate for the associated climate damages and environmental and racial injustices.

This raises the question of what compensation might mean for Indigenous peoples – a question that could hardly be addressed in the absence of dialogue.[11] Given the central role of land in Indigenous resistance to colonialism, in Indigenous continuance and survivance (Whyte et al. 2018; Vizenor 2008),[12] and in Indigenous accounts of intergenerational relationality, it is clear that there can be no decolonization without the rematriation of land (see Whyte and Meissner 2021). Such rematriation would belong to a broader strategy that is neither focused on the past (as dreams of rectifying a wrong often are) nor on the future (as reconciliation projects tend to be). Rather, in line with spiraling time, the overall idea would be to understand compensation as part of a "constructivist" account of reparations, in the sense Táíwò has recently given to this word (Táíwò 2022). Accordingly, reparation means overcoming a world built on the destructive foundations of primitive accumulation by constructing a just world. My hope is that asymmetrical reciprocity and the gift, as understood

[11] In the Canadian context, see, for example, https://redpaper.yellowheadinstitute.org/.

[12] "'Continuance' here refers to Indigenous survival and flourishing in the face of change, including change stemming from oppression" (Whyte, Caldwell, Schaefer 2018, 153).

To my knowledge, Gerald Vizenor coined the term "survivance" to combine the senses of (i) survival with (ii) the sense of the endurance of a language and culture against oppression, and (iii) with the older meaning of intergenerational succession after the death of the previous holder of an office or estate (Vizenor 2008, 19; Breinig 2008, 39–40).

here, can play a role in this project. They call for the recognition of and resistance to the bloody history of colonial violence, in response to which visions of the future are to be demarginalized.

Bibliography

Adorno, Theodor W. 2005. "Progress." In *Critical Models. Interventions and Catchwords*, translated by Henry W. Pickford, 143–160. New York, NY: Columbia University Press.

Arendt, Hannah. 1961. "The Concept of History." In *Between Past and Future. Eight Exercises in Political Thought*. 41–90. New York, NY: Viking Press.

Arrondel, Luc, and André Masson. 2006. "Altruism, Exchange or Indirect Reciprocity: What Do the Data on Family Transfers Show?" In *Handbook of the Economics of Giving, Altruism and Reciprocity: Applications Volume 2*, edited by Serge-Christophe Kolm and Jean Mercier Ythier, 971–1053. Amsterdam: Elsevier.

Baucom, Ian. 2020. *History 4° Celsius: Search for a Method in the Age of the Anthropocene*. Durham, NC: Duke University Press.

Benjamin, Walter. 2003. "On the Concept of History." In *Selected Writings, Volume 4*, edited by Howard Eiland and Michael W. Jennings, 389–411. Boston, MA: Harvard University Press.

Breinig, Helmbrecht. 2008. "Native Survivance in the Americas." In *Survivance: Narratives of Native Presence*, edited by Gerald Vizenor, 39–60. Lincoln, NE: University of Nebraska Press.

Caputo, John D. 1988. *Radical Hermeneutics. Repetition, Deconstruction, and the Hermeneutic Project*. Bloomington, IN: Indiana University Press.

Clarkson, Linda, Vern Morrissette, and Gabriel Regallet. 1992. *Our Responsibility to the Seventh Generation: Indigenous Peoples and Sustainable Development*. Winnipeg: International Institute for Sustainable Development (www.iisd.org/publications/our-responsibility-seventh-generation)

Climate Action Network International. 2022. "ECO: No Climate Justice Without Human Rights." *ECO 4, COP 27*, https://climatenetwork.org/resource/eco-4-cop27/.

Coulthard, Sean Glen. 2014. *Red Skin White Mask. Rejecting the Colonial Politics of Recognition*. Minneapolis, MN: University of Minnesota Press.

Dillon, Grace L. 2012. "Imagining Indigenous Futurisms." In *Walking the Clouds: An Anthology of Indigenous Science Fiction*, edited by Grace. L. Dillon, 1–15. Tucson, AZ: University of Arizona Press.

2016. "Indigenous Futurisms, Bimaashi Biidaas Mose, Flying and Walking towards You" *Extrapolation* 57, no.1–2: 1–6.

Eliade, Mircea. 1963. *Myth and Reality*. Translated by Willard R. Trask. New York, NY: Harper & Row.

1971. *The Myth of the Eternal Return: Cosmos and History*, translated by Willard R. Trask. Princeton, NJ: Princeton University Press.

Foster, John Bellamy, Brett Clark, and Richard York. 2010. *The Ecological Rift. Capitalism's War on the Earth*. New York, NY: Monthly Review Press.

Fritsch, Matthias. 2005. *The Promise of Memory: History and Politics in Marx, Benjamin, and Derrida*. Albany, NY: SUNY Press.

2017. "'La justice doit porter au-delà de la vie présente': Derrida on Ethics Between Generations." *Symposium* 21, no. 1: 231–253.

2018. *Taking Turns with the Earth*. Stanford, CA: Stanford University Press.

2020a. "Asymmetrical Reciprocity in Intergenerational Justice." In *Future Design: Incorporating Preferences of Future Generations for Sustainability*, edited by Tatsuyoshi Saijo, 17–36. Berlin: Springer.

2020b. "Response to Critics of Taking Turns with the Earth" *Etica & Politica/Ethics & Politics* XXII, no. 2: 557–588.

2021. "Why Indigenous Voices Are Particularly Important for Canada at UN Climate Change Negotiations." *The Hill Times*, https://bit.ly/3MiP5zp.

Gadamer, Hans-Georg. 1989. *Truth and Method*, 2nd rev. edn., revised translation by J. Weinsheimer and D.G. Marshall, NY: Crossroad.

Gardiner, Stephen. 2011. *A Perfect Moral Storm: The Ethical Tragedy of Climate Change*. Oxford: Oxford University Press.

Gosseries, Axel. 2009. "Three Models of Intergenerational Reciprocity." In *Intergenerational Justice*, edited by Axel Gosseries and Lukas H. Meyer, 119–146. Oxford: Oxford University Press.

Harjo, Laura. 2019. *Spiral to the Stars. Muskoke Stories of Futurity*. Tucson, AZ: University of Arizona Press.

Heidegger, Martin. 2008. *Being and Time*, translated by John Macquarrie and Edward Robinson. New York, NY: Harper Perennial.

Indigenous Climate Action. 2021a. *Decolonizing Climate Policy in Canada: Report from Phase One*. http://bit.ly/3MiOXQr.

2021b. *The Risks and Threats of "Nature-based Climate Solutions" for Indigenous Peoples – Sneak Peek*. https://bit.ly/46ZyI2E.

Indigenous Environmental Network. 2021. *No to Nature-Based Solutions Dispossessions!* www.ienearth.org/sign-the-statement-no-to-nature-based-dispossessions/

Jamieson, Dale. 2014. *Reason in a Dark Time. Why the Struggle Against Climate Change Failed – and What It Means for Our Future*. Oxford: Oxford University Press.

Jojola, Ted S. 2013. "Indigenous Planning: Towards a Seven Generation Model." In *Reclaiming Indigenous Planning*, edited by Ryan Walker, Ted Jojola, and David Natcher, 457–472. Montreal: McGill-Queens University Press.

Kimmerer, Robin Wall. 2013a. *Returning the Gift. What Does Earth Ask of Us*? Center for Humans and Nature. (www.humansandnature.org/earth-ethic-robin-kimmerer).

2013b. *Braiding Sweetgrass: Indigenous Wisdom, Scientific Knowledge and the Teachings of Plants*. Minneapolis, MN: Milkweed Editions.

2018. "*Mishkos Kenomagwen*, the Lessons of Grass: Restoring Reciprocity with the Good Green Earth." In *Traditional Ecological Knowledge. Learning from Indigenous Practices for Environmental Sustainability*, edited by Melissa K. Nelson and Daniel Shilling. 27–56. Cambridge: Cambridge University Press.

Kolm, Serge-Christophe. 2006. "Reciprocity: Its Scope, Rationales and Consequences." In *Handbook of the Economics of Giving, Altruism and Reciprocity, vol. 1*, edited by Serge-Chrisophe Kolm and J. Mercier Ythier, 371–541. Amsterdam: Elsevier.

Lakhani, Nina. 2021. "'A Death Sentence': Indigenous Climate Activists Denounce COP26 Deal." *The Guardian*, https://bit.ly/4979npl

Maffie, James. 2014. *Aztec Philosophy. Understanding a World in Motion.* Boulder, CO: University Press of Colorado.

Marx, Karl. 1992. *Capital Volume 1*, translated by Ben Fowkes. London: Penguin.

Mauss, Marcel. 2002. *The Gift*, translated by W.D. Halls. London: Routledge Classics.

National Geographic Society. 2018. *Indigenous Peoples Defend Earth's Biodiversity—But They're in Danger.* National Geographic News Article. www.nationalgeographic.com/environment/article/can-indigenous-land-stewardship-protect-biodiversity-.

Nichols, Robert. 2020. *Theft is Property! Dispossession and Critical Theory.* Durham, NC: Duke University Press.

Scott, Conrad. 2016. "(Indigenous) Place and Time as Formal Strategy: Healing Immanent Crisis in the Dystopias of Eden Robinson and Richard Van Camp." *Extrapolation* 57, no. 1–2: 73–93.

Shotwell, Alexis. 2019. "Claiming Bad Kin." *Bearing* no. 3: 8–11, http://archive.blackwoodgallery.ca/publications/SDUK_03-Bearing.pdf

Simpson, Audra. 2017. "The Ruse of Consent and the Anatomy of 'refusal': Cases from Indigenous North America and Australia." *Postcolonial Studies* 20: 18–33.

Singer, Peter. 2002. *One World: The Ethics of Globalization.* New Haven, CT: Yale University Press.

Stewart-Harawira, Makere. 2005. *The New Imperial Order: Indigenous Responses to Globalization.* London: Zed Books

2016. "Returning the Sacred: Indigenous Ontologies in Perilous Times." In *Radical Human Ecology: Intercultural and Indigenous Approaches*, edited by Lewis Williams, Rose Roberts and Alastair MacIntosh, 73–90. London: Routledge.

Táíwò, Olúfẹ́mi O. 2022. *Reconsidering Reparations.* Oxford: Oxford University Press.

Tuck, Eve and C. Ree. 2013. "A Glossary of Haunting." In *Handbook of Autoethnography*, edited by Stacey Holman Jones, Tony E. Adams, and Carolyn Ellis, 639–658. Walnut Creek, CA: Left Coast Press.

Tuck, Eve and K. Wayne Yang. 2012. "Decolonization Is Not a Metaphor" *Decolonization: Indigeneity, Education & Society* 1, no. 1: 1–40.

Tully, James. 2020. "On Resurgence and Transformative Reconciliation." In *Plants, People and Places: The Roles of Ethnobotany and Ethnoecology in Indigenous Peoples' Land Rights in Canada and Beyond*, edited by Nancy Turner, 402–418. Montreal: McGill-Queen's University Press.

Veracini, Lorenzo. 2015. *The Settler Colonial Present.* Basingstoke: Palgrave Macmillan.

Vizenor, Gerald, ed. 2008. *Survivance: Narratives of Native Presence.* Lincoln, NE: University of Nebraska Press.

Warnke, Georgia. 2011. "The Hermeneutic Circle Versus Dialogue." *Review of Metaphysics* 65, no. 1: 91–112.

Whyte, Kyle Powys. 2017. "Our Ancestors' Dystopia Now: Indigenous Conservation and the Anthropocene." In *The Routledge Companion to the Environmental Humanities*, edited by Ursula K. Heise, 206–15. London: Routledge.

2018. "Indigenous Science (Fiction) for the Anthropocene: Ancestral Dystopias and Fantasies of Climate Change Crises." *Environment and Planning E: Nature and Space* 1, no. 1–2: 224–242.

2020. "Too Late for Indigenous Climate Justice: Ecological and Relational Tipping Points." *WIREs Climate Change* 11: doi: 10.1002/wcc.603

2021. "Against Crisis Epistemology." In *Routledge Handbook of Critical Indigenous Studies*, edited by Hokowhitu, Brendan, Aileen Moreton-Robinson, Linda Tuhiwai Smith, Chris Andersen, and Steve Larkin, 52–64. Abingdon, Oxon: Routledge.

Whyte, Kyle, Chris Caldwell, and Marie Schaefer. 2018. "Indigenous Lessons about Sustainability Are Not Just for 'All Humanity.'" In *Sustainability. Approaches to Environmental Justice and Social Power*, edited by Julie Sze, 149–179. New York, NY: New York University Press.

Whyte, Kyle, Jared L. Talley, and Julia D. Gibson. 2019. "Indigenous Mobility Traditions, Colonialism, and the Anthropocence." *Mobilities* 14, no. 3: 319–335.

Whyte, Kyle, and Shelbi Nahwilet Meissner. 2021. "Without Land, Decolonizing American Philosophy is Impossible." In *Decolonizing American Philosophy*, edited by Corey McCall and Phillip McReynolds 37–61. New York, NY: SUNY Press.

Yusoff, Kathryn. 2018. *A Billion Black Anthropocenes or None*. Minneapolis, MN: University of Minnesota Press.

3

Intergenerational Justice and the Environment in Africa

Workineh Kelbessa

1 Introduction

Very few authors have studied the nature of intergenerational relations in Africa (Wiredu 1994; Murove 2004; Kelbessa 2011; Behrens 2012, 2013; Mbonda and Ngosso 2021; Dennis 2022). Among those that have, some have focused on the nature of moral obligations to future generations of humans, while others have emphasised that the fact that the African worldview recognises the interdependence of all natural entities means that intergenerational justice in Africa recognises justice among different species.

Taking some examples from different parts of Africa, this paper explores how Africans envision their futures and promote intergenerational justice. Africa is not a homogenous geographical unit, and nor does it have a single, unified African worldview or overarching view of life and the universe. We can find different conceptions of the role of the current generation's responsibility for the future generation in different parts of Africa. Nonetheless, different cultural groups have much in common, and I will examine how some African cultural groups view life and the universe and care about future generations. In particular, I will examine the question: what kind of world should the present generation leave to future generations in Africa?

In Section 2, I will investigate ways in which Africans fulfil their obligations to future generations. I will explore whether non-human animals have a place in Africa's conception of intergenerational justice in Section 3. In Section 4, I will examine the relationship between intergenerational justice and sustainability in Africa. I will provide concluding remarks at the end of this chapter.

An earlier version of this paper was presented at the International Conference on Justice Between Generations: Asian, African, Indigenous, and Western Perspectives held in Montreal at Concordia University, from 29 September to 1 October 2021. I would like to thank those present for their questions and comments. Furthermore, I am grateful to the Africa Oxford Initiative, University of Oxford, for its support.

2 Moral Obligations to Future Generations

2.1 The African Concept of Time and Intergenerational Justice

John Mbiti, a Kenyan Theologian, argues that Africans lack the concept of the distant future. For traditional Africans, time is just a two-dimensional phenomenon with a long past, or *Zamani*, and a present, or *Sasa*. He maintains that people are not interested in events that lie in the future beyond, at most, two years from now (Mbiti 1996, 70). He stresses that the future is not real because it has not yet been experienced. Alexis Kagame (1996) holds a similar view. The French philosopher, sociologist, and anthropologist, Lucien Lévy-Bruhl, states that primitive people lack any concept of the future because of their inability to abstract from a series of experiential events to conceive a unilinear order of succession in which such events occur (1923, 123–24, 445–46). A critical examination of the African conception of time shows that this is not true. As I have argued elsewhere, 'If we let this view stand, the Oromo [and other African cultural groups] could not have any concept of the future' (Kelbessa 2011, 97–98).

Yet, Africans and other Indigenous people in the world use many different signs, including atmospheric conditions, changes in wind direction, higher than normal ambient temperatures, behavioural changes of animals, phonological changes in plant species, the dropping of immature fruits by certain tree species, the appearance of insects, astrological phenomena, the migration of birds, and the flowering of plants (see Shoko 2012; Sanni et al. 2012; Ayal et al. 2015) to understand local environmental and climate changes, and predict the future, organise their lives around seasonal calendars, and deal with future events.

2.2 Intergenerational Justice in Africa

Various cultural groups in Africa recognise the moral obligation of the present generation to future generations. For instance, the Oromo people of Ethiopia, the largest ethnic group in the country, have developed intergenerational justice that requires the current generation to provide adequate life prospects for future generations, including future human *and* non-human generations. The present generation is required to leave a healthy environment for the generations to come. But what is the basis of the Oromo people's obligations to future generations?

It is the responsibility of the present generation to protect and preserve the land and pass it on to future generations. This obligation is based on the idea that the destruction of the land will jeopardise the prospects of future generations. The Oromo people not only care about their children's vital interests, but also about the survival of human beings in the world.

It is worth noting that Oromo ethics in particular, and African ethics in general, do not require the current generation to pay attention to the rights and interests of future individuals but, rather, to those of future communities.[1] Therefore, it is not necessary to know the exact nature and needs of autonomous individuals, since the focus is on groups, that is, generational communities. Thus, the current generation can have obligations to anyone who will be a member of the future generations' community. The Oromo of Ethiopia believe that we know enough about the well-being of people in the future to act responsibly on their behalf, because, like people today, people in the future are people and, as such, need a healthy environment (Kelbessa 2011). Consequently, those countries that irresponsibly aggravate climate change ought to learn from this ethical principle, which highlights the intergenerational dimensions of global climate change, and to pay attention to the well-being of future generations over and above their own current interests.

The other important basis of obligation is divine punishment. It is believed that *Waaqa* (God) will punish those who disturb the cosmic order and needlessly degrade the land beyond recovery:

> The land is a blessing and the source of survival. *Waaqa* allows humans and other creatures to use the land. Accordingly, the people should not ravage the actual purpose of *Waaqa* and the whole history and order of things. Thus, the Oromo people believe that if one does not look after the land, one is not only frustrating his own desire instrumentally to have good land in the future but is also undermining future generations and the cosmic order. (Kelbessa 2011, 79)

Therefore, to a certain extent, religion is the basis of obligations to future generations. The Oromo do not view land as mere property that can be used by humans without restrictions. The land has intrinsic value and deserves respect and protection.

The Oromo term *handhuuraa* also shows the responsibility of a father towards a newborn baby. *Handhuuraa* means umbilical cord. During the

[1] Likewise, Edith Weiss stressed the need to focus on group rights rather than the individual rights of people in the future. "Intergenerational planetary rights may be regarded as group rights, as distinct from individual rights, in the sense that generations hold these rights as groups in relation to other generations-past, present and future. They exist regardless of the number and identity of individuals making up each generation. When held by members of the present generation, they acquire attributes of individual rights in the sense that there is identifiable interest of individuals that the rights protect. However, those interests derive from the fact that those living now are members of the present generation and have rights in relation to other generations to use and benefit from the planet" (Weiss 1990, 203). Richard Slaughter (1994, 1084), for his part, argues that our organic continuity with future people through our shared genetic material can help us to talk about their rights.

name-giving ceremony, the father gives his newborn baby a heifer (Kelbessa 2011, 98). His child will use this heifer in the future, so the father cannot take the heifer back. Furthermore, *finna* – the term for social development – stands for 'the legacy of the past which each generation inherits from its forefathers and which it transforms; it is the fertile patrimony held in trust by the present generation which it will enrich and bequeath to future generations…' (Kassam, as cited in Jalata 1996, 112).

The African worldview recognises intergenerational solidarity among the dead, the living, and the yet-to-be-born (see Herskovits 1967; Wiredu 1994, 46; Murove 2004, 184; Behrens, 2012, 203 and 2018, 53–54).[2] In Africa, the current generation has direct and indirect obligations to future generations. First of all, past, present, and future generations communally own the land. One generation doesn't have an absolute ownership right over the environment. Africans see land as a communal or shared resource. They subscribe to a diverse collective ownership of land. In Cameroon, for example, the people see land as a gift from God, owned by the entire community whose every member community should have a place to live and farm (Mbonda and Ngosso 2021, 11). No generation can be the sole owner of the land. The next generation should be guaranteed the ability to live upon and to live off the land, as well as to make a living from it (Mbonda and Ngosso 2021, 11). According to Ernest-Marie Mbonda and Thierry Ngosso, the current generation has three obligations for future generations: to ensure the best birth conditions, to ensure the best education, and to preserve the planet (Mbonda and Ngosso 2021, 7). In the African worldview, individuals may privately own livestock and chattels (van Rooy 1997, 102).

[2] Intergenerational ethics is not unique to Africa. The seventh-generation principle common in Indochina and the Americas (Goodwin 1994; Terreblanche 2018, 182) states that current decisions should lead to a sustainable world for the next seven generations. Edmund Burke, Anglo-Irish statesman and philosopher, held a similar view in *Reflections on the Revolution in France (1790)*:

> [Society] is a partnership in all science; a partnership in all art; a partnership in every virtue and in all perfection. As the ends of such a partnership cannot be obtained in many generations, it becomes a partnership not only between those who are living, but between those who are living, those who are dead, and those who are to be born. (Burke 2003, 81–82)

Daniel Callahan, an American philosopher (1981), put forward a similar point of view. "That we exist at all puts us in debt to those who conceived us – our parents – and in debt to the society in which we were born, without which we might have been conceived but could not have survived (for our parents were not sufficient unto themselves). We could not exist had not someone and some society taken some responsibility for our welfare" (1981, 76–77). For Callahan, the provisions of past generations make the existence of the present generation possible. "To live at all is to be linked in an inextricable way to the past, and to be a determinant of future generations" (Callahan 1981, 77).

In African worldviews, contemporary people should respect their ancestors and leave a healthy and usable environment for future generations. They ought to preserve an environment which is rich in biodiversity for posterity. In addition, the current generation ought to be grateful to, and follow the example of, past generations in regard to leaving behind a healthy land. This indicates an indirect moral obligation to future generations.

As Kwasi Wiredu rightly points out, one can use some of the resources of this one system of reality to support human life. But two major considerations determine the practicality of this activity: first, whether it is animate or inanimate, no object that may be under the control of a super-human force or power can be overexploited; second, land – an important resource that does not belong to an individual but to an entire clan – should be protected and passed down from generation to generation (Wiredu 1994, 46).[3] So, land is not just a resource that can be exploited without restriction, but is also a resource for living in harmony. In traditional Africa, if the chief or head of a clan misappropriated or squandered public or communal funds, the public could remove him from office and choose another person to take his place (Gyekye 1996, 101). Also, as I have pointed out elsewhere (Kelbessa 2011), the Oromo – Ethiopia's largest ethnic group – uses the ethical principle of *saffuu* or *ceeraa fokko* (mutual relationship in the cosmic order) to govern the use of natural resources. No one can needlessly exploit his fellow human beings and natural resources. As Kwasi Wiredu persuasively argues:

> [o]f all the duties owed to the ancestors, none is more imperious than that of husbanding the resources of the land so as to leave it in good shape for posterity. In this moral scheme the rights of the unborn play such a cardinal role that any traditional African would be nonplussed by the debate in Western philosophy as to the existence of such rights. In the upshot there is a two-sided concept of stewardship in the management of the environment involving obligations to both ancestors and descendants which motivates environmental carefulness, all things being equal. (Wiredu 1994, 46)

Following in the past generation's footsteps, the present generation should pass a healthy environment onwards to future generations. It should avoid the mismanagement and unsustainable use of natural resources.

In their work on *ukama* (relationality), Benezet Bujo (2001), a diocesan priest from the Democratic Republic of the Congo, and Munyaradzi Felix

[3] Likewise, for Native Americans, 'the Earth does not belong to human beings; Human Beings belong to the Earth.' 'This we know: the earth does not belong to man: man belongs to the earth. … Whatever befalls the earth, befalls the sons of the earth. Man did not weave the web of life: he is merely as strand in it. Whatever he does to the web, he does to himself' (Chief Seattle, cited in Weiss, 1990, 198).

Murove (2004), a Zimbabwean scholar, hold similar views. *Ukama* is a Shona word that means relatedness. According to Murove, *ubuntu* is a concrete expression of *ukama*. However, *ukama* traces our human relationality to the natural environment through totemism or what Murove (2009) calls totemic ancestorhood. *Ukama* shows humanity's connectedness to the non-human world. Totemic ancestorhood drives this connectedness. After discussing the role of *ubuntu* and *ukama*, Lesley Le Grange identifies two claims about *ukama* (*ubuntu* and *botho*) as an ecophilosophy/ecosophy:

> The first is that beliefs about ancestors entail a sense in which past, present and future generations are all part of the moral community. The second is that the fundamental relatedness of beings encapsulated by *ukama* includes a sense of relatedness with other natural entities, not just persons. (Le Grange 2015, 306)

The first claim reminds the current generation to fulfil its obligation to future generations. Relatedness to all-natural entities also helps us promote environmental well-being. For Le Grange, it is 'because it has intrinsic value – that nature needs to be cared for in the now/ present. Such as ecophilosophy/ecosophy is consistent with the DEM [Deep Ecology Movement] platform principles' (Le Grange 2015, 307).

Ukama has some connection with the primordial existence of ecophylia in African traditional thought which, strangely enough, is somewhat supported by Charles Darwin's theory of evolution – most especially in his later book, *The Descent of Man,* first published in 1871, wherein Darwin demonstrates the common origins of humanity and nature (Murove, personal communication, 29 September 2015). Murove claims that while *ukama* recognises human nature based on ontological relationality, the totemist element inherent in this relationality embraces cosmological or ecological relationality as inseparable from what it means, to be human. For this reason, an authentic understanding of African ontology and cosmology will be based on the assumption that the existence of beings is facilitated by the existence of other beings. In this regard, a genuine understanding of the community would have to postulate the primacy of relatedness and interrelatedness as the enduring principle of existence. According to Murove:

> [t]he life experience of the current generation is understood as being grounded in the past, and ... the present will contribute to its own existence into the future when it has become the past. Through anamnestic solidarity, the communal life of the living (the present) and that of the ancestors (the past) is re-enacted as a gift to be shared and passed on to posterity. (Murove 2004, 184)

Anamnestic solidarity is solidarity with future generations based on the memory of the past. According to Gelfand, 'ukama is an articulation of anamnestic solidarity because a person "owes his (sic) personality and character to his mudzimu (ancestor)'" (Gelfand 198, 18; quoted in Le Grange 2015, 306). Bujo also recognised anamnestic solidarity in African ethics 'which involves remembering one's ancestors' (2001, 34). The concept of anamnesis is used to show the oneness of past, present, and future generations.

In short, what is important in Africa's intergenerational justice is that although future generations cannot directly pay back what the current generation does for them, they incur the duty to respect their obligations to the generations that preceded them, and to do the same thing for the generations to come. According to Kevin Gary Behrens, the backward-looking concept of responsibility to future generations is probably one of the most important 'contributions African thought can make to our conception of moral obligations to the future' (Behrens 2012, 187).

Certain African proverbs show the responsibility of the current generation for future generations: 'The world is not ours, the earth is not ours. It's a treasure we hold in trust for future generations.' This proverb is common among various cultural groups in Africa. '*Rigita thi wega; ndwaheiruio ni aciari; ni ngombo uhetwo ni ciana ciaku*. You must treat the earth well; it was not given to you by your parents; it is loaned to you by your children.' (Kikuyu proverb.) Native Americans, the Oglala Sioux people, have a similar proverb: 'Treat the earth well. We do not inherit the earth from our ancestors. We borrow it from it from our children.' Another African proverb emphasises the need to take care of children. 'The child who is not embraced by the village will burn it down to feel its warmth.' This African proverb suggests that rural communities need to love, educate, and listen to young people. Otherwise, uneducated and neglected young people can threaten the survival of the village community.

In the African worldview, individuals can only be human beings, survive, and be complete, in their respective communities with others (Munyaka and Motlhabi 2009, 68; Dolamo 2013, 8). In other words, '[i]ndividuals cannot survive outside of their respective communities in as much as fish cannot survive outside of water' (Dolamo 2013, 8). In many cultural groups in Africa, the community embraces past, present, and future generations. According to the African worldview, currently living human and non-human beings, ancestors, the as-yet unborn, and the natural world, are interconnected. The living elders of the clan and ancestors can influence the thought, feelings, and behaviour of the people.

Here, one might wonder if the three generations belong to the same community, or if they are discrete communities, such that there is a relationship of responsibility not only within but between them. The response to this issue depends on the conceptualisations of existing physical and nonphysical beings. Children – the future generation – will soon be the current generation, and in a few years, the present generation will be the ancestors. There is no clear distinction between the physical and metaphysical. So, the ancestral community is not the same as the living community, but the two interact. Regarding the future generation, the basic idea is that humans are the guardians of a world that is not theirs. Therefore, they are under an obligation to take care of it and pass it on to the next generation.

It is worth noting that *ubuntu* includes restorative justice and intergenerational ethics (Terreblanche 2018). The term *ubuntu* in Nguni languages (in Zulu and Xhosa), the term *botho* in the Sotho languages, and the term *huhnu* in some of the languages of Zimbabwe have a similar meaning: humanness. It is present in almost all African languages in South Africa under a variety of different names. '*Ubuntu* is from "IsiNguni"; in Sesotho it is *Botho*; in XiTsonga the word is translated as *Vumunhi*; while in TshiVenda it is *Uhuthu*' (Munyaka and Motlhabi 2009, 63–84; see also Dolamo 2013, 1–10). *Ubuntu* ethics teaches us how human beings are related to one another, as well as our duties to different generations, both human and non-human (Le Grange 2015, 304).

One of the ethical axioms of *ubu-ntu* is 'avoid killing, promote life'. If these two are combined, then the living have an ethical obligation to make life liveable for the next generation. This cannot be fulfilled without concern and care for the environment. Similarly, Puleng LenkaBula insists that the following Sesotho aphorism shows the relationship between human life and ecological life: '*motho ke motho ka batho ba bang*: no person is complete in him/herself; s/he is fully human in as far as s/he remains a part of the web of life, including creation and the earth' (2008, 378).

3 Do We Have Moral Obligations to Non-Human Animals?

Some writers argue that the African worldview is anthropocentric, and that Africans have direct responsibilities or obligations only to fellow human beings. For these authors, respect for persons, and the importance of community, character, and morality, are some of the components of *ubuntu*. According to Penny Enslin and Kai Horsthemke:

> [s]ome of the values and principles claimed to be emphasised by *ubuntu* are dubious. For example, the assertion that it fosters 'respect for the environment' is questionable. A concern for the environment could be fostered only based on human benefits and would therefore not amount to an acknowledgement of the intrinsic value of nature or the environment, let alone 'respect.' In fact, in focusing exclusively on human beings, *ubuntu* is by definition speciesist. (Enslin and Horsthemke 2004, 548; see also Horsthemke 2015 and 2017)

Kai Horsthemke maintains that animals lack the prerequisite humanness and *ubuntu* ethics cannot prove that human beings have a direct obligation to animals. For him, '*ubuntu* does not, indeed cannot, concern animals directly-obviously not as moral agents, but not as moral recipients either' (Horsthemke 2017, 133). So, his conclusion is that, in *ubuntu* ethics, humans have indirect concerns about non-human animals.

On the other hand, while *ubuntu* seems to be anthropocentric on the surface, various scholars have shown that *ubuntu* ethics does not exclude non-human animals and the natural environment (Ramose 2002; Le Grange 2015; Etieyibo 2017). For them, human beings cannot exist outside physical nature, while u*buntu* both prohibits the irresponsible exploitation of the environment or natural resources, and requires humans to protect the environment. Le Grange also argues that '*ubuntu*/*botho* has great promise as an ecophilosophy/ecosophy … an anthropocentric reading of *ubuntu* is flawed and that by definition it means relatedness to (or embeddedness in) the web of life' (Le Grange 2015, 308).

Thaddeus Metz for his part argues that African modal relationalism, *ubuntu* ethics, is not speciesist, because 'the reason for favouring human beings, in cases where their urgent interests are at stake, is not the mere fact that they are human' (Metz 2017, 169). Metz finds that, unlike mainstream anthropocentrism, African modal relationalism conceives moral status in 'the act that typical human beings have certain abilities to commune as subjects'. Human beings and 'beings such as chimps, elephants, and dolphins do share this capacity' (2017, 169) although not to the same degree.

One can also raise the following question to the critics of African animal ethics: what do Africans do when their livestock get sick? Do they kill them? Africans do their best to try to treat sick animals. Surely, dogs used for hunting were not left to die when they were ill. Also, some Ethiopians do not sacrifice the animals they raised because they consider them their own children. They sell them in the market and buy other animals to sacrifice for various purposes. The Oromo people of Ethiopia also believe that humans have obligations to non-human animals. They have formulated animal ethics and laws that protect the rights of animals. Animals are not merely resources for the benefit of human beings but have the right to live, and ought not to be harmed or killed for no reason. In Borana, southern Oromia, owners who overexploit, injure, and kill their livestock are punished (for details see Kelbessa 2014, and 2018a and b). Likewise, wild animals have the right to live and to drink water. It is not considered right to go hunting at night at water sources. Furthermore, for the Oromo and Kom people of Cameroon, it would be wrong to deplete a species (Kelbessa 2011; Tosam 2019, 179).

The Oromo conception of justice is extended to both human beings and animals. The traditional version of Oromo social ethics teaches that no one deserves to be abused. The Oromo not only view justice, integrity, and respect as human virtues that apply to human beings, but extend them to non-human species and Mother Earth.

In general, African worldviews emphasise the interconnectedness and interdependence of human beings, non-human species, and ecosystems:

> African worldviews regard human beings and the nonhuman world as extensions of each other. They do not regard the earth as a commodity, as the source of survival. In African worldviews, well-being is relational, as the well-being of humanity cannot be achieved without the well-being of the earth. They are related. They are part of the same whole. In African worldviews, human beings are in nature and part of nature in balance with the whole. When human beings see themselves as outside of nature, it is purely for purpose of conceptual need. The purpose here is to engage in conceptual analysis. Even here humans are still in nature. (Kelbessa 2018b, 321)

The interrelatedness of the components of the natural environment is not limited to, but transcends, generations. The interconnected web of life is the basis of our environmental moral obligations to future generations. We also have a moral obligation to protect the environment for present and future generations.

4 Intergenerational Justice and Sustainability in Africa

The United Nations World Commission on Environment and Development (WCED) defined the term 'sustainable development' as follows: 'Sustainable development is development that meets the needs of the present without compromising the ability of future generations to meet their own needs' (WCED 1987, 43). Does this definition meet the African conception of sustainable development?

As I argued elsewhere (2021 and 2024), the African worldview values and supports the sustainable use and conservation of natural resources. Intergenerational ethics in Africa teaches that it is the responsibility of the present generation to protect the environment in order to ensure the survival of both current and future generations. It also teaches that when there are no middle-aged people in the family, the younger generation should support the elderly (Jecker 2021).

Some cultural groups in Africa have used the ethical principles of caring, sharing, and cooperation to address intra-generational injustice. To mention a few examples, the Oromo of Ethiopia, the Akan people of Ghana, and *ubuntu* societies in Southern African countries have formulated fine laws and ethical principles that require the members of the communities to support individuals in need (for details, see Kelbessa 2024; Tutu 1999; Makward 2007; Gyekye 2011). Failure to make one's fair contribution is reproachable and punishable by law. In *ubuntu* ethics, one cannot realise one's true self by exploiting and deceiving a fellow human being. *Ubuntu* ethics discourages self-centredness and promotes mutual support. It would be wrong to be greedy and selfish.

The people in different parts of Africa have used proverbs to encourage their children to conserve resources for future use. Consider the following proverbs:

- 'He who eats an egg foregoes a future meal of chicken soup.' '*Ikusasa liyabekelwa*: always store some for the future' (Ndlovu and Ncube 2014, 211), (Ndebele proverb, Zimbabwe).
- '*Ifaan guurratanii, dukkanaan daakkatan*: one who collects crops in daylight will grind during the night' (Oromo proverb).
- '*Ol kaayan malee olka'aniif hin fuudhan*: if you don't save anything, you cannot pick it up when you stand up from sitting' (Oromo proverb).

This last Oromo proverb implies that one can only take away tomorrow what s/he puts away today.

In the African worldview, development is not only about economic growth. Material well-being, physical well-being, mental well-being, spiritual well-being, social well-being, and environmental well-being are the necessary components of development. It is worth noting that some Western philosophers have also argued that economic growth is not the ultimate goal of development. It is one means that is important to improve one's life. For example, Denis Goulet emphasises that, despite the need for an increase in the number of goods and services (1997, 24, 1168; 2002, 22, 29), the real indicator of development is qualitative human enrichment, *not* an increase in production or material well-being. Likewise, John Stuart Mill (1848a, b) and John Maynard Keynes (1930) do not consider economic growth as an end in itself. According to Mill:

> [i]t is scarcely necessary to remark that a stationary condition of capital and population implies no stationary state of human improvement. There would be as much scope as ever for all kinds of mental culture, and more and social progress; as much room for improving the Art of Living, and much more likelihood of its being improved when minds ceased to be engrossed by the art of getting on (1848b, 756).

Keynes (1930) also stresses that when we reach a certain material standard of living, we should focus on the art of living rather than the means of life.

Africa's conception of sustainable development does not ignore the interests of non-human generations but focuses on the interests of human and non-human generations and the well-being of the environment. So, this view differs from the WCED's definition of the term 'sustainable development', which emphasises the needs of human beings. But the stark reality is that African governments have not paid sufficient attention to African perceptions of the needs of future human and non-human generations. They have not established strong institutions that can play a role in protecting, preserving, and defending the interests and needs of future generations (Olawuyi 2021, 641). There is no agency or commission directly responsible for protecting the interests and needs of future generations in Africa.

Certain governments have used the linkage approach to protect, preserve, and defend the interests/needs of present and future generations in accordance with the existing political systems and institutions. They established the Ministry of Environment in the 1990s and after to address the concerns of both current and future generations. The concerns of future generations are indirectly implemented by institutions, such as through environmental protection (Olawuyi 2021, 647).

However, as Damilola Olawuyi (2021) notes, the linkage approach has not been efficacious. Real progress has not been made by the prevailing paradigm of incorporating intergenerational equity as part of the broader mandate of environmental protection and sustainable development in Africa: 'Lack of continuity, low levels of transparency, inadequate funding, limited engagement with youth, lack of functional independence, lack of coordination, and lack of commitment' (Olawuyi 2021, 649) have hampered the linkage approach to intergenerational justice in its various efforts to make a difference in the protection and defence of the concerns of future generations. The establishment of a focal institution or office to provide holistic assessment, review, and monitoring of various intergenerational equity issues for future generations is important if intergenerational equity issues are to be addressed. As Olawuyi (2021) correctly states, appointing distinct 'Parliamentary Commissioners for Future Generations' or 'Ombudsmen for the Environment or Future Generations' is necessary if the job of institutionalising sustainable development in policy-making is to be undertaken successfully. This measure can help African governments to revive and implement Indigenous African intergenerational justice.

On the other hand, the destruction of cultural heritage will hamper the needs of future generations in Africa. Various militant and terrorist groups, including the Boko Haram group in West Africa, the Al Shabaab in East Africa, the Ansar Dine in the historic Malian city of Timbuktu, the Tigray People's Liberation Front in Ethiopia, and the like, have destroyed cultural sites, stolen cultural artefacts, and killed the custodians of cultural heritage, which in turn will have negative impacts on future generations in Africa. 'The destruction of cultural heritage might mean that future generations may never be able to enjoy the benefit of shared cultural identity showcased through ancient African museums, mausoleums, and cultural sites' (Olawuyi 2021, 641). So, African governments ought to do their utmost to protect and preserve cultural heritage for the benefit of present and future generations. They should also protect forests and national parks that can help current and future generations of animals survive.

5 Conclusion

Unlike some environmental ethicists who believe that only obligations to posterity and not the value of non-human creatures matter, Africans have a deep concern for both humans and non-human creatures. They have developed moral principles that deal with future generations (both future human and non-human generations) and the preservation of the natural environment and its resources throughout their history. According to African worldviews, the present generation is under an obligation to maintain the basis on which the survival of future generations depends. The excessive use of natural resources beyond their limits is wrong and reduces the chances of survival for future generations. Therefore, members of the current generation should behave responsibly toward the environment.

Since holistic thinking and the ethical obligations of the present to future human and non-human generations are central aspects of the African worldview, an African worldview can promote sustainable development that takes into account economic, social, and environmental aspects. African policymakers should be cognisant of African perceptions of the moral obligations of the present to future generations and environmental well-being. They should aim at the critical appropriation of Indigenous knowledge and the integration of Indigenous and modern scientific knowledge to promote environmentally and socially sound development.

Bibliography

Ayal, Desalegn Yayeh, et al. 2015. "Opportunities and Challenges of Indigenous Biotic Weather Forecasting among the Borena Herders of Southern Ethiopia." *SpringerPlus* 4, no.1: 617.

Behrens, Kevin Gary. 2012. "Moral Obligations towards Future Generations in African Thought." *Journal of Global Ethics* 8, no. 2–3: 179–191.

2013. "Interspecific, Intergenerational Justice in African Thought." In *Is Planet Earth Green?* edited by Gabriela Mádlo, 90–99. Oxford: Inter-Disciplinary Press.
2018. "An African Account of the Moral Obligation to preserve Biodiversity." In *African Philosophy and Environmental Conservation*, edited by Jonathan O. Chimakonam, 42–57. London: Routledge.
Bujo, Benezet. 2001. *Foundations of an African Ethic: Beyond the Universal Claims of Western Morality*. New York, NY: The Crossroad Publishing Company.
Burke, Edmund 2003. "Reflections on the Revolution in France (1790)." In *Reflections on the Revolution in France*, edited by Frank M. Turner, 81–82. New Haven, CT: Yale University Press.
Callahan, Daniel. 1981. "What Obligation Do We have to Future Generations?" In *Responsibilities to Future Generations*, edited by Ernest Partridge 73–88. Buffalo, NY: Prometheus Books
Dennis, Otto. 2022. "African Environmental Intuitionism and the Obligation to Posterity." In *African Philosophy in an Intercultural Perspective*, edited by Anke Graneß, Edwin Etieyibo, and Franz Gmainer-Pranzl, 181–190. Stuttgart: J. B. Metzler.
Dolamo, Ramathate. 2013. "*Botho/Ubuntu*: the Heart of African Ethics." *Scriptura* 112: 1–10.
Enslin, Penny and Kai Horsthemke. 2004. "Can Ubuntu Provide a Model for Citizenship Education in African Democracies?" *Comparative Education* 40, no. 4: 545–558.
Etieyibo, Edwin. 2017. "Ubuntu and the Environment." In *The Palgrave Handbook of African Philosophy*, edited by Adeshina Afolayan and Toyin Falola, 633–657. New York, NY: Palgrave Macmillan.
Goodwin, Brian. 1994. *How the Leopard Changed Spots: The Evolution of Complexity*. Princeton, NJ: Princeton University Press.
Goulet, Denis. 1997. "Development Ethics: A New Discipline." *International Journal of Social Economics* 24, no. 11: 1160–1171.
2002. "What is a Just Economy in a Globalized World?" *International Journal of Social Economics* 29, no. 1–2: 10–25.
Gyekye, Kwame. 1996. *African Cultural Values: An Introduction*. Accra: Sankofa Publishing Company.
2011. "African Ethics." In *Stanford Encyclopedia of Philosophy*, edited by Edward Zalta. http://plato.stanford.edu./entries/african-ethics/.
Herskovits, Melville J. 1967. *Dahomey: An Ancient West African Kingdom, Vol. I*. Evanston, IL: Northwestern University Press.
Horsthemke, Kai. 2015. *Animals and African Ethics*. London: Palgrave Macmillan.
2017. "Animals and the Challenges of Ethnocentrism." In *Animals, Race, and Multiculturalism*, edited by Luis Cordeiro-Rodrigues and Les Mitchell, 121–146. Cham: Palgrave Macmillan.
Jalata, Asafa. 1996. "The Struggle for Knowledge: The Case of Emergent Oromo Studies." *African Studies Review* 39, no. 2: 95–123.
Jecker, Nancy S. 2021. "Intergenerational Ethics in Africa: Duties to Older Adults in Skipped Generation Households." *Developing World Bioethics* 00: 1–10, doi.org/10.1111/dewb.12325.
Kagame, Alexis. 1996. "The Empirical Apperception of Time and the Conception of History in Bantu Thought." In *African Philosophy: A Classical Approach*, edited

by Parker English and Kibujjo M. Kalumba, 82–90. Upper Saddle River, NJ: Prentice Hall.

Kelbessa, Workineh. 2011. *Indigenous and Modern Environmental Ethics: A Study of the Indigenous Oromo Environmental Ethic and Modern Issues of Environment and Development. Ethiopian Philosophical Studies, Vol. I.* Washington, DC: The Council for Research in Values and Philosophy.

2014. "Can African Environmental Ethics Contribute to Environmental Policy in Africa?" *Environmental Ethics* 36, no. 1: 31–61.

2018a. "The Moral Status and Well-being of Animals in the Oromo Culture." In *Africa and Its Animals: Philosophical and Practical Perspectives*, edited by Rainer Ebert and Anteneh Roba, 129–144. Johannesburg: University of South Africa.

2018b. "Environmental Philosophy in African Traditions of Thought." *Environmental Ethics* 40: 309–323.

2021. "African Worldviews, Biodiversity Conservation and Sustainable Development." *Environmental Values* doi: 10.3197/096327121X16328186623922.

2024. "African Environmental Philosophy and the Quest for a Sustainable Future." In *The Sage Handbook of Global Sociology*, edited by Gurminder Bhambra, Lucy Mayblin, Kathryn Medien, and Mara Viveros-Vigoya, 507–522. Thousand Oaks, CA: Sage Publications.

Keynes, John Maynard. 1932. "Economic Possibilities for Our Children." In *Essays in Persuasion*, 358–373. New York, NY: Harcourt Brace.

Le Grange, Lesley. 2015. "Ubuntu/Botho as Ecophilosophy and Ecosophy." *Journal of Human Ecology* 49, no. 3: 301–308.

LenkaBula, Puleng. 2008. "Beyond Anthropocentricity – Botho/Ubuntu and the Quest for Economic and Ecological Justice in Africa." *Religion and Theology* 15: 375–394.

Lévy-Bruhl, Lucien. 1923. *Primitive Mentality.* Boston, MA: Beacon Press.

Makward, Edris. 2007. "African Culture in the Context of a Global World." *Présence Africaine* 175–177:630–645.

Mbiti, John S. 1996. "The Concept of Time." In *African Philosophy: A Classical Approach*, edited by Parker English and Kibujjo M. Kalumba, 66–80. Upper Saddle River, NJ: Prentice Hall.

Mbonda, Ernest-Marie and Thierry Ngosso. 2021. "Intergenerational Justice: An African perspective." In *The Oxford Handbook of Intergenerational Justice*, edited by Stephen M. Gardiner. New York, NY: Oxford University Press.

Metz, Thaddeus. 2017. "How to Ground Animal Rights on African Values: Reply to Horsthemke." *Journal of Animals Ethics* 7, no. 2: 163–174.

Mill, John Stuart. 1848a. *The Collected Works of John Stuart Mill, Volume II – The Principles of Political Economy I.* Toronto: Toronto University Press.

1848b. *The Collected Works of John Stuart Mill, Volume III – The Principles of Political Economy Part II.* Toronto: Toronto University Press.

Munyaka, Mluleki and Mokgethi Motlhabi. 2009. "Ubuntu and Its Socio-Moral Significance." In *African Ethics: An Anthology of Comparative and Applied Ethics*, edited by Munyradzi Felix Murove, 63–84. Scottsville: University of KwaZulu-Natal Press.

Murove, Munyaradzi Felix. 2004. "An African Commitment to Ecological Conservation: The Shona Concepts of Ukama and Ubuntu." *Mankind Quarterly* XLV: 195–215.

2009. "An African Environmental Ethic based on the Concepts of Ukama and Ubuntu." In *African Ethics: An Anthology of Comparative and Applied Ethics*, edited by Munyaradzi Felix Murove, 314–331. Scottsville: University of KwaZulu-Natal Press.

Ndlovu, Mbulisi and Bhekezakhe Ncube. 2014. "The Philosophy of Sustainable Development as Depicted in the Proverbs of Amandebele." *Journal of Emerging Trends in Educational Research and Policy Studies (JTERAPS)* 5, no.8: 209–213.

Olawuyi, Damilola. 2021. "Embedding Intergenerational Justice across Government: Regional Trends in Africa." In *Intergenerational Justice in Sustainable Development Treaty Implementation: Advancing Future Generations Rights through National Institutions*, edited by Marie-Claire Cordonier Segger, Marcel Szabó, and Alexander R. Harrington, 638–655. Cambridge: Cambridge University Press.

Ramose, Mogobe B. 2002. *African Philosophy through Ubuntu (revised edition)*. Harare: Mond Books.

Sanni, Shukurat Adunni, Kolapo Olatunji Oluwasemire, and Nnadozie Okonkwo Nnoli. 2012. "Traditional Capacity for Weather Forecast, Variability and Coping Strategies in the Front Line States of Nigeria." *Agricultural Sciences* 3, no. 4: 625–630.

Shoko, Kampion. 2012. "Indigenous Weather Forecasting Systems: A Case Study of the Biotic Weather Forecasting Indicators for Wards 12 and 13 in Mberengwa District Zimbabwe." *Journal of Sustainable Development in Africa* 14, no. 2: 92–114.

Slaughter, Richard A. 1994. "Why We Should Care for Future Generations Now." *Futures* 26, no. 10: 1077–1085.

Terreblanche, Christelle. 2018. "Ubuntu and the Struggle for an African Eco-Socialist Alternative." In *The Climate Crisis: South African and Global Democratic Eco-Socialist Alternatives*, edited by Vishwas Satgar, 168–189. Johannesburg: WITS University Press.

Tosam, Mbih Jerome. 2019. "African Environmental Ethics and Sustainable Development." *Open Journal of Philosophy* 9: 172–192.

Tutu, Desmond. 1999. *No Future without Forgiveness*. New York, NY: Random House.

van Rooy, J. A. 1997. "Scriptural Ethical Principles and Traditional African Ethics." *In die Skriflig* 31, no. 1–2: 93–106.

Weiss, Edith Brown. 1990. "Our Rights and Obligations to Future Generations for the Environment." *The American Journal of International Law* 84, no. 1 (Jan.): 198–207.

Wiredu, Kwasi. 1994. "Philosophy, Humankind and the Environment." In *Philosophy, Humanity and Ecology. Vol. I. Philosophy of Nature and Environmental Ethics*, edited by Oruka H. Odera, 30–48. Nairobi: ACTS Press and AAS.

World Commission on Environment and Development. 1987. *Our Common Future*. Oxford: Oxford University Press.

4

Reasonabilism, Homeostasis and Intergenerational Justice in African Thought

Joseph C. A. Agbakoba

1 Introduction

In this paper, I explore the conception of reasonability and harmony (especially homeostasis) and the notion of justice, and the related notions which they undergird (especially the aspect of intergenerational justice) from an African intercultural philosophical perspective that integrates a trans-colonial constructivist approach. I focus mainly on their nature and their evolutions from pre-colonial times in order to consider how they might be enriched by extant philosophical resources. I do not intend simply to exhume and exhibit pre-colonial African notions of reasonability, harmony, justice and related notions; rather, I seek also to reconceptualize them in a manner that is influenced or inspired by contemporaneous challenges and problems, as well as local and global knowledge resources.[1] My end, given the above, is to elucidate the idea of reasonability, harmony, justice and related ideas as developed in the contemporaneous African context of a dynamic market of ideas and influences occasioned by technology, globalization, post-independence, colonial history and pre-colonial or traditional philosophical resources, focusing mostly on the Igbo.

Reasonability emerges specifically from the African context, in which crucial limitations and inadequacies of the rationality of modernity were exposed as a result of their permitting or sponsoring the exclusion of non-Western humans: both in terms of the limitations of reason itself and in terms of the limitations of the conceptions of reason as a clinical and sanitized capability detached from affectivities, the conatus and concrete living.[2] However, one can

[1] For more details on this approach see Agbakoba 2021, 15–32 and Agbakoba 2019, 326–342.

[2] Reason conceived in this way permitted, or is compatible with, the instrumental treatment of the other, and accounts for various philosophers, such as Hume and Kant, combining both enlightenment and racist views, and for the rise of systems of instrumental reason, such as Nazism, fascism and bolshevism, through their sponsoring of the mass destruction and killings of, in some cases, millions of racial, political or ideological others.

see the tendency in traditional (pre-colonial) African society to reasonabilism, which is the notion – as we shall see – that consciousness and the capacities of the conscious human are both substantivities and relationalities, optimized in a specific reason-conatus/affect cluster that is necessarily alloyed in such a way that the presence of one aspect necessarily involves the presence of other aspects. The wholesomeness of the human being as a person manifests this unity and balance. It is for this reason that the good life is to be found in the middle (mean) in some type of Aristotelian sense. The Igbo express this thus: 'obulu uzo, obulu uzo onwu; o kpeazu nwa akanri; etiti nwa onyeoma.' Literally translated this means: 'the one running in front would die first; the laggard is a dwarf; the one in the middle is a child of a good person.' Properly interpreted, the maxim says that running ahead without restraint or the control of reason leads to an early death (the Igbo society is highly achievement-based so they do not mean by any means that coming first in any respectable field of endeavour is to be deplored; indeed, they work hard to come first in all fields of endeavour); the laggard is a cretin in terms of their emotions, will or intellect, or in their development; the middle is the offspring of a good person and so is a good person or personifies goodness, in the manner of Igbo conceptions of goodness (Agbakoba 2019, 39). There is, thus, a fundamental sense of, and need for, complementarity and harmony based in reason, the conatus and affects in Igbo thought. We see this, for instance, in Ezeudu's and Obierika's perspective on Okonkwo's participation, as demanded by a divinity of the land, in the ultra-retributive execution of Ikemefuna in Chinua Achebe's masterpiece *Things Fall Apart* (1958/1962, 40–43). Ezeudu advises Okonkwo to stay away from the party of executioners because the young man Ikemefuna calls him father (or in other words, he has taken him as his father and sanctuary). He should not, therefore, be a party to the violation of the principle of security that is central to fatherhood and the overarching responsibility for life and sanctuary it incurs. And, when Okonkwo tries to justify his participation on the grounds that it was ordered by a deity of the land, Obierika rejects his reasoning on the grounds that the deity did not name anyone as executioner and that he should not have volunteered, the implication being that those without personal ties of friendship, filiality or responsibility, may volunteer, if they like (Achebe, 40–47).

In order to see how this idea of complementarity and harmony grounds the Igbo notion of justice – including its intergenerational aspects – I shall go further into the metaphysical, and the related epistemological, foundations that underpin these key notions, with the further aim of reconfiguring and enriching them in the light of certain dimensions of contemporaneous philosophical knowledge, lived experiences and developmental expectations of Africans, as indicated.

First, let us note that it appears that without concrete historical embodiment in which its forms and contours, laws and structures are laid out, reason is highly germane to the logical order (the order of thought) but not to the order of material existence. However, when we want to consider reason in concrete terms – to historicize it, so to say – then we have to consider it as being embodied in stuff or matter (in this case humans), in which and through which concrete trains of thought and actions ensue. In a unified way, thoughts and actions become the subjects of reason or irrationality, as the case may be. Logical patterns of thought have to imbue, and are in turn imbued by, other dimensions of the psychological, spiritual and social forces that make up a human being – especially a human being engaged in action. In this regard, consciousness – the first and basic substratum of the embodiment of reason – becomes important.

2 Consciousness and Reasonability

Our consciousness is manifested to us in many ways on account of our self-consciousness. Through the introspective power of our self-consciousness, we apprehend in a basic way the rational, perspicacious, desiring, aspiring, imaginative, dynamic and volitional dimensions of our individual consciousness and, intentionally and reflexively, can engage these as well as our self-consciousness itself, thereby providing for our creativity and freedom (including radical existentialist freedom). Further, as individuals and as subjects of consciousness and self-consciousness, we have the power inherent in these subjectivities to control, act upon and order or structure our world according to rational patterns. Indeed, it seems we necessarily do so in accordance with various rational patterns that differ in intensity in their resemblance to pristine reason, that is, the principle of consistency or transcendental reason.

In other words, as consciousness, being – the subject of consciousness – is an irreducible given, to which reason belongs. However, being does not manifest itself only as reason and as the striving for acceptable structures of reason (including structures or forms of justice). Rather, being also manifests itself as emotions which enable us to have positive pro-sentiments towards, among other things, the structures of justice and the persons or things involved; and as imagination, which enables us to visualize better alternatives to strive for and worse alternatives to avoid. Being is also more than these manifestations because it makes them possible as acts of given, unified, holistic subjectivities or consciousnesses (the unities of consciousness express realities of beings over and above their specific acts or faculties). This is the dimension of the conatus or will, which is apprehended via intuition as the subject-self or ego, and which has full self-ordering capabilities (freedom and choice, including in the radical Sartrean sense).

As self-ordering entities, humans are capable of ordering and structuring experiences of external impressions and objects according to rational patterns in intrinsic or instrumental ways, that is, according to transcendental reason (according to the perception of the ultimate innate structure of one's perceptive power/consciousness, which is the principle of consistency) or, in the case of instrumental reason, according to an excitatory experience within one's general consciousness – even if this is the experience of one's being or the subjective power of one's being (or, in other words, the ego as distinct from the inner structure of this subjectivity or ego). The Igbo seem to recognize and invest their notions of morality, community organization and the good life in this self-ordering capacity of humans because, as we shall explore further, the notion and person of a Nze, which is a title conferred on the upright and successful person, expresses a person who imposes order on chaos.[3]

In this construal, two ultimate possibilities compete for dominance in our self-understanding and in the ways in which we generally interpret and organize the experiential and cognitive world in relation to ourselves: the perception of the ego and the perception of the innate structure of the subjective self or ego (the principle or form of consistency/reason), both of which compete for ultimacy and to be deployed as supreme cognitive organizing principle(s) in at least some basic ways.

In the latter model, the form or principle of reason in itself is the leading/ultimate organizing principle around which all the other powers of being coalesce, and so the 'progress' of reason can be considered in terms of the dynamics that produce refinement in reason both in itself and in the ways in which it sifts, refines and coalesces with the mutually enabling powers of consciousness and subjectivity. This is the reasonabilistic tendency. In the former model, being as the ego, asserts itself and then affirms whatever rational structure such

[3] "Nze and its attributes occur in the Afa system in the following symbols: OtunukpaIjite, which means abundance of grip, and hence discipline. This Afa symbol says that events, states, things are governed by the power of 'holding', that is control, order, law(s), discipline; phenomena and existence are law-governed; and the Nze is the visible and living manifestation of law, regularity, discipline (including self-control) that govern the universe, hence also truthfulness and justice; it expresses discipline and law-like regularity… Ose Okala: Ose ordinarily is exertion by way of pulling or separating and it evokes motions that arise based on this sort of exertion. It thus means here the exertion or imposition of Okala (events) and thus the involvement of order and control. It depicts the Ozo and hence also Nze as an organizer and imposer of law and order in his environment regarding humans, living and non-living things; the reproducer of the true cosmic order in personal and communal existences, given the understanding of the personality of the Nze, as a personification of the cosmic order, truth and justice; the desirable end of man." See Agbakoba 2019, 40.

affirmation of being implies – here, existence as the 'egoistic' power of being truly precedes essence in terms of structure. In the dynamics of its refinement, this mode of organizing reality primarily around and in favour of the ego can only mean a diminishing of the form or principle of reason in itself in the relations internal to subjectivity (consciousness) and in relations with the objective world. This, ironically, would mean the progressive diminishing of forms of awareness, empathy, affect and so on: in short, progressive grossness and apathy. This is the insensibilistic tendency.[4]

I have discussed this fundamental nexus from a more metaphysical angle elsewhere; let it suffice to say in this regard that the subject-self, if it is to remain or be maintained in accordance with the principle of consistency, would have to contend with internal and external sources of flux (with itself as a being of flux) in changing relational situations (Agbakoba 2019, 83–114). This requires that the powers of consistency be aligned with other dynamic principle(s) that are compatible, complementary and mutually reinforcing, such that, together, an evolving reasonabilistic harmony can be achieved. Actually, it appears that reason exists or survives in the context of the range of psychological states that constitute background actuating affectivities; otherwise, the subject-self and its reason could be overruled or diminished by negating passions that lead to irrationalities. Reason in the subject-self has to be alloyed with supportive passions in order to be a dominant force in a dynamic reality. The summation of such compatible and supportive principles and forces is what I have referred to as ontological beneficence – including, but not limited to, freedom and choice (based on the primal 'restraint' of nature from imposing on us humans, fully deterministically); creativity; equality, equity and justice; solidarity and charity; and other-regarding attitudes generally. Beneficence may also be used interchangeably with empathy here, in the sense of taking care of others and their interests. The being of reason (consistency) and beneficence are inextricably bound to one another in ways that are mutually reinforcing, so that one can go from one to the other. For instance, one can assert that the more there is ontological freedom, the more there is reason and a tendency towards the fullness of reason (reasonabilism), and that the converse is the case with a tendency towards insensibility (irrationality) and apathy (insensibilism). And, where reasonabilism is a life-affirming and expansive harmony of being, insensibilism is a life-denying, diminishing and narrowing circle of harmony of being in both the general and specific senses of consciousness and being.

Before going further let me point out that, as indicated above, this notion of a unified consciousness of active, mutually reinforcing faculties (components)

[4] For more details see Agbakoba 2019, 83–114.

features in, and is compatible with, a major dimension of the African metaphysical outlook. The Igbo, as already indicated, think in terms of relatedness and relationalities, not simply in terms of forms of relations, but also in terms of associational dynamics that influence, if not wholly determine, the specific manifestation of the being of a thing. Hence, the Igbo say, 'ife kwulu, ife akwudebe ya', which translates into English as, 'whatever is (stands), there is something else that exists (stands) in close proximity to it'. In other words, nothing in the universe is in isolation. Existence, thus, becomes one huge network of interconnected entities in which the specific manifestation of a thing is not to be considered in isolation from the relationalities that underpin its existence. So, reason is not to be considered in isolation but, rather, together with the realities of our consciousness that maximize or diminish its existence. In this way we see, already, at the fundamental metaphysical level of Igbo thought, the importance of association and relationality in material, formal or functional dimensions. And, as things exist in proximity, they relate complementarily, agonistically and so on. I would say here that those who may think that traditional African thought was founded principally or solely on the complementarity of binaries or opposites while Western thought was founded on the antagonism of opposites or binaries, might be overgeneralizing: African thought reflects both complementary and agonistic relations, even if it may tend to favour complementarity and harmony.[5]

This ontology, apparently, naturally favours enhancements of awareness in aid of the comprehensive and holistic perception of associations and relationalities. Thus, ethical positions are reached not only via ethical reasoning, but also via 'pure' intuitions. By way of dilation in this regard, a human being as a subject-self shows its knowing capabilities via the faculties of reason, sense perceptions and intuition. Reason and the senses are particular faculties closely tied to specialized organs and parts of the brain. On the other side, intuition – which, properly speaking, is a faculty or capacity for information gained without direct recourse to reason and the senses – is rather different. It is tied to the unifying faculty that makes unity of consciousness possible, namely, the will

[5] I would agree broadly with Sophie Oluwole's qualified generalization on this matter based on the fact that one may make, for instance, a distinction in African thought between the oppositionality of being and the complementarity of functionality within a larger context of existence, in which case one may still encounter the irreconcilable oppositionality of certain fundamental categories, such as being and nothingness. Secondly, severe punishment, such as death, total banishments and so on, in African systems are apparently due to the failure to see the complementarity of being and/or functionality in legal cases. Thirdly, I would also agree that African thought is predominantly (not exclusively) complementarian because I think that there is an implied sense of methodological complementarianism: Africans might favour the path of complementarity in identifying and solving problems, both theoretically and practically. See Oluwole 2014, 152–183.

or conatus, which, perforce of unifying specific perceptual or cognizing faculties (among other things), has to share in the qualities of awareness and perception as a faculty or capacity in its own right. Thus, inhering in the will, along with the energy or reality that is subjectively established as the self or ego, are the perceptual capacities. Contrary to Hume, this will is not perceived by the subject-self as the particular experiences of the self but as the subject to which such experiences belong (Hume 1994, 304).[6] Therefore, its cognizing cannot depend on the sources of such particular experiences (namely, the senses and reason) but on itself as a holistic entity, that is, on pure intuition without direct recourse to the senses or reason. The nature of this ego is in dispute: whether, for instance, it is a mental substance, a long-enduring self or fleeting existents that give an illusion of permanence as in the Buddhist notion of impermanence. Whatever the case may be, it is clear that the ego and the conatus that emerges from it integrate all the elements of the self, both mental and physical, into a single functional unit. Thus, it is an integrating capacity which, though more than the sum of its parts, would share in some way in the parts; this is the domain of pure intuition, as already indicated. There, possibility, nature and the faculty of pure intuition in Western philosophy are disputed in ways that may not occur in other philosophical traditions, such as the African philosophical tradition. However, Democritus and Epicurus, in classical times, were of the view that, 'infra' and 'ultra' human sensuous stimuli (composed of rarefied atoms) reach our subconscious or unconscious mind and are cognized via pure intuition. Democritus and Epicurus were atomists, and anticipated sub-atomic particles that operate beyond or unnoticed by the senses, but which impact our being and are cognized by us (Odia 2018); unheeded by the senses these particles interact directly with the will as a perceptual faculty, as indicated above.

To appreciate the significance of this, one has to recognize that as conscious and self-conscious beings, among our fundamental dimensions is our intentionality: our aboutness, the connectedness of awareness to other things, of which our intentionality is, thereby, about (Brentano 1970, 109–129). This aboutness exists in two basic modes: aboutness in relation to things external to the self, and aboutness in connection to internal states of the self, focusing on one's experiencing of one's self, from specific experiences of the self to the self in-it-self or, in other words, the self as a holistic conatus. We experience the self in this way always, but we seldom pay attention to it, so this depth of selfhood exists as subliminal consciousness. Only occasionally, when we pay special attention, do we have full consciousness of our long-enduring selfhood

[6] Hume tries and fails to establish the existence of the subject-self via introspection; this is because the subject-self may be perceived only via pure intuition: see Hiriyanna 1978, 20–21.

or subject-self (and this is always an intuitive experience). From out of this subject-self emerge reason, imagination, emotions and other dimensions of our mind, according to Descartes' demonstrations and his cogito ego sum.

There is, then, complementarity between the conatus as a perceptual faculty and the faculties of reason, imagination and the emotions, such that intuitive perceptions of harmony (or otherwise) of or within the internal and external environments aid rational impressions, expressions and imaginations in more or less factual, counterfactual or subjunctive ways; and these are reinforced or further complemented by positive reason and harmony-affirming affects, such as contentment, joy, conviviality, tolerance, respect and so on, or are diminished by their opposites, as the case may be. Thus, our perceptions and emotions (affects) may aid our development of reasonability or diminish it in favour of insensibilism (apathetic inconsistency) and, therefore, our perception of, and responsibility for, justice: especially, as we shall see, justice conceived fundamentally as a state of homeostasis or dynamic harmony, as among the Igbo (Odia 2018).

The human being, therefore, has to pay attention, not only to the cultivation of rational capacities (ratiocination and mental operations), but also to the cultivation of complementary reasonabilistic and beneficent affects, the imagination and pure intuition regarding the orientation of the will towards harmony. All these things go together, complementarily, in apprehending, establishing and extending harmony, which, as already indicated, is the basis of justice in Igbo (African) thought. The Igbo notion of justice, which I have expounded and built upon, is grounded and justifiable in the framework of aspects of Igbo ontology and epistemology discussed above. Let me now turn to African notions of justice and intergenerational justice in the context of homeostasis, given the foregoing ontological and epistemological background.

3 Justice in African Thought: the Case of the Igbo

In addressing justice in African thought, as indicated above, I shall dwell mostly on Igbo thought; generalizations about Africa may only be made as might be appropriate. Justice in traditional Igbo thought flows from the metaphysics and epistemology of the traditional worldview, certain outlines of which have been sketched above. In this regard, a thing is what it is on account of both its substantive nature and its manifestation due to relationalities. Substantively, things have their essences or udi (i.e., types), and inherent power or ike, but whether these will manifest themselves or not, and their degree of manifestation, are matters of the relationalities in which a thing is ensconced. Justice, therefore, is the relationality that permits or enables the optimum manifestation of the nature of a being, that is equilibrium. Thus, justice is harmony or ndokwa: the appropriate balance of relationalities, that exhibits a fair order in the sense of being in accordance with the inherent nature of things.

In this regard, the Igbo generally will accept that there are objective laws governing nature and natural harmony; that harmony with the true nature and order of things is achieved by understanding these objective laws as they are manifest in given contexts and by conforming to them; and, that the harmony so achieved produces the wellbeing of the terms and parties involved. For this reason, there are different levels or types of harmony and, thus, justice. Fundamental metaphysical and natural harmony is the most basic type of justice. At this level, everything in reality has its natural place, which makes for cosmic harmony:

> Justice, taken as fair entitlement and disentitlement is the universal principle governing the relationship between things in the universe: animate and inanimate, natural and supernatural. Justice is [thus] the principle that sustains the cosmic and social order. (Agbakoba and Nwauche 2006, 78)

If, for any reason, a thing goes against this natural order then it must be 'punished' by whatever means will restore the natural order (Alutu 1986, 317). It is important to note here that the pan-psychic underpinning of traditional Igbo thinking furnishes the Igbo assumption that everything has some type of mind, some type of cognitive and affective capacities, and is alive in some way. And, thus, everything is responsible, even if only in a tiny way, for their position in the vast web of relations, harmony or disharmony. Therefore, all things are deserving of 'punishment', if they are to be associated with disharmony, for all things have spirits that should intuitively understand and respect cosmic harmony, and are, thus, liable to punishment for infractions (Agbakoba and Nwauche 2006, 79).

The order in human relations (social order and harmony) reflects some of the exactitude and rigidity of the patterns of the natural cosmic order. However, being the sphere of human relations, it is more complex, fluid and complementarian. The human being is expected to be in complementary (harmonious, reasonable or reasonabilistic) relations with connected peoples, whether they are living, dead or yet to be born. Anyone, real or potential, that may have bearing on a person's life or afterlife, in the present or the future, is looped into the web of relationalities and socio-centric considerations. This is because the Igbo believe in life after death in a way that is largely founded on the continuity of life on earth in the afterlife with its biological, social and theological ties. Justice in Igbo thought is, thus, harmony, or ndokwa, in this web of relationalities; and this harmony is the objective basis of fairness and of justice as fair order that is impartially and non-arbitrarily founded and maintained. As I mentioned elsewhere, the Igbo have words for particular acts of justice or just judgements, namely ikpemkwuma-oto (just judgement, which literarily combines ikpe), an act of legal judgment, with mkwuma-oto, which means 'standing straight or an act of standing straight, a just act'; but they have no word for justice as a concept (Agbakoba and Nwauche 2006, 77). However, this appears to be due to the way in which the concept of justice is subsumed under the concept of harmony, thereby evoking the Socratic notion of justice, but going beyond it to incorporate cosmic dimensions.

The traditional Igbo society which espoused this notion of justice is to be found in communal – and usually agrarian – republican towns (village clusters) in which people are bound together by consanguinity and ancestry, common religious worship and family relations: this is the umunna (literarily, father's children). Umunna is the locus of ethical living and moral development, as well as the basis of the characterization of the ethics and normative expectations of the society. Justice in the context of umunna is similar to ubuntu (a Southern Bantu equivalent, more or less). Mogobe Ramose presents justice in the context of ubuntu as 'seeking the restoration of disturbed equilibrium regardless of the time when the disturbance occurred' and emphasizing 'that truth must be constantly found through attunement to be-ing' (Ramose 2002, 94–95).

A key challenge to ndokwa (justice) conceived in this way is contextual inadequacy given the transformative impact of modernity upon agents, spaces, environment and relationalities, for with its diverse spheres and mutations and other factors, modernity has expanded and transformed knowledge of reality, the world and its contents, including human nature and possibilities. I address this challenge by pursuing a trans-colonial constructivist path which allows me to reconceptualize the notion of harmony in a manner that overcomes these limitations by drawing on the elastic nature of Igbo thought, as well as various enrichments from other sources. Let me point out immediately, in this regard, that the Igbo notion of ndokwa can escape the insularity, rigidity and insufficiency of its traditional conceptualisation because of the elements of openness to knowledge (cognitive progressivism), contextual realism and dynamism in Igbo thought.

Going further, in this respect, the possible rigidity and inhumanity or parochiality of notions of harmony – especially when conceptualized and imposed by knowledge and power elites on the rest of society for the sake of creating or protecting privilege – is reduced because, for the Igbo, conceptions of harmony in given contexts need not be taken as absolute ideas and arrangements cast in stone, but rather as open verisimilitudes subject to progressive veridic changes as better knowledge and attitudes are developed. Therefore, ndokwa is open to dynamism and so can be seen as a dynamic harmony or homeostasis. This is based on the Igbo notions of cosmic flux, cognitive progressivism and the life and responsibilities of the upright person (nze) or the way of the upright person (amanze).[7]

To a greater extent, the Igbo think of the world, or reality, in terms of flux and in a rather Heraclean manner, for the Igbo say 'enu bu oda: the world is like a river current' (Bosah ca. 1975, 195). Like a twisting, twirling current, the world changes and is in constant transformation; yet, there are, nonetheless, structures and more enduring (long enduring) substantivities and relationalities. The challenge of human beings is to discover these enduring structures of the world, the changing patterns and their basis, and to seek out harmony based on such knowledge, thus engendering cognitive progressivism. The Igbo notion of cognitive progressivism is expressed in the saying, 'ama odo enu: no one knows the world and destinies of humans' and 'uche na bia abia: wisdom grows in a person'. In other words, no one has complete knowledge of the universe or reality, and a person's wisdom grows over time. This view concerns the ordinary folks or ogbodi (those uninitiated into the mysterious cults of knowledge) regardless of rank (that is whether they are community nobles or people of lower status). Thus, the ordinary Igbo is open to knowledge acquisition and, especially, new and better ideas and knowledge of the universe and humans, and with these comes the possibility – and, indeed, reality – of better ideas of harmony. Therefore, a nze or amanze should equip himself/herself with information and knowledge about the world and be open to learning, because s/he is expected to discover and pursue the path of reasonability which leads to homeostasis in the changing but increasingly cognizable world (Agbakoba 2019, 208–211). This is a fundamental basis upon which to attribute responsibility and culpability to humans: one cannot escape moral responsibility on grounds of ignorance unless it is shown that such ignorance is not wilful and stems neither from an absence of the right efforts to know nor from opting to ignore unpleasant facts, and so on.

The objective of this harmony, which is the basis of its comprehensibility to human beings, hinges on the primacy of life or ndubisi (life is supreme) and the wellbeing of the living, which are only achievable within a community. So, in its struggles with the basic problems of human relations, traditional Igbo society tended to maximize the wellbeing of communities, thus, favouring socio-centricity.

[7] The word nze, literarily, is avoider of wrongdoing; thus, it connotes living uprightly, implying the traditional system of ethics; Nze is a title given to some persons who have supposedly achieved uprightness. For some details on this and related issues, see Agbakoba 2019, 153–265.

In addition to the notions of relationality and interconnection expressed in their traditional metaphysics, the Igbo give further expression to the interconnectedness of peoples and to the necessity of solidarity with the notion of 'ometuta imi, ometuta onu' (if the nose is affected, the mouth would also be affected). In other words, the fate, survival and wellbeing of community members are so strongly intertwined that whatever affects one member affects all members: hence, one for all, all for one, which is the basic principle of umunna, ubuntu and ujamaa – as communalism is known in Eastern Africa. Consequently, solidarity and the different levels of meanings within it become important:

- first, the recognition of shared circumstances;
- second, a recognition of the sociality of actions and inactions, and of human existence generally; and, thus, the notion that a human being can only exist in the human web of sociality/community;
- third, a recognition of the individual as an embodiment of the community, and the community as composed of such embodied individuals: there is no individual life outside the community, and no community without the individuals who embody it.

Therefore, the sociality (as opposed to the asociality or unsociality) of an action which affirms the existence of community also affirms the existence of the individual. Hence, again, the maxim of unity: one for all, all for one.

This web of sociality is also understood as extending over a long and open temporal frame. Because the individual is not conceived in an atomistic or monadic sense, relations may be traced as widely as necessary over geographical and temporal spaces and in past, present and future configurations, as Ramose has indicated (see earlier in this section, Ramose 2002). Further, great emphasis is placed on collective responsibility. It is said, for instance, 'ofu nkpisi aka luta manu ozue nkpisi aka ndi ozo' (literarily: 'when one finger is smeared with oil other fingers will eventually have marks of oil'), or, in other words, the culpability of one member of a social unit spreads to the other members (Bosah, ca. 1975, 189). Thus, space and time hold special significance in the conceptualization of justice in practical terms, especially because of the aspects of complementation in which justice involves restitution, restoration, transformation or mobilization (as the case may be) in order to achieve equilibrium and harmony.

In addition, as I tried to show elsewhere, this socio-centric and complementarian foundation of justice is amenable to – and, indeed, may be clarified by – the classification of practical justice into two parts: negative practical justice and positive practical justice. Negative practical justice is achieved via some type of subtraction from a person's wellbeing or total worth, such as the loss of freedom, property or life, the infliction of pain and so on, while positive practical justice is achieved through the processes of cultivating people and their potentials by enhancing or maximizing their socially beneficial talents and capabilities so as to enable them to contribute to society in a manner that offsets their liabilities and offences, and, thereby, achieving harmony. This form of justice is eminently expressive of restorative and transformative justice.

Furthermore, and importantly, positive justice is founded to some extent on pro-active solidarity and initiative justice that is both a mode of solidarity in which care for the other is proactively expressed, and also specific initiatives by people to establish fairer orders of harmonious relations (justice), especially with the aid of forbearance, pro-active solidarity and even renunciation or abnegation (Bosah, ca. 1975, 189). By way of illustration, if on account of hard work, diligence and resourcefulness in his/her business, a person becomes successful and rich, such a person need not wait for poorer upcoming relatives or associates to solicit his/her help. If such a person is to be considered a good person (or, in other words – if we take Menkiti's correct assessment that personhood is achieved by meeting certain ethical standards), then they should initiate the process of empowering their less fortunate relatives or associates with knowledge, skills, capital and other things that would help them to become successful in life (Menkiti 2006, 324–327). This is the basis of the success of the famed Igbo apprentice system, which has enabled young people to gain the necessary skills and capital to start their own businesses. The basis of this practical initiative-justice is not only solidarity, but also a complementarian web of reciprocities that bind people in communities. The traditional extended family and clan served, among other things, as a welfare system; so, in the contemporary African state, where state-sponsored welfare programs and policies are very sparse or non-existent, the traditional welfare system continues to cushion the hardships, uncertainties and misfortunes of life. In this regard, as it is said, a wealthy person surrounded by poor and unsuccessful relatives and associates, cannot ever be really wealthy, because such a person will have so many dependents and so many obligations and demands from them that, sooner or later, they too will become poor. Therefore, one has to empower others to rise out of poverty in order to help sustain one's community; and, one is expected to be proactive in this regard, in order to activate the imperative which places obligations on others to act reciprocally in solidarity, fairness and responsibility and, thus, to establish a present and future order of harmony (justice).

There is of course the possibility of abuse, in that some beneficiaries of proactive solidarity and initiative justice may fail in reciprocity and their obligations; nevertheless, people are expected to reach these levels of personal responsibility for the good of themselves and their community, in spite of the vulnerability to abuse, on a number of grounds:

1. Affordability: such an investment is often affordable, even if it requires the application of a frugal lifestyle (denying oneself certain luxuries) alongside the investment of one's time and energy in beneficial projects and the deployment of one's expendable resources.
2. Prudence: one must also think of securing a self-reliant future for oneself, in case others fail in their reciprocal obligation to do so.
3. One has to look out for, and embed, ways and means of enforcing contracts and obligations in proactive initiatives of positive practical justice.
4. One may seek recompense in cosmic justice, and here, spiritual intelligence and supreme beliefs and values become important. In this regard, Christianity, which is the new dominant religious philosophy in Igbo land, seems – at least nominally – to be well placed to support those who, without being adherents of traditional religious philosophy, have nonetheless retained a good deal of its ethical outlook.[8]

This socio-centric and complementarian system prioritizes emotional intelligence, social and collective identity, communitarian ethics and so on, in addition to responsibility and initiatives for justice. Consequently, people might be expected not only to be careful to avoid disharmony, but also to be proactive in seeking homeostasis. In this regard, an intuitive understanding of people's emotions, dispositions, interests and aspirations and of how to harmonize them becomes important. Achieving justice is not simply a matter of understanding and applying abstract formal rules or the structures of predetermined relations (that are supposedly good or desirable), but – and as reasonabilism demands – of ensuring that within the context of the lived realities of relationalities and the provenances of agents, harmony is achieved. The intuitionist apprehension and understanding of contexts thus helps agents

[8] Christianity came to Igbo land in the mid-nineteenth century. Evangelization preceded colonization by decades in Igbo land and was the main vehicle of modernity in Igbo land, as in some other lands in the southern part of West Africa. However, progress was slow for many reasons. The Igbo nevertheless welcomed the education and learning, science and technology that came with Christianity. Even though some, like Olufemi Taiwo, think that colonization pre-empted the healthy growth of modernity that was associated with Christian evangelization, and even though the colonial personnel were in some ways hostile to evangelization, nevertheless, evangelization was boosted with colonization because the colonial government defused the traditional state and powers that would have otherwise forcibly prevented the spread of Christianity. The modern colonial state also created a modern sector where the people educated in missionary institutions could be employed, giving converts economic security and status, see Taiwo 2010, 1–17. And for colonial opposition to evangelization, see Basden 1982, 297–306.

to avoid rigid formalism, to arbitrate and reconcile people or harmonize relations in situations where the laws and mores are not clear or applicable, and also to act anticipatorily to provide grounds for future harmonious relations – and this is important for different types of informal, semi-formal and formal relations, especially in respect of positive practical justice and initiatives of justice. Some of these things will become clearer when we take a look at intergenerational justice. However, before I move on to this, let me point out that for the Igbo, harmony is the greatest social good. This is expressed in the maxim, ndokwaka (harmony is greater).[9]

4 Intergenerational Justice

From the foregoing discussion, one may see that all the perceptual capabilities of humans (including pure intuition) play complementary roles in our perception, understanding, construction and maintenance of harmony in the changing situations of agents and in the changing contexts of our complex web of relationalities. In addition, the upright person (nze), who has the responsibility of bringing harmony into existence and perpetuating it, should seek knowledge freely, interculturally, conscientiously and steadfastly, to avoid culpable ignorance, including affected ignorance and akrasia, and to be able, thereby, to achieve the maximization of the good, that is, of harmony. Furthermore, in this regard, the ideal moral agent, (a nze – adept avoider of wrong-doing) does not simply act in an orderly way or follow a set of rules; rather, a nze imposes order, harmony (justice) and should be conceived as a person who brings harmony to a chaotic, unjust and disharmonious place, as the situation demands (Agbakoba 2019, 32–48). So, there is a hugely active, existentialist and creative aspect to the discharge of personal responsibility for harmony (justice), and this encourages initiative to be taken towards the viable practical administration of justice including, and especially, short- and long-term positive practical justice that carries intergenerational implications.

Generally, in respect to building harmony intergenerationally and holistically for a society, the Igbo vision incorporates the living, the dead (ancestors) and future generations (the yet-to-be-born). Traditionally, ancestors are the living-dead; they are venerated and propitiated as the link to the world of divinities, protectors and providers for their living descendants, and also

9 Re Bosah ca. 1975, 209: this text shows that an age-grade organization (incorporating those born from 1904 to 1906) at Onitsha chose to be named Ndokwaka. Age-grade organizations usually choose the name they bear according to what the community finds significant in their lives.

as the enforcers of morality, among other things (Oguejiofor 2001, 83–84). These ancestors return to the world of the living via some type of reincarnation (ibia uwa or ino uwa) and, in so doing, perpetuate their own life through their lineages (descendants). In a sense, immortality is believed to be the continued existence of a person through his/her descendants, some of whom are supposed to be actual incarnations, while others are full, partial or potential sites of embodiments and cohabit with the living. The living and the dead are, thus, intimately bound with and interested in the lives of one another. This relationship is governed formally by standards of propriety (codes of religion and morality centring on care, reciprocity, solidarity and responsibility, including the proactive discharge of responsibility), which are supposed to ensure mutual care and harmony. We see this surmised clearly in aspects of traditional funeral ceremonies wherein mourners address the dead person thus: 'bulu anya anyi na muo, ka anyi bulu anya gi na madu' ('be our eyes on the spirit side of the world' – that is, watch out for our welfare in the netherworld, while we be your eyes on the human side of the world – that is, while we watch out for your welfare in the world of humans).[10] In a more or less elaborate way, this nexus between the living and the dead, and the standards of propriety built around it, also govern the relations and expectations of harmony between the living, and also between the living and the 'yet-to-return-ancestors', that is, the yet-to-be-born.

In looking at intergenerational justice among the living and between the living and future generations, I shall look generally at the relations between the elderly (those of retirement age), active adults (including relations between generations of older and younger active adults), children and expected children/ descendants. A basic way by which the aforementioned and nodal relatedness of things (relationalities) is made harmonious is the exposition and maintenance of the complementarity of difference, opposites and diversity. This is expressed in the saying: 'mili kwudolu ncha, o we'e gbor' (literarily: 'water stood by and in support of soap, that is how soap came to foam'; in simple terms: 'without water, the soap will not foam'). Without people complementing each other there will be no bubble; in terms of our mutual flourishing, the various roles we play in life and in society are unique, invaluable and irreplaceable. This is at the heart of the socio-centricity of the conception of society and justice.

In keeping with this, we have always to seek out the complementary role played by an expanding set of relationalities in the making of a given state of harmony and existential realization. In this regard, the harmony (justice)

[10] In Onitsha, this is usually pronounced in the Ikpu Akwa rites during burials by the Isi Ada (a clan or family's most senior daughter and presiding official in this ceremony) on behalf of people who come to pay their last respects to a deceased as s/he lies in state.

between generations is based on complementarity. The elderly are supposed to be the wise intermediaries between the living and the dead. At this stage in life, they are supposed to be living examples of what propriety or impropriety has in store for the younger generations who are supposed to be taking care of their welfare. However, this is only possible if the elderly have worked for it by investing in raising worthy children and family members (because in the traditional society and, more broadly, up till now, welfare for the elderly rests in the family and extended family: the state is virtually non-existent in this sphere). This leads directly to the question of responsibility and leadership in intergenerational relations.

Leadership is seen ideally as the security of life provided by fatherhood and the continuity of life provided by motherhood. They are complementary principles, even though most Igbo communities are ultimately patriarchal, while a few are matriarchal. Adults in positions of leadership are supposed to provide physical, psychological, economic, environmental and other forms of security and wellbeing; in the process, equity (olulu-onye), numerical equality (nraanya) and equal opportunities (nraanya enyemaka) are expected to be discharged impartially and non-arbitrarily intergenerationally as well as intragenerationally. Their followers, such as the youth and the unborn, are generally the guarantors of their future welfare, their immortality and their existential status, in this world and the hereafter. In relation to intergenerational justice, the leader is informed and guided by such notions and maxims as nkiruka (the future is greater, in terms of the wellbeing of a person and his/her family or a group of people: this expresses hope and faith in a better future and a certain type of progressivism); azuka (future generations will be greater: another expression of hope and faith in a better future and a form of progressivism); 'egbebelu, ugobelu nkesi ibeya ebena nku kwaya' (a proverbial affirmation of tolerance, which literally translates thus: 'let the kite perch [on a tree] and let the eagle perch [on the same tree], anyone of them who says the other should not perch should get a broken wing').

In general, in return, the younger generation and future generations are supposed to provide loyalty, respect, manpower and other types of support. The Igbo summarize the obligations of their youth and descendants in general thus: 'onye fe'e eze, eze elue ya' (those who discharge their obligations to their leader with propriety are rewarded with leadership positions someday, in their own time, by divine providence or people's choice, as the case may be). In this way, the generation that holds leadership needs the youth and the generations that follow – and vice versa. This relation of reciprocity and complementarity also extends to the unborn and future generations, because they are the future youths, leaders and elders. Even though they exist in the present as potentialities, one has to prepare the best of grounds for their flourishing so that they, in turn, will be fully obligated to one as an elder or ancestor. In this regard, the Igbo notion of nkiruka (the future is greater or better) and azuka (the coming generations are greater or better) become significant across spheres of existence that include the environment. There are, thus, traditional notions that support active concern for future generations and efforts to ensure the conditions of their flourishing; hence, the responsibilities (and other issues of justice) which the present generations have for the unborn.[11]

Within this framework, an Igbo person ought to provide as complementarian a solution as possible to philosophical problems in justice. For example, the tension between impartiality and partiality in the discharge of justice may be resolved by 'impartialitude', which is the achievement of as much impartial justice as possible while conserving the bonds of reciprocity and emotional ties of close-knit groups (significant social-selves and identities) that would have been otherwise brushed aside by dispassionate impartiality.[12] For instance, faced with the dilemma of choosing between exposing the crime of a close relative with whom one is bound in complex reciprocal relations (say a father) and concealing such a crime, an African approach to the pursuit of justice as harmony is likely to suggest that one may choose neither but, instead, quietly and adequately compensate the victim (out of court arbitration, direct/indirect settlements, for instance) and, at the same time, seek to ensure, by various means, that the offender does not engage in any future crimes. The success of this option depends on the adequacy of the compensation and success in preventing future crimes. However, in some cases, optimal levels of compensation, crime prevention, or both may not be achieved. Nevertheless, a reasonable approximation of impartiality is likely to be achieved, while at the same time the nested relations of close social units are preserved: this would be 'impartialitude'. There is much that can be said for and against this notion, but let it suffice to say here that impartialitude and harmonization may not be applicable, acceptable or adequate in some more complicated cases of crime, especially when the state is involved as the prosecutor and executor of the law. This, nevertheless, would not deter from its value in the more common and less complex situations of crime, conflict and so on.

In a similar vein, practical justice as harmonization is very open to adopting, adapting and generating the means of positive practical justice – that is,

[11] It should be noted that names take on extraordinary significance in oral cultures (oratures) because this is one of the means by which such communities encoded, preserved and communicated significant ideas.

[12] Circumstances that could elicit "impartialitude" are discussed in more detail in Agbakoba 2019, 179–182.

justice that is achieved without recourse to punishments that inflict pain, loss (including loss of life, limbs, property, freedom, etc.) or otherwise significantly diminish the life of the putative offender by subtractions to wellbeing (negative justice) but, instead, achieves harmonization by additive values (which add to wellbeing), positively capacitating putative offenders, making them better and more wholesome contributors to social units/society and, thus, able to compensate for their previous wrongdoing, lapses and omissions by the increase in their present and newly laudable contributions. A clear example of positive justice on a global scale is the United States' (US) Marshall Plan, which poured billions of US dollars into Germany and Japan for the reconstruction of these aggressor countries and their economies after the Second World War. This was a complete reversal of the punitive, retributive (negative) justice seen in the policies of reparations imposed on Germany after the First World War, which crippled the German economy and greatly contributed to the rise of Hitler and the Nazis, and to their initiation of the Second World War. Thus, through positive practical justice, the USA brought peace that has endured for over 75 years in the developed capitalist world and augmented its soft power, while Germany and Japan have become respectable democracies and contributors to global peace. From this, it can be seen that positive practical justice goes beyond restorative and transformative justice (on account of the restrictions of the latter to what are predominantly individual criminal cases – especially as alternatives to extant penal and carceral systems), and extends to all types of formal, semi-formal and informal relations in which there might be injustice (imbalances) and the need for harmonization (justice). But, as already indicated, it also has its limitations.

5 Conclusion

In this chapter I have tried to explicate the complementarian foundations of African metaphysical and epistemological thinking, especially that of the Igbo, and to show how these undergird notions of harmony, justice and intergenerational justice. In the process, and in keeping with my intercultural, trans-colonial constructivist approach, I mediated traditional African thought, reconfiguring, expanding and transcending it. My reflections point to a way of looking at justice, including intergenerational justice, as a dynamic homeostasis that needs to be constantly built, rebuilt and maintained, based on reasonabilism (an alloyed combination of the principle of consistency and ontological beneficence) and an attitude of cognitive progressivism that is ever open to interculturality and hybridity.

Bibliography

Achebe, Chinua. 1958/1962. *Things Fall Apart*. Essex: Pearson Education Limited.

Agbakoba, Joseph C. A. 2019. *Development and Modernity in Africa: An Intercultural Philosophical Perspective*. Köln: Rüdiger Köppe Verlag.

2021. "On the Kantian Influence in African Thought and the Notion of Trans-colonization." *Estudos Kantianos, Marília* 9, no. 2: 15–32.

Agbakoba, Joseph. C. A. and Enyinna S. Nwauche. 2006. "African Conceptions of Justice and Responsibility." *The Cambrian Law Review* 37: 78.

Alutu, O. John. 1986. *Nnewi History*. Enugu: Fourth Dimension Publishers.

Basden, G. T. 1982. *Among the Ibos of Nigeria*. Abagana: University Publishing.

Bosah, S. I. 1975. *Groundwork of the History and Culture of Onitsha*. Onitsha: No.1 Bosah Street.

Brentano, Franz. 1970. "The Distinction between Mental and Physical Phenomena." In *Introduction to Philosophy of Mind*, edited by H. Morick, 109–129. Glenview, IL: Scott, Foresman and Co.

Hiriyanna, Mysore. 1978. *Essentials of Indian Philosophy*. London: George Allen and Unwin.

Hume, David. 1994. "A Treatise of Human Nature." In *From Plato to Wittgenstein: the Historical Foundations of Mind*, edited by Daniel Kolak, 304. Belmont, CA: Wadsworth Pub. Co.

Menkiti, Ifeanyi A. 2006. "On the Normative Conception of a Person." In *A Companion to African Philosophy*, edited by Kwasi Wiredu, 324–327. Oxford: Blackwell Publishing.

Odia, Sylvester I. 2018. "From Democritus' Atoms to Quantum Mechanics: Towards an Epistemology of the Subconscious Mind." Address given at the inaugural departmental lecture of the Philosophy Department, Seminary of Saints Peter and Paul, Bodija, Ibadan for the 2018/2019 academic session, 23 November 2018.

Oguejiofor, Josephat Obi. 2001. "Non-universalizability of Traditional Moral Values and Corruption in Nigeria." *Bigard Theological Studies* 21: 83–84.

Oluwole, Sophie B. 2014. *Socrates and Orunmila*. Lagos: Ark Publishers.

Ramose, Mogobe. 2002. *African Philosophy Through Ubuntu*. Harare: Mond Books

Taiwo, Olufemi. 2010. *How Colonialism Preempted Modernity in Africa*. Bloomington, IN: Indiana University Press.

PART II

Intergenerational Ethics in Dialogue with Confucianism and Daoism

5

Ghosts and Intergenerational Justice

A Confucian Perspective

Yat-hung Leung and Mario Wenning

The Prince of Jin 晉 dreamed of a huge vengeful ghost with disheveled hair hanging to the ground. It beat its chest, leapt up and down, and said, 'For you to murder my descendants was unjust (buyi 不義). I have the god's (di 帝) approval [of my request for revenge]!' It smashed the main gate and the door to his private quarters and made its entry. Terrified, the lord entered the inner chamber, and the ghost smashed that door also. The lord woke up and summoned the shaman of Sangtian. What the shaman described corresponded exactly to the dream. The lord said, 'What then?' He replied, 'You will not eat the grain of the new harvest!'

The lord fell seriously ill and sought a physician from Qin 秦. The Liege of Qin sent a physician named Huan to treat him. Before he arrived, the lord dreamed that his illness assumed the form of two boys, who said, 'He is a skilled physician. I fear he will harm us. Where can we escape?' One of them said, 'If we lodge above the diaphragm and below the heart (huang zhi shang, gao zhi xia 肓之上、膏之下), then what can he do to us?' The physician arrived and said, 'There is nothing to be done about the illness. It is above the diaphragm and below the heart, where it can neither be overcome with heat treatment nor reached through acupuncture. Medicine will not get to it. There is nothing to be done.' The lord said, 'He is a good physician.' He gave him handsome gifts and sent him back.

In the sixth month, on the bingwu day, the Prince of Jin wanted to taste the new grain. He had the official in charge of sacrificial grains present it and the cook prepare it. He summoned the shaman of Sangtian, showed him the new grain, and had him killed. When he was about to eat, he became bloated, went to the privy, fell in, and died. A eunuch had dreamed in the morning of ascending to heaven with the lord on his back. By midday, he was carrying the Prince of Jin out of the privy. And then he was killed to attend his lord after death. (*Zuo Commentary*, Lord Cheng 10.4)[1]

[1] Adapted from Durrant, Li, and Schaberg (2016, 787).

1 Introduction

This 'ghost story' from the *Zuo Commentary* dates back to the Spring and Autumn Period (771–476 BCE) and is rich in allusions. It recounts a horrific episode epitomizing the belief in vengeful ghosts that has been common in classical Chinese civilization and that continues to this day to have an impact. Appeals to ghosts (*gui* 鬼) and spirits (*shen* 神) persist in spite – or in the midst – of modernization processes. The story depicts a haunting ghost taking revenge on Lord Jing 景 of Jin 晉, who killed the ghost's descendants. We know that Lord Jing wiped out the Zhao lineage because he believed in the – false – accusation made by Zhao Zhuang Ji 趙莊姬, according to which the Zhaos were going to rebel (see Durrant, Li, and Schaberg 2016, 787). The ghost in the story, presumably an ancestor of the Zhao lineage, first appeared in Lord Jing's dream, claiming that it was unjust for the Lord to murder Zhao's descendants and that he has divine approval for revenge. The shaman's prediction that Lord Jing's fate was already sealed turns out to be true, even if too late to save this messenger of bad news from being killed at the order of the Lord. The ghost caused the Lord to catch a disease. The disease appears in the form of two boys – presumably murdered descendants of the ghost – who, afraid of being caught and hurt by the physician, decide to lodge above their host's diaphragm and below his heart, where the attempt to employ medicine and acupuncture fail to ward off the danger. The famous idiom '*bing ru gaohuang*' 病入膏肓, meaning that an incurable malady is one that 'has entered the space between the diaphragm and the heart' (see Durrant, Li, and Schaberg 2016, 786), originates in this passage. This idiom, which is still in use today, denotes a problem that does not have a solution.

In spite of its supernatural dimension, this story is relevant to the theme of this volume since it addresses intergenerational justice. Victims of injustice engage, as ghosts, in retributive acts within the world of the living. Most importantly, the story ascribes agency to a spirit world that responds to the violent interruption of intergenerational continuity. Their acts were thought to have an impact on both the present and the future. We argue that the belief in revengeful ghosts was superseded by a moral evolution contributing to an increase in humanism in China. However, in contrast to Max Weber's thesis of a disenchantment (*Entzauberung*) that accompanies the processes of rationalization and leads to a disappearance of the spirit world (Weber 1963), in the Chinese tradition ghosts continue to play an important role, even if the relationship to them undergoes a transformation. The chapter starts by tracing the transition from a bargaining relationship with ghosts to a Confucian conception of combining moral cultivation with respect to the spirit world (Section 2).

This transformation is concomitant with what we call 'spiritual humanism' (Section 3). As we will suggest in the concluding section, spiritual humanism in the Confucian tradition is based on an ethics between generations that does not entail the disappearance of a belief in the spirit world. According to our reading, Confucius' spiritual humanism stakes a middle ground that evades, on the one hand, the dismissal by secular humanism of the existence of a spirit world, and, on the other hand, religious dogmatism with its claims to understand the operating mechanisms of the world of spirits (Section 4).

2 The Intergenerational Bond with Ancestor Ghosts

In the *Zuo Commentary*, there are numerous stories depicting victims of the violence inflicted by humans who return as ghosts in order to take revenge.[2] In the following section, we focus on the conception of ancestor ghosts, which sheds light on the intergenerational bond with the spirit world that was interrupted, in our story, by the violent acts of Lord Jin.[3]

2.1 Ancestor Ghosts

In the ancient Chinese tradition, the existence of ghosts is presumed, while the question of how to relate to them is a topic of debate. As Max Weber argued, 'In historical times the most fundamental belief of the Chinese people has been to ascribe power to ancestral spirits, not exclusively but predominantly to the spirits of one's own ancestors' (Weber 1959, 87). Confucius is credited with the recommendation to 'attend to the coming (generation) and remember the remote (ancestors)' (cited in Leong and Tao 2019, 75).[4] Commenting on this passage, Leong and Tao state:

> One can hardly find a better expression to interpret the Chinese mind. Ancestor-worship is therefore far from being an idolatrous worship, a worship of ghosts and goblins; it is a respect to the past, gratitude to what the past has handed down to us, admiration to the good example of the past. Since relationships and

[2] For instance, Shensheng 申生 of Jin returned as a ghost threatening to take revenge on the Jin family that pushed him to suicide (see Lord Xi 10.3 in Durrant, Li, and Schaberg 2016, 301). For details of haunting ghosts from pre-Qin to Han, see Lin (2005).

[3] We refer mainly to the *Zuo Commentary*, Confucius, and Zhu Xi 朱熹 (1130–1200).

[4] While we are not aware of the passage, in the *Analects* 9.23 Confucius claims that 'We should look upon the younger generation with awe' (*housheng kewei* 後生可畏) (in Slingerland 2003, 94), while in the *Analects* 1.9, Zengzi states, 'Take great care in seeing off the deceased and sedulously maintain the sacrifices to your distant ancestors, and the common people will sincerely return to Virtue' (in Slingerland 2003, 4).

> ancestral heroes count so much, it is but natural that ancestor-worship has become paramount in importance and great in potential force. The altruism by which a man would share his last penny with his family … shows how much stress the Chinese lay on common descent. (Leong and Tao 2019, 73 & 75)

The belief that one's ancestors, as well as strangers, would become ghosts and spirits that engage in communication with the visible world, even if primarily in dreams – as in the story – was widely spread and harboured significant consequences. Already, early in the Shang 商 dynasty (c. 1600–c. 1046 BCE), we witness the emergence of the cult of ghosts, ancestors (*zuxian* 祖先) and gods (Wolf 1974); this is succeeded by the Zhou 周 (1046–256 BCE) – a period that overlaps with that covered by the *Zuo Commentary* (722–468 BCE). The term '*gui*', as well as compounds such as *guishen*, can refer to spirits in general (including gods, spirits of ancestors, and even animal and plant spirits). This generic usage was later to become differentiated. Accordingly, *gui* 鬼 increasingly referred to the spirits of the dead and *shen* 神 and *di* 帝 to spirits and gods (Poo 2022).

Particularly important for the emergence of an intricate pantheon of spiritual beings was the Chu 楚 religion, which was significantly influenced by Indigenous beliefs with shamanic elements in South-West China (Hu 2020). The spirit world was divided into different kinds of ghosts that corresponded to different functions. Most common is the appeal to human ghosts (*rengui* 人鬼), which are predominantly ancestor ghosts (*zuxian gui* 祖先鬼). Human ghosts are thought to possess the capacity to return (*gui* 歸) which, phonetically, resembles the concept of ghost (*gui*). It is in the nature of ghosts that they return to the world of the living, even if, over time, they move upward and become indifferent to and detached from the realm of current (living) human affairs. The task of the living consisted in appeasing those antagonistic ghosts to whom one was not related, and transforming those to whom one was related into pliable ancestors. The means of taming or domesticating capricious ghosts consisted in a sophisticated set of ritual rules and practices that 'were a never-ending attempt to keep spirits at bay' (Puett 2011, 227; see also Puett 2019). In classical China, ghosts and spirits were thought to have desires analogous to human desires and, as the ingenious ghost boys from our opening story who hide in their host's body demonstrate, ghosts were afraid of suffering. Most importantly, ghosts needed to be nourished. As Thomas Wilson puts it, they 'linger after the death of the body and … they must be nurtured through pious feasting rites of cult sacrifice' (Wilson 2014, 186). Gifts to ancestors do not only include food, but may also include money offerings or, in contemporary Chinese communities, replicas of commodities ranging from cars and houses to symbols of prostitutes.

Human ghosts can be further divided into hungry ghosts, blameless ghosts, and sad ghosts, depending on how they have lived and been treated while alive, how they died, and whether or not they were properly remembered after death. Ghosts were thought of as being extremely dangerous, becoming malicious if they suffered injustice before death, if they did not have offspring, or if they were neglected (Harrison 2021, 344). In particular, hungry ghosts are thought to possess the capacity to channel their ghostly anger, jealousies, and frustrations into acts of revenge. Importantly, ghosts do not need to have been previously human: other kinds of ghosts include non-human ghosts, such as nature ghosts, that can be further divided into animal ghosts (e.g., bug ghosts), plant ghosts (e.g., bush ghosts), ghosts corresponding to natural elements (e.g., wind and wildfire ghosts), and location ghosts (e.g., hill ghosts and stove ghosts).

More generally, the Confucians – who primarily, even though not exclusively, discuss obligations towards formally human ghosts – share an assumption that spirits stay, at least for some time, after the body has died. While Confucius himself refused to speculate on the nature of ghosts, later Confucians such as Zhu Xi thought that a human being has two components namely, a *hun* 魂 and a *po* 魄. The *po*, which is the corporeal component, *yin* and static in nature, comes first; whereas the *hun*, the anima, *yang* and active in nature, comes next (see Zhu 1986, 40–41).

2.2 The Evolving Relationship with Ancestor Ghosts

The relationship between humans and ghosts underwent an evolution. In the ghost stories from the *Zuo Commentary*, descendants worship their ancestor ghosts, while the ancestor ghosts offer protection and assistance to the descendants.[5] For instance, whenever they undertook a journey the rulers had to 'report to the temple' (*gaomiao* 告廟) where their ancestors were enshrined and worshipped (see *Zuo Commentary*, Lord Huan 2.7 in Durrant, Li, and Schaberg 2016, 81). People believed that they should have their ancestors close to them. This is one of the reasons why millions of Chinese continue to migrate to their ancestral hometowns during significant festivities such as tomb-sweeping day. Even fleeing from a political persecution, Kong Kui 孔悝 of Wei nonetheless made an attempt to bring the ancestral tablet (*shi* 祏) with him (see *Zuo Commentary*, Lord Ai 16.4 in Durrant, Li, and Schaberg 2016, 1945). The ancestors are said to be able to communicate with their descendants

[5] This paragraph on ancestor ghosts and human interaction draws on Chen (1996, 64–66).

via dreams and divinations[6] and to be able to intervene in human affairs.[7] While Confucius continued the tradition of ancestor worship and did not call into question the existence of ghosts and spirits, he emphasized the importance of moral self-cultivation, rather than prudential considerations and bargaining with ghosts for favours, altering the way in which human beings were to interact with the ancestor ghosts.

On the one hand, Confucius seems to be agnostic concerning the status of the existence of dead people. When asked what wisdom (*zhi* 智) is, Confucius said, 'Working on what is right (*yi* 義) for the common people, respecting (*jing* 敬) the ghosts and spirits while keeping them at a distance (*yuan zhi* 遠之) – this might be called wisdom' (*Analects* 6.22 adapted from Slingerland 2003, 60).[8] Besides, when a student asked about how to serve ghosts and spirits, Confucius replied, 'you are not able even to serve man. How can you serve the ghosts?' When further asked about death, Confucius replied, 'You do not understand even life. How can you understand death?' (*Analects* 11.12 adapted from Lau 2000, 99).[9] These quotations have been interpreted to suggest that Confucius was a secular humanist who dismissed concern for the spirit world. However, in contrast to this interpretation, Confucius did emphasize sacrifices, and takes ghosts into consideration as if they exist. Indeed, the previous quotations could also be interpreted to mean that it is first necessary to understand human affairs before turning to the – we may infer – more complex spiritual matters. In Karl Jaspers' view, Confucius reveals a limit consciousness – a sophisticated understanding and acknowledgment of the boundaries of human cognition and human control – that makes him a truly paradigmatic individual (*maßgebender Mensch*). In analogy to the other paradigmatic individuals – Buddha, Socrates, and Jesus – Confucius refuses to be a god or even a sage and insists on being a finite human. Concerning Confucius' relationship to the spirit world, Jaspers writes: 'Ancestor cult and sacrifice were for him an essential reality. But in

[6] For instance, Han Jue 韓厥 had dreamed of his father telling him: 'Tomorrow morning, avoid the right and the left!' That was why he stood in the center and avoided death in the war (see *Zuo Commentary*, Lord Cheng 2.3; in Durrant, Li, and Schaberg, 2016, 717).

[7] For instance, it is recorded that a deceased father showed his gratitude to the family of his daughter's husband by helping the latter in a war. In the war, that ancestor ghost turned into an old man tying knots of grass to block the enemy's way. 'Tie knots of grass' (*jiecao* 結草) has now become a common idiom for repaying a favour (even after death) (*Zuo Commentary*, Lord Xuan 15.6; in Durrant, Li, and Schaberg, 2016, 682–683).

[8] The first line of Slingerland's translation that reads 'Working to ensure social harmony among the common people' is loaded with further elaborations. The text more directly means what is right or appropriate (*yi* 宜) to common people (see Zhu 1983, 89; Qian 2011, 167–168).

[9] It is also said that Confucius did not speak of topics of 'prodigies (*guai* 怪), force (*li* 力), disorder (*luan* 亂) and spirits' (*Analects* 7.21 adapted from Lau 2000, 61). While here we discuss ghosts and gods generally as spiritual beings, gods are of another kind than ghosts. For a reconstruction of the religious pantheon of early Chinese thought see Clark and Winslett 2023.

all his dealing with these matters he showed a remarkable aloofness and freedom from superstition.' For Jaspers, the Confucian relationship to spirits is, in the last instance, ambivalent and leaves open the crucial question, 'Should one keep a respectful distance from the gods or ignore them as much as possible?' (Jaspers 1966, 54).

Following Michael Puett, one can consider Confucius' attitude to the spirit world as a subjunctive mode (Puett 2008). In terms of linguistics, subjunctive statements express a possibility and are often accompanied by a desire, a wish, or other emotional states, including fear. We propose to explain the apparent contradiction between Confucian humanism and the Confucian emphasis on the importance of ritual practices as signalling a crucial innovation. Confucius transformed the meaning of sacrifice from a bargaining model, as one finds it in archaic religions, to a moral one. Henceforth, Confucians could no longer hope to bribe ghosts, but needed to focus on becoming virtuous human beings.[10] This transformation implies not only a recognition that, to use Herbert Fingerette's phrase, 'the secular is sacred' (Fingerette, 1972) – not only in the suggestion that human beings have quasi-sacred ethical commitments within secular forms of interaction, but also in the expansion by spiritual humanism of the scope of the ethical community so as to include the dead and the unborn. What is required by spiritual humanism is a transformed perception of, and comportment towards, the spirit world. For a Confucian reflection on what it means to be human (*ren* 人) and what is meant by humanity (*ren* 仁), it was crucial to relate oneself in the proper way to those who were human in the past and, as we will suggest in the conclusion, those who will be human in the future. For Confucius, the sacrifice to our ancestors is no longer aimed at seeking protection, curing one's ailments or asking for blessings from them, which reflected the bargaining model. Rather, respecting the spirit world is motivated by one's moral feelings towards ancestors who are acknowledged as one's origin or root (*ben* 本). That is, the sacrifices are, as Xu Fuguan 徐復觀 (1904–1982) contends, an extension of sincere filial piety (*xiao* 孝) (see Xu 1969, 82). This is shown when Confucius claims, 'I can find no fault with Yu 禹. Sparing in his food and drink, he yet extended (*zhi* 致) filial piety to the ghosts and spirits' (*Analects* 8.21 in Lau 2000, 74; translation consulting Xu 1969, 82).[11] In Xu's explanation, the sincere sacrifice of Yu

[10] Drawing on Karl Jaspers' axial age hypothesis, Karen Armstrong identifies this 'great transformation' as the origin of religion (Armstrong 2007). We prefer to speak of spiritual humanism instead of religion to avoid debates about theological assumptions and organized religion that were of no concern in the classical sources.

[11] Heiner Roetz has highlighted the potential significance of a critical reconstruction of filial piety in the Confucian tradition for addressing intergenerational justice in times of ecological crisis (2023).

was to extend his filial piety to his parents, to ghosts and spirits. Conversely, for Confucius such acts of reverence would fail in either one of two ways: (1) if they are committed insincerely in the sense of half-heartedly; or (2) if one takes a dogmatic stance towards the metaphysical nature of the spirit world and moves from a subjunctive mode to an indicative, assertive, or dogmatic mode. Confucius considered the gratitude to and appreciation of the ancestors' virtues and meritorious deeds as the central meaning of sacrifice. Accordingly, as Xu states, 'through sacrifice, one connects one's own spirits with those which one's life comes from and succeeds' (Xu 1969, 82).

This implies a profound conversion of our perception of the spirit world, particularly concerning the status of spiritual beings, in that, although ghosts and spirits are not taken to be non-existent, neither are they held to exist as causal agents that can influence the living, as archaic people used to think. More specifically, it is owing to our moral virtues, especially the moral affections towards our ancestors (i.e., our roots or origins), that Confucius did not deny the existence of ghosts and spirits but suggested that they are to be thought of as being present. In dealing with those now dead, if one treats them as if they were entirely dead and past, one would reveal a lack of humanity (*ren* 仁) and should, thus, avoid any such attitude towards them; however, if one treats them as if they were entirely alive as the living are, that would reveal a lack of wisdom, and should, thus, also be avoided (see Sun 1989, 216). One shows a lack of humanity and affection if one takes the dead as having ceased to exist (rather than having changed their form), whereas it shows a lack of wisdom if one takes the dead as existing in the same way as the living do, that is, as continuously present, spatio-temporal organisms with whom one can interact outside of dreams and subjunctive ritual reality.

Tang Junyi 唐君毅 (1909–1978) provides support for what we consider to be a Confucian middle view. He thinks that we have reason to hold that things – or, in our case, persons – are present unless there is concrete evidence to the contrary; it is not unreasonable (and in fact it is natural) to hold that these things still exist, even if one does not perceive them with one's senses in ordinary life. If so, given the lack of concrete evidence that the spirits of the dead do not exist, it is still reasonable to regard their existence as possible (see Tang 1986, 137–140). Thus, essential for the subjunctive mode is the idea of *ru* 如, which means 'as if', and appears most notably in the *Analects* 3.12: 'Sacrifice as if they were present means to sacrifice as if the spirits were present. But the Master said, "If I can't take part in the sacrifices, it's as though I haven't sacrificed at all"' (adapted from Watson 2007, 28). Although they are not existent in the same way as the living are, the ghosts and spirits are not entirely non-existent. It would also be unwarranted to imagine them in a certain way, as was done, often in an artistic manner, by archaic society. They are 'as if' present when one sincerely takes part in ritual exercises. That is, they 'exist' only during our transference (*gantong* 感通), or, in other words, when we are aware of our connection to them and our shared feelings and sense of resonance with them. This transference happens because of the virtues of humanity (*ren* 仁), sincerity (*cheng* 誠), and respectfulness (*jing* 敬) towards the dead. That is, we only aim at the resonance and express our gratitude to the dead, as illustrated above by Xu. Therefore, Tang thinks that such an 'as if' presence or the subjunctive existence of ghosts and spirits is a kind of 'pure presence' (or 'pure existence') (*cuncai* 純在), which means a mere presence without any particular determination concerning the exact status of these beings. We remain agnostic as to whether they have the same human appearances, or need to eat and drink, and so on. This stance is, first, rational, given our lack of evidence to the contrary; and is, second, a result of our moral awareness that we are not seeking any benefit from the ghosts and spirits, and, therefore, have no need to dwell upon their status of existence or their power to affect the world (see Tang 1986, 142–146).[12] It is because of the necessity of our moral feelings towards the dead in constituting the transference and the 'as-if' presence of the dead that Confucius was of the view that, unless he can sincerely take part in the sacrifices, it's as though he has not sacrificed at all.[13]

Given that Confucius transformed the central meaning of sacrifice from seeking benefits from, to expressing gratitude and respect to, the dead, then the idea of ancestor ghosts as a stand-in for justice in the story of the *Zuo Commentary* at the beginning of our paper may appear as primitive.[14] While

[12] This is an instance where Xunzi, an important Confucian in the pre-Qin period, showed some disagreement with other Confucians, for he, as Sor-hoon Tan notes, denied the existence of supernatural beings such as ghosts or spirits (*Xunzi* 19.11, 21.8 in Knoblock 1994, 72–73, 108–110), despite his appreciation of the positive impact of the mourning rituals on the emotions and ethical life of the mourners and its beneficial consequences in sustaining social order (see Tan 2015, 250).

[13] Zizhang 子張 said, when a gentleman (*shi* 士) is 'at a sacrifice, he thinks of respectfulness (*jing* 敬); at a funeral, he thinks of grief. If he does this much, he will get by' (*Analects* 19.1 adapted from Watson 2007, 134). On the relationship between religious thought and practices in the *Analects*, see also Cline 2013.

[14] Later, Confucians developed this view of Confucius. For instance, Zhu Xi used the concept of vital force (*qi* 氣) to explain the existence of ghosts and transference. The offspring can have transference (Zhu called it *gange* 感格) with the ancestors because they share the same vital force (see Zhu 1986, 47). For example, he said, 'The offspring bears the numerous achievements of their ancestors, and so their heart-mind are connected with their ancestors' heart-mind' (Zhu 1986, 46–47). The emperors' sacrifice to heaven (*tian* 天) is explained in the same vein: 'The son of heaven (*tianzi* 天子) [i.e., the emperor] encompasses the world and bears everything in it; he is related to it and his heart-mind is connected to it; so, his heart-mind can be connected to the world' (Zhu 1986, 46); 'The son of heaven is the host (*zhu* 主) of the world …, and when one is the host of [the world], and the world's vital force is encompassed by him, then there is the relation' (Zhu 1986, 47).

the story reveals a connection to justice, it also insists on the significant influence that spirits could exert on the world of the living, whereas Confucius suggested that we view the spirit world via a moral perspective that emphasizes connectedness and wisdom rather than causal interaction.

3 The Transformation of the Human–Ghost Relationship

The transformation in our perceptions of ancestor ghosts, the meaning in sacrifice, and, more broadly, our perception of the spirit world outlined above, are in fact concomitant with, or manifestations of, the emergence of humanism. They signal a transition from an archaic anxiety and faith in bargaining with ghosts to a reflective moral relationship. In primitive religion, people attributed some sense of morality to the spirit world. This can be seen in the ancestor ghost of the Zhaos accusing Lord Jing of unjustly killing Jin. But it is interesting to see that Zhao still required the approval of the god (*qing yudi* 請於帝) for exercising his revenge via the two skilful ghost boys. Here, we can witness the seeds of a transformation of the spirit world and the emergence of a moral awareness in and between human beings, that is, the emergence of humanism which, at the same time, is spiritual in that it continues to take obligations to ancestors for granted.

Chinese culture starts with experiences of the spirit world without, however, insisting on distinguishing religion from what is now called philosophy. According to Vincent Shen, the ancient Chinese people conceived the ultimate reality to be the high god (*shangdi* 上帝) or god (*di* 帝) in the Shang dynasty, or heaven (*tian* 天) in the Zhou dynasty, although always in an uncontested polytheistic context. The high god evolved from the Shang people's cult of ancestry. It 'dominated over a pantheon of divinities composed of natural powers (like the sun, Yellow River, mountains, etc.)' (Shen 2013, 24), whereas heaven, in Zhou, evolved from a reference to god 'into a more universal power symbolized by the physical sky covering universally all

Therein, Zhu continued to defend the idea of 'as-if' presence. When asked whether 'performing sacrifices to the heaven-and-earth and the mountains and rivers' that involve expensive gifts of animal victims and alcohol 'is merely to express the sincerity of one's heart-mind' or is really invoking something, Zhu replied that 'If nothing comes to enjoy the things, who are we performing the sacrifice to? What is it from the above that generates the feelings of reverence and awe? However, it would be absurd (*wangdan* 妄誕) to say that this something arrives in a cloud chariot' (Zhu 1986, 51; see Sommer 2020, 533–534). For Zhu's view on ghosts and spirits, see Zhu 1986, 33–55; for explications, see Azuma 2017, 141–155, Wilson 2014, and Wu 2013.

things under it' (Shen 2013, 24).[15] In the Shang dynasty, the idea of a mandate (*ming* 命) justified the power of the political leaders. The Zhou people, needing to justify their revolution against King Zhou 紂 of Shang, believed that the mandate 'was always assured by the kings' virtues' (Shen 2013, 25).[16] The Shang people were spiritual in the sense that they conducted divinations before taking major actions. They obtained approval or disapproval from the high gods.[17] There is a parallel within the pantheon of the spirit world to this reliance on, if not obedience to, god that can be found in the request of the Zhao ancestor ghost in our story, which, according to Chen Qian 陈謇, reflects the presence of the hierarchical relationship between human ghosts (*rengui* 人鬼) and the high gods (see Chen 1996, 65). The hierarchy of the spirit world mirrors the primitive hierarchy between humans and the emperor as the son of heaven.

But, as Shen suggests, the transformation that saw the ultimate reality shift, in human understanding, from being that of god to being that of heaven, also saw the very idea of heaven itself being 'changed to a more humanistic interpretation' (Shen 2013, 30).[18] There was, in fact, a decline in political theology, according to which only the ruler had been able to mediate between the spirit world and the people. This decline gave way to the emergence of a humanistic sense of moral obligation and capacity for deliberation whose nascent and most prominent manifestation is called by Xu the 'consciousness of anxiety' (*youhuan yishi* 憂患意識).[19] This awareness no longer denotes the anxiety in the face of ghosts and spirits, but the anxiety springing from a sense of responsibility when facing difficulties that are yet to be overcome (see Xu 1969, 20–21). The emergence of the idea of seriousness (*jing* 敬) – the moral virtue of bearing responsibility and trying our best when dealing with difficult

[15] In English, it may thus be better to translate '*tian*' as 'heavens' rather than heaven to refer to an impersonal physical sky. The plural avoids associations with a personal god or a paradise as one finds in Christianity. At the same time, the common translation of '*tian*' as 'heaven' in the singular better captures the universal normative dimension associated with the term in classical China, which is why we decided to continue to use 'heaven' in the singular.

[16] For instance, the *Book of Odes* reads, 'The mandate of heaven is not constant' (*tianming mi chang* 天命靡常) and the *Book of Zhou* reads, 'Great Heaven has no partial affections; it helps only the virtuous (*wei de shi fu* 惟德是輔).'

[17] For instance, there are texts reading: 'The King makes the divination and says: the result is auspicious, with the approval of *di* [*wang zhan yue: Ji di ruo* 王占曰：吉， 帝若]' (quoted in Shen 2013, 26).

[18] Xu also thinks that '*Di* 帝, *tianming* 天命, *tian* 天 are originally used interchangeably; however, the odor of a personified god that the term *di* represents is especially strong' (Xu 1969, 39). But with the more frequent emphasis on *tian*, the vanishing of personification has become clear.

[19] There were external factors that facilitated such a decline, such as the separation of historians from the diviners, the ambiguities of the divinatory results, and so on (see Shen 2013, 30–32).

affairs – marks a crucial transition.[20] Also, the idea of ritual propriety (*li* 禮) is essential in the cultivation of morality, because it provides the basic norms of action.[21]

Confucian spiritual humanism highlights the idea that morality is internal to human deliberation and character formation. Confucius asks: 'What can a man do with the rituals who is not humane?' (*Analects* 3.3 adapted from Lau 2000, 19). According to Xu, by focusing more on one's character rather than the objective norms in the social world, morality becomes the dimension in which one perfects one's personhood (see Xu 1969, 69–70). If one makes an effort, one can achieve humanity and be a genuine human being.[22]

This shows the rise of moral awareness in human beings. The second dimension of this development towards humanism is the 'humanization of heaven' (*tian de renwenhua* 天的人文化).[23] Heaven, which has drawn people's focus away from ghosts, gods, and numerous spiritual beings, is no longer seen as a personified ultimate reality that is only communicated with, if not ultimately interpreted, by the emperor. Rather, heaven, and the related concepts like that of heavenly mandate (*tianming* 天命) and heavenly way (*tiandao* 天道) are 'transformed from abstract external ideas into symbols denoting various forms or states of inner moral substance' (Rošker 2017, 286). Thus, for Confucius, heaven symbolizes concrete moral principles, which in fact carry implications for human behaviour. On the one hand, the heavenly mandate or heavenly way expresses what human beings should do. With his unceasing moral practice, Confucius gradually came to recognize the universality and perpetuity of morality, which he found expressed by heaven. That is why he said he 'recognized the heavenly mandate when he turned fifty' (*Analects* 2.4 adapted from Lau 2000, 11) and that a gentleman (*junzi* 君子) should stand in awe of (*wei* 畏) – or in other words, should respect – the heavenly mandate (see *Analects* 16.8 in Lau 2000, 165). On the other hand, there is an affinity and interconnectedness between heaven and human beings. Especially after his recognition of the existence of a heavenly mandate, Confucius vividly felt the interconnectedness of his life with heaven: facing assassination, he did not

20 The term *jing* 敬 can have different dimensions. Here, it is about a solemn attitude when dealing with important affairs, which is a bit different from a respectful feeling towards ancestors.

21 For instance, 'Ritual propriety is the marking line of superior and inferior, the warp and woof of heaven and earth, and the basis for the people's livelihood. That is why the former kings esteemed it' (*Zuo Commentary*, Lord Zhao 25.3; in Durrant, Li, and Schaberg 2016, 1639); brought to our attention by Xu (1969, 49).

22 Confucius says, 'Is humanity really far away? No sooner do I desire it than it is here' (*Analects* 7.30; adapted from Lau 2000, 65).

23 A phrase that Jana S. Rošker uses in describing Xu's elaboration on Confucius (Rošker 2017, 286).

show signs of fear and believed that 'heaven has implanted this virtue (*de* 德) in me. Huan Tui – what can he do to me?' (*Analects* 7.22 in Watson 2007, 50). This confidence in facing a challenge is due to a virtue that he understood to have come from heaven. He also emphasized the possibility of moral ascent: 'I start from below and get through to what is up above (*xiaxue er shangda* 下學而上達). If I am understood at all, it is, perhaps, by heaven' (*Analects* 14. 35 in Lau 2000, 143). The 'perhaps' signals that Confucius was never secure that he could claim morality or interpret heaven correctly. However, he also resisted the tendency to base morality on the recognition of others. Instead of recognition, he strived to be worthy of recognition. When we consider these two aspects together, we can say, with Xu, that 'his recognition of the heavenly mandate is the complete self-awareness and self-recognition of the nature of himself, the moral nature of his heart-mind (*xin* 心)' (Xu 1969, 88). His respect for heaven and for the heavenly mandate is a moral insight reflected in moral and religious emotions: 'the highest moral emotion is always a homogenous mental state with the highest religious emotion' (Xu 1969, 88).[24]

Morality has its root in human beings.[25] The quest for justice originates in human relationships to others, including currently non-living generations, and to ourselves. We may always fall short in fulfilling our obligations to other humans, including those present in the spirit world. That an ancestor ghost acts as a stand-in for retribution may, again, seem primitive. However, the above explorations into intergenerational bonds, moral authority, and a respectful awareness of the spirit world reveal a progression, in that a humanist ethics that includes obligations to a subjunctively conceived spirit world replaced a somewhat unreflective religion of instrumental transactions between the human and the dogmatically conceived spirit world. Meanwhile, despite this evolution, we see a peculiar preservation and transformation of a form of non-dogmatic spiritual sentiment in Confucianism. It consists in an awareness that heavens and the spirit world are connected to humans while, at the same time, being mindful to maintain caution towards ghosts.

[24] Later, Confucians like Mencius claim that human nature is good and this nature is endowed from heaven (*Mencius* 6A6 in Lau 2003, 247) and that 'For a man to give full realization to his heart-mind is for him to understand his own nature, and a man who knows his own nature will know heaven' (*Mencius* 7A1 adapted from Lau 2003, 287). The Song-Ming Neo-Confucians even explicitly developed the idea of 'interpenetration between heavenly way, nature, and mandate' (*tiandao xing ming xiang guantong* 天道性命相貫通), meaning that heaven and human nature share the same moral content (see Mou 2003, 27).

[25] For instance, Confucius said, 'The practice of humanity depends on oneself alone, and not on others' (*Analects* 12.1; adapted from Lau 2000, 109).

4 Conclusion

In this chapter, we have reconstructed the conception of spirits and ghosts in classical China from a perspective informed by Confucianism. We have argued that Confucius maintained neither that ghosts exist in the same way as humans and other living entities, nor that they are relegated to a world beyond this world. Ultimately, he was convinced that we know neither what ghosts are, nor what they want or need from humans. However, the Confucian texts do not reject belief in ghosts and spirits altogether. The existence of ghosts was taken for granted in China, and ghosts were a common reference point in classical debates among Confucian philosophers.

We have also pointed out that there has been an evolution towards moral reasoning that emphasizes the importance of showing sincere respect to dead people, especially ancestors. Confucius advocated keeping a proper distance and focusing on honouring, or at least respecting, the dead while caring for the living, especially the elderly as well as the young. In Erin M. Cline's view, Confucius promulgated the notion of maintaining an appropriate distance from ghosts (as well as one's children) 'because he disapproves of attempts to curry the favour of the spirits in order to further one's own selfish ends' (Cline 2015, 49). In addition to dismissing a naïve and egoistic conception of negotiations with the spirit world, we also believe that Confucius suggested cultivating a sense of respectful caution in light of our limited understanding of transcendent spirits. To consider this account as an evolution away from the older bargaining model is not to deny that the negotiation of relations with the spirit world persisted, or that it continues as a significant factor in the folk religions – not only, but especially, in East-Asian contexts (Reader and Tanabe 1998). We have presented Confucius' 'as if' concept as a viable alternative to both religious dogmatism and secular humanism. It sidesteps the Scylla of having knowledge of or acquaintance with the spirit world and the Charybdis of reducing human obligations to the perceivable here and now of currently living generations.

What implications does this spiritual humanist view have for environmental justice between generations? While there have been some attempts to make Confucianism fruitful for environmental concerns, China's 'green religion' is usually associated with Daoism (Miller 2017). Yet, Daoism has little to say about the core Confucian concern for harmonious intergenerational relationships. While the human-generation-oriented basis of classical Confucian ethics does not hold nature, including nature ghosts, at its centre, there are occasional references to 'the sun and the moon, the mountains and rivers' as forming part of the 'hundred spirits' who, according to *Mencius* 5A5, enjoy the sacrifices performed by humans. Confucian ethics can contribute to a rethinking of environmental justice between generations. Among the duties of being properly human, Confucians argue, is that of allowing the natural environment to continue to sustain human flourishing into the future. There is no doubt that human flourishing, for Confucians, depends upon our achieving long-term inter-generational continuity. This implies a need for both backward-looking as well as forward-looking relations.

The contemporary Confucian humanist Tu Weiming has emphasized the potential contributions of Confucianism to the mobilization of an ecological turn. This attempt is echoed by the current political rhetoric of transforming China into an environmental civilization. Discussing modern Confucian-inspired attempts to draw on the ancient vision of a harmonious unity of heaven and humanity (*tian ren heyi* 天人合一), Tu recalls that early-twentieth-century Confucians developed an 'anthropocosmic' (as opposed to anthropocentric) worldview. They 'did not wish merely to honor their ancestors but also to show that they cared for the well-being of future generations' (Tu 2001, 247). Such relations are conceptualized not primarily as relationships of fairness and intergenerational transactions, but as harmonious relationships in which future generations build upon the achievements of their ancestors, while the dignity of these ancestors rests in part on the actions of current and future generations.

The implications for intergenerational justice of the Confucian conception of an 'as-if' relationship towards the spirit world, as outlined above, are significant. According to this conception, humans need to acknowledge both their interconnectedness with the past and the future as well as their existential limitations. The presently living generation is not all that there is. It lives within a web of dependencies involving ancestors and future people 'as if' they were present. Currently living people have an obligation to keep in mind the consequences of their actions for both past and future people. If they fail to do so, they are, in a sense, failing to be properly human.

As James Miller argues in this volume, Confucians have devoted much energy to emphasizing pious relationships with paternal ancestors. Yet, we also witness more recent attempts to rescue Confucianism by modernizing it, as the contributions to this volume by Jing Iris Hu and Marion Hourdequin attest. Mencius' claim that the failure to have children is radically un-filial (*Mengzi* 4A26) seems hopelessly outdated in today's world. Not only does it clash with basic individual rights, but, in the face of a global population of eight billion people, the notion of an obligation to have more children ignores the finitude of our planet. Yet, the possibility of enabling future people to live and flourish is an intrinsic value and one that is not only for the future. From a Confucian perspective, future people are, at least in part, desired to extend human relationships and allow ancestors to be recalled and nourished in a dignified manner. As Heiner Roetz has argued, Confucian ethics invites us to interrupt the self-assertive tendency of the presently living generation by remembering (*erinnern*) and pausing (*innehalten*) since '*we do not have the right to devastate the earth, the only place for remembering the dead*; it does not only "belong" to us and to future people, but also to them' (Roetz 2024). One could add that, conversely, past, living and future generations also belong to the earth, which forms the natural habitat that allows for human co-existence in space and across time.

In contemporary China, visitors are often surprised by the extent of concern for – and fear of – ghosts. Returning to the opening ghost story, we venture the hypothesis that, in contexts where there are significant degrees of injustice and an absence of accountability, hungry ghosts serve as stand-ins. They may turn into agents of revenge for past and present wrongs when nobody else does. Ghosts thus fulfil an important function as reminders that might is not right. As the story reveals, medicine, religion, and politics may not help when injustice has been committed. The ghost boys can enter the space between the diaphragm and the heart that is beyond the reach of scientific solutions. Confucius has good reason to recommend that we keep ghosts at a respectful distance and focus on doing what is right.

Bibliography

Armstrong, Karen. 2007. *The Great Transformation: The World in the Time of Buddah, Socrates, Confucius and Jeremiah*. London: Atlantic Books.

Azuma, Juji 吾妻重二. 2017. *A New Study of the Learning of Master Zhu 朱子學の新研究*, translated into Chinese by Fu Xihong 傅锡洪 et al. Beijing: Commercial Press.

Chen, Qian 陈骞. 1996. "A Tentative Discourse on *Zuozhuan*'s View on Ghost and Gods" 试论《左传》鬼神观. *Journal of Yuxi Teachers College (Social Science Edition)* 玉溪师专学报（社会科学版）12, no. 1: 62–68.

Clark, Kelly James and Justin Winslett. 2023. *A Spiritual Geography of Early Chinese Thought*. London: Bloomsbury.

Cline, Erin M. 2013. "Religious Thought and Practice in the *Analects*." In *The Dao Companion to the Analects*, edited by Amy Olberding, 259–291. New York: Springer.

2015. *Families of Virtue: Confucian and Western Views on Childhood Development*. New York, NY: Columbia University Press.

Durrant, Stephen, Wai-yee Li, and David Schaberg, trans. 2016. *Zuo Tradition / Zuozhuan: Commentary on the "Spring and Autumn Annals."* Seattle, WA: University of Washington Press.

Fingerette, Herbert. 1972. *Confucius: The Secular as Sacred*. New York, NY: Harper and Row.

Harrison, Victoria S. 2021. “What if the Dead Are Never Really Dead?” *The Monist* 104, no. 3: 337–351.
Hu, Qiong. 2020. Defining Chu Religion: Gods, Ancestors and Ghosts. University of Macau PhD thesis, unpublished.
Jaspers, Karl. 1966. *Socrates, Buddha, Confucius, Jesus (from The Great Philosophers. Volume I)*. New York, NY: Harper Collins.
Knoblock, John, trans. 1994. *Xunzi: A Translation and Study of the Complete Works*. Stanford: Stanford University Press.
Lau, D. C. trans. 2000. *The Analects*. Hong Kong: The Chinese University Press.
2003. *Mencius*. Hong Kong: The Chinese University Press.
Leong, Y. K. and L. K. Tao. 2019. *Revival: Village and Town Life in China 1915*, reprinted. London: Routledge.
Lin, Su-chuan. 林素娟. 2005. “Exploration to Customs of Vengeful Ghosts and Solutions of Facing them in the Pre-Chin and Han Dynasty” 先秦至漢代禮俗中有關厲鬼的觀念及其因應之道. *Journal of Chinese Literature of National Cheng Kung University* 成大中文學報 13: 59–94.
Miller, James. 2017. *China’s Green Religion: Daoism and the Quest for a Sustainable Future*. New York, NY: Columbia University Press.
Mou, Zongsan 牟宗三. 2003. *The Problems and Development of Song-Ming Neo-Confucianism* 宋明儒學的問題與發展. Taipei: Linking.
Poo, Mu-Chou, 2002. *Ghosts and Religious Life in Early China*. Cambridge: Cambridge University Press.
Puett, Michael. 2008. “Ritual and the Subjunctive.” In *Ritual and its Consequences: An Essay on the Limits of Sincerity*, edited by Adam B. Seligman, Robert P. Weller, Michael J. Putt, and Bennett Simon, 17–42. Oxford: Oxford University Press.
2011. “Sages, the Past, and the Dead.” In *Mortality in Traditional Chinese Thought*, edited by Amy Olberding and Philip J. Ivanhoe, 225–248. Albany, NY: State University of New York Press.
2019. “Life, Domesticated and Undomesticated: Ghosts, Sacrifice, and the Efficacy of Ritual Practice in Early China.” *Hau: Journal of Ethnographic Theory* 9, no. 2: 439–460.
Qian, Mu 錢穆. 2011. *A New Explication of the Analects* 論語新解. Taipei: Dongda.
Reader, Ian and George J. Tanabe Jr. 1998. *Practically Religious: Worldly Benefits and the Common Religion of Japan*. Honolulu, HI: University of Hawai’i Press.
Roetz, Heiner. 2023. “An Overlooked Dimension of Intergenerational Justice? A Note on Filial Piety in the Age of Ecological Crisis.” In *Confucianism for the Twenty-First Century*, edited by Chun-chieh Huang and John A. Tucker, 197–208. Göttingen: Brill.
2024. “China—eine ‘ökologische Zivilisation’?” In *Nachhaltigkeit: Chinas Umgang mit Umwelt und Nachwelt in Vergangenheit und Gegenwart, Jahrbuch der Deutschen Vereinigung für Chinastudien 19*, edited by Lena Liefke and Angelika Messner. Wiesbaden: Harrassowitz.
Rošker, Jana S. 2017. “Is Confucianism a Religion? Modern Confucian Theories on the Ethical Nature of Classical Discourses.” *Asian Philosophy* 27, no. 4: 279–291.
Shen, Vincent. 2013. “The Fading of Political Theology and the Rise of Creative Humanism.” In *The Dao Companion to Classical Confucian Philosophy*, edited by Vincent Shen, 23–51. Dordrecht: Springer Netherlands.

Slingerland, Edward, trans. 2003. *Confucius Analects: With Selections from Traditional Commentaries*. Indianapolis, IN: Hackett Publishing Company, Inc.

Sommer, Deborah. 2020. "Zhu Xi's Philosophy of Religion." In *Dao Companion to Zhu Xi's philosophy*, edited by Kai-chiu Ng and Yong Huang, 523–541. Cham: Springer.

Sun, Xidan 孫希旦. 1989. *Collected Explanations of the Book of Rites* 禮記集解. Beijing: Zhonghua shuju.

Tan, Sor-hoon. 2015. "Xunzi and Naturalistic Ethics." *Journal of Value Inquiry* 49, nos. 1–2: 247–265.

Tang, Junyi 唐君毅. 1986. *Origins of Chinese Philosophy: The Dao*. Vol. 1. 中國哲學原論: 原道篇. 卷一. Taipei: Xuesheng shuju.

Tu, Weiming. 2001. "The Ecological Turn in New Confucian Humanism: Implications for China and the World." *Dædalus* 130, no. 4: 243–264.

Watson, Burton, trans. 2007. *The Analects of Confucius*. New York, NY: Columbia University Press.

Weber, Max. 1959. *The Religion of China*. New York, NY: The Free Press.

1963. *The Sociology of Religion*. Boston, MA: Beacon.

Wilson, Thomas. 2014. "Spirits and the Soul in Confucian Ritual Discourse." *Journal of Chinese Religion* 42, no. 2: 185–252.

Wolf, Arthur P. 1974. "Gods, ghosts, and ancestors." In *Religion and Ritual in Chinese Society*, edited by Arthur P. Wolf, 131–182 Stanford, CA: Stanford University Press.

Wu, Chan Liang 吳展良. 2013. "An Interpretation of Zhu Xi's Theory of Ghostly and Godly Existence" 朱子之鬼神論述義. *Chinese Studies* 漢學研究 31, no. 4: 111–144.

Xu, Fuguan 徐復觀. 1969. *The History of the Chinese Philosophy of Human Nature: The Pre-Qin Period* 中國人史論史：先秦篇. Taipei: The Commercial Press.

Zhu, Xi 朱熹. 1983. *Collected Arrangements and Annotations of the Four Books* 四書章句集注. Beijing: Zhonghua shuju.

1986. *Classified Sayings of Master Zhu* 朱子語類. Beijing: Zhonghua shuju.

6

Intergenerational Ethics and Sustainability

A Confucian Relational Perspective

Marion Hourdequin

1 Introduction

We live in an interconnected world that is facing important global and intergenerational environmental challenges, from pollution to climate change. These challenges are intertwined with issues of ethics and justice. For example, what would a just transition from fossil fuels to renewable energy look like, and how might this transition be achieved? What social, economic, and environmental burdens might an energy transition create, and how might these burdens be alleviated? Related questions arise in relation to land management and the use of natural resources. Is it possible to manage land and natural resources in ways that sustain people today, maintain healthy ecological systems, and provide for the future, and if so, how?

Discourses of sustainability seek to address some of these questions, including their intergenerational dimensions. The 1987 World Commission on Environment and Development (WCED) report, *Our Common Future*, for example, defined sustainable development as development that "meets the needs of the present without compromising the ability for future generations to meet their own needs" (p. 24), and the report stressed the importance of prioritizing "the essential needs of the world's poor" (p. 54) and of living "within the world's ecological means" (p. 55). The characterization of sustainable development in *Our Common Future* is fundamentally hopeful: "[S]ustainable development is a process of change in which the exploitation of resources, the direction of investments, the orientation of technological development[,] and institutional change *are all in harmony and enhance both current and future potential to meet human needs and aspirations*" (WCED 1987, 57, emphasis added). The idea of harmonizing institutions, technology, and use of natural resources to sustain current and future people is not new, and diverse cultures throughout history have sought to realize similar ends. Interestingly, the aspiration articulated in

Our Common Future largely aligns with the core values of a philosophy with roots in China more than two millenia ago. Early Confucianism – as exemplified in the thought of Confucius (Kongzi), Mencius (Mengzi), and Xunzi – also expresses a vision in which people's basic needs are met and leaders and institutions support both human sustenance and social harmony.

However, as the WCED report itself notes, sustainability, harmony, and equity can be difficult to achieve, especially when people do not view their interests as aligned. As the report explains, "All would be better off if each person took into account the effect of his or her acts upon others. But each is unwilling to assume that others will behave in this socially desirable fashion, and hence all continue to pursue narrow self-interest" (WCED 1987, 58). *Our Common Future* offers some suggestions through which interests may be better aligned, emphasizing that the common good may be best realized when equity is prioritized and ecological limits are respected. Nevertheless, although the overall vision of the WCED report emphasizes mutual flourishing, the discourses of sustainability that emerged in subsequent decades focused strongly on tradeoffs, accentuating the idea that in a world of limited resources, more for one group implies less for another.

In this chapter, I contend that certain conventional discourses of sustainability, along with related frameworks for intergenerational ethics, create conceptual barriers to realizing the goals of genuine sustainability and intergenerational flourishing. Moreover, although it might seem an unlikely source of insight for contemporary challenges, early Confucianism provides a model of intergenerational ethics that may better align with these goals. In particular, early Confucianism offers a relationally grounded ethics that conceptualizes community diachronically and emphasizes the importance of building and sustaining harmonious, flourishing human communities over time. These Confucian ideas resonate with relational and communitarian approaches to intergenerational ethics and sustainability more broadly, which can helpfully supplement existing frameworks for intergenerational ethics by emphasizing shared values and concerns, including commitments to common intergenerational projects.

2 Common Approaches to Intergenerational Ethics and Sustainability

To see more clearly what early Confucian perspectives may add to certain common contemporary approaches to intergenerational ethics and sustainability, it may be helpful to start by examining these latter approaches and their limitations.

Take sustainability first. Although *Our Common Future* describes sustainability as mutual flourishing through time, the report's characterization of sustainability as "[meeting] the needs of the present without compromising the ability for future generations to meet their own needs" can also be interpreted as setting present and future needs in tension with one another. Picking up on this tension, subsequent discussions tended to conceptualize sustainability as a distributive problem requiring tradeoffs between present and future wellbeing (see, e.g., Beckerman and Pasek 2001). If sustainability involves sharing or apportioning limited resources over time, then the question becomes, "How much must *we* (current generations) save for *them* (future generations)?"

This question, in turn, led to debates over *what*, specifically, to save, and these debates turned on the distinction between *strong sustainability* and *weak sustainability*. Proponents of *strong* sustainability argued that each generation should conserve a steady supply of natural capital for the next. According to this view, sustainability requires maintaining forested areas at their current levels, ensuring a non-declining supply of fresh water, and, more generally, conserving natural resources for future generations. Proponents of strong sustainability envision sustainability as involving the transmission of a basket of goods from one generation to the next: According to this view, the key to sustainability is a steady supply of resources, or "stuff."

In contrast, weak sustainability theorists suggests that it is *welfare* that should be sustained, and that sustaining welfare across generations may *not* require a constant supply of natural resources. As Bryan Norton explains: "The key theoretical divide here is over the question of substitutability of types of capital: weak sustainability theorists assume there are no limits on substitutability among resources and pay attention only to welfare changes, whereas strong sustainability theorists believe there are limits on such substitutions and specify stuff instead of welfare" (Norton 2005, 313). In other words, weak sustainability theorists tend to think that welfare can be maintained even if certain resources decline, because new resources can substitute the old, or because wealth or technology can compensate for resource declines.

Regardless of the view one takes on strong versus weak sustainability, the focus of the debate is on how many resources current generations can use without impinging on the wellbeing of those who will live in the future. More specifically, the discourse focuses on the kind of stuff current generations owe to future generations and whether different kinds of stuff are commensurable with one another or not. Do we need to save forests for future people? Or can we just give them money instead?

In my view, this approach is limiting. First, it focuses too much on resources, or stuff, ignoring other aspects of intergenerational ethics, such as the value of cultivating and passing on stable institutions, a just legal system, certain forms of knowledge, or positive relations with others and with the natural world. Second, debates over strong versus weak sustainability – insofar as they foreground tensions between current and future consumption or current and future welfare – presuppose scarcity and tradeoffs, suggesting that sustainability is a matter of a given generation making sacrifices for those that follow.

An emphasis on intergenerational conflict and tradeoffs also appears in dominant conceptions of intergenerational justice that focus on resource distribution over time. As Lukas Meyer (2021) explains:

> One of the legitimate claims of future generations vis-à-vis present generations appears to be a claim of distributive justice: Depending on the understanding of the relevant principles of distributive justice to be applied, if there is an intergenerational conflict of interests, present generations may be obligated by considerations of justice not to pursue policies that impose an unfair intergenerational distribution of costs and benefits.

This framing suggests that intergenerational justice involves dividing up goods and burdens across generations, and the underlying assumption seems to be that the good of each generation is distinct from – and potentially in tension with – that of others. This reinforces the idea that providing for future generations means taking something away from present generations, and vice versa.

Intergenerational justice is also often framed in terms of the *rights* of future people: Do future generations "[hold] legitimate claims or rights against present generations"? (Meyer 2021). And if so, what do future generations have a right *to*? Is there a right to some threshold level of welfare, or to some level of welfare relative to present generations? There are clearly multiple ways to answer questions about the rights future generations can claim in relation to present ones, and about what current generations owe to the future. However, as is the case with the sustainability discourses discussed earlier, these framings tend to conceive the rights of future generations and obligations to future generations as *constraints* or *limitations* on the behavior of present generations, again foregrounding the potential for intergenerational conflict.

Common discourses of sustainability and intergenerational justice both frame intergenerational ethics as a distributive problem, where the key challenge is to balance rights or fairly divide a limited pool of resources. Distributive justice does, of course, matter. However, it is not the only way to think about intergenerational ethics and can be limiting as the sole lens. In particular, starting from a position that foregrounds scarcity and tradeoffs can crowd out other possibilities. If we *assume* tradeoffs, we may fail to ask whether tradeoffs are necessary, or explore ways in which tradeoffs might be avoided. Perhaps there are ways to meet everyone's needs without significant tradeoffs, and to ease potential conflicts of interest between present and future generations. In the following sections, I explore the possibility that a Confucian relational perspective on intergenerational ethics might reshape perspectives so that putative tradeoffs are less prominent. This perspective does not deny that people have diverse and sometimes conflicting desires and needs, nor that an important aspect of ethics is to harmonize these desires and needs, but it does not frame this challenge primarily in terms of tradeoffs.

3 Distributive Justice, Rights, and the Common Good

To get an intuitive feel for the Confucian perspective, we can consider the workings of a well-functioning family. Families sometimes encounter situations in which the needs of one family member and another are in tension. Perhaps one child likes to listen to music while they do homework, while the other prefers a quiet environment. Or perhaps different family members have different dietary needs. These tensions could be viewed as requiring tradeoffs: Music or no music in the background? Meet one person's dietary needs or meet those of the others? However, it is not necessary to approach the goal of meeting family members' needs through a distributive justice or tradeoffs-centered frame. Instead, family members might try to make sure that everyone has what they need, adjusting their values and priorities to enable that, such that the distinction between one person's interests and those of another are not so sharp. For example, attending a child's sporting events or musical performances when one otherwise could have been relaxing at home is not necessarily something that many parents would view as a "tradeoff," because their concern for their children and desire to support them has been integrated into their own thinking in a way that softens any putative conflicts. That is not to say that conflicts never arise, just that the overarching goal that guides the resolution of tensions ideally reflects each individual's consideration of the good of others and the possibility of finding harmonious ways of supporting each person's needs (Wong 2020). This process of reconciling diverse desires and needs may involve modulating one's own goals and desires in order to harmonize with those of others (see Wong 2020 for related discussion).

In a discussion of Confucianism and individual rights, Craig Ihara (2004) describes a similar view. He suggests that there are certain contexts "where individual rights are out of place" (Ihara 2004, 11). Dance and sports teams are key examples: When a soccer player frequently hangs on to the ball too long and fails to pass to teammates, one would not generally say that the teammates' *rights* have been violated, even though the ball-holder can be criticized. As Ihara explains, framing the problem in terms of rights is unlikely to help:

instead, introducing rights-talk into sports "changes the game in a fundamental way. It reconceptualizes the activity in a way that makes basic the individual, and not the team" (Ihara 2004, 12). Ultimately, Ihara argues that in communities that share a common goal, the idea of individual rights has little role to play. This is not because individuals need to sacrifice themselves for the common good, but because the common good is conceptualized in a way that incorporates concern for each individual and seeks harmonious ways of meeting everyone's needs. Ihara acknowledges that rights can provide important protections for individuals, but he suggests that their importance enters the picture primarily when something has gone wrong and shared goals and values have been lost. Moreover, insofar as traditional Confucian thought lacks a conception of individual rights or focuses little on rights-based ethical reasoning, this reflects Confucianism's community-centered ethos, which holds that "human beings have intrinsic value" as "constitutive parts of an intrinsically valuable whole" (Ihara 2004, 24; see also Fingarette 1972).

Although these examples focus on ethics among contemporaries, Confucian ethics has an important diachronic dimension, emphasizing that "we are creatures of time," situated in relation to others within and beyond our own lifetimes (Hourdequin and Wong 2021). This provides a way of grounding intergenerational ethics that understands persons as embedded in networks of connection across space and time, and that sees moral personhood as developing through intergenerational relations. As I explain below, rather than focusing on tradeoffs *between* present and future generations, early Confucian philosophy emphasizes the shared intergenerational project of building and sustaining flourishing communities *across* generations.

4 A Confucian Approach to Intergenerational Ethics

Confucianism is a many stranded and dynamic tradition.[1] Over centuries and millennia, Confucianism has blended with Buddhism and Daoism, and it has been adapted in various political traditions and contexts. Significant developments include the rise of Neo-Confucianism in the Song and Ming Dynasties and the emergence of New Confucianism in the twentieth century. My goal here is not to do justice to the many facets of Confucianism, nor to reconcile early Confucianism with its diverse contemporary manifestations throughout the world. Instead, my modest aim is to suggest that early Confucianism – as exemplified in the text of the *Analects of Confucius*, as well as in the *Mengzi*

[1] This section draws on and extends a number of ideas in Hourdequin and Wong (2021).

and *Xunzi* – can offer some important insights with respect to intergenerational ethics, as well as a coherent alternative or complement to approaches that focus primarily on intergenerational ethics and sustainability as problems of distributive justice.

Early Confucianism provides a relational perspective on intergenerational ethics in which gratitude, reciprocity, and learning across generations play a central role. This relationally grounded intergenerational ethics is knit together by shared commitments to building and sustaining flourishing communities over time. Although early Confucian ethics emphasizes *human* communities, it also situates humans in a broader triad of Heaven, Earth, and humanity (for discussion, see Li 2014, ch. 10), and Mengzi and Xunzi explicitly recognize the interdependence between humans and the broader environment. Thus, building especially on later neo-Confucian ideas, Confucian intergenerational ethics may be extended to foreground this interdependence and encompass care for socioecological communities over time.

Before exploring in more detail the elements of a Confucian approach to intergenerational ethics, it may be helpful to briefly describe the context in which Kongzi's thought – as well as that of his successors, Mengzi and Xunzi – emerged. Confucianism developed during the late Zhou dynasty in ancient China, during a period of significant social turmoil. The centralized rule of the early Zhou dynasty had broken down, and local rulers vied for land and power. Rather than provide for the needs of the people, many of these rulers sought to amass wealth for themselves. Dismayed by this situation, Kongzi (Confucius) argued for a return to virtuous rule, and to the traditions and rituals, or *li*, that he saw as providing structure for ethical relations and societal harmony. Kongzi also emphasized the important role of the family in moral learning: Through family relationships, children develop respect, gratitude, reciprocity, and empathy, then apply these qualities in broader settings. For this reason, Kongzi suggested that filial piety is the root, or foundation, of *ren*, the central Confucian virtue (*Analects* 1.2).[2] This key virtue is what enables kings and other leaders to rule well, and to sustain a harmonious and flourishing society.

From the beginning, Confucian ideas were situated in multigenerational time. Amidst social and political chaos, Kongzi looked back across centuries for moral models that could guide social renewal. He found such models in the ancient sage-kings – Yao, Shun, and Yu – who were known as humane and virtuous rulers (*Analects* 8.18, 8.19, 8.21), and in the rulers of the early Zhou dynasty (*Analects* 3.14, 8.20), whom he saw as benevolent leaders who presided during times of relative peace and prosperity. Kongzi was dismayed by

[2] All passages quoted from the *Analects* are translated by Ames and Rosemont (1998).

the fractiousness of the late Zhou dynasty, but remained hopeful that the *Dao* would be restored. Over shorter timescales, early Confucianism emphasized the role of intergenerational relationships and learning, beginning from a relational conception of persons that situates individuals in networks of connection, both synchronically and diachronically.

Confucian intergenerational ethics can be conceptualized in terms of three key elements: (1) a relational conception of persons and their good; (2) a sense of gratitude toward those who have supported one's development and positively shaped one's life and identity; and (3) a shared commitment to a sustained and flourishing human community (Hourdequin and Wong 2021). These elements are linked, as gratitude is intertwined with the relational conception of persons central to Confucianism, and a commitment to collective flourishing through time grows out of a relationally grounded, intergenerational sense of community. The sense that one is part of a community that is extended in time helps to diminish conflicts between individuals and between generations. In early Confucian philosophies, ethical self-cultivation develops persons who can contribute to the shared project of building harmonious communities, and to sustaining and revitalizing those communities through time. Rather than viewing generations as distinct entities with disparate interests, the Confucian conception of community is transgenerational. The goal is not to enable a single generation or time-slice of the human community to flourish, but to support the flourishing of the temporally extended whole.

To fill out this sketch, we can begin with the relational conception of persons central to early Confucianism. According to this view, persons are understood as embedded in networks of relations across space and time, and these relations shape persons' identities, responsibilities, and moral development (Rosemont 1991; 2006). Early in life, children (ideally) learn to relate well to others in their immediate family, then apply these lessons in new contexts as they grow. In Confucian ethics, responsibilities are often linked to specific roles – as a parent, child, teacher, student, minister, or ruler – though the overarching virtue of humaneness, or *ren*, is one that can find expression across all the roles people occupy (see Ames 2011, ch. IV). Another important aspect of Confucian self-cultivation involves the sociality of moral development itself: "We are born human … but we are given our *humanity* by and with others" (Olberding 2019, 56). In other words, "persons come into being in families and communities that sustain them, and they grow into moral personhood through their contributions to the growth and sustenance of others" (Hourdequin and Wong 2021). As such, Confucian persons are not conceptualized as isolated individuals; instead, they are persons-in-relation, whose "identities and welfare are deeply bound up with those of others" (Hourdequin and Wong 2021).

This relational conception of persons is tied to gratitude, a key Confucian virtue that weaves people together into communities that extend backward and forward in time. The paradigmatic source of gratitude in early Confucianism lies in family relationships, and especially in relationships between parents and children. The *Analects* emphasizes that parents provide years of nurture for their dependent children (*Analects* 17.21), and that good parents nurture children not only physically, but emotionally, socially, and morally. In the family, children learn how to relate to others and how to fulfill responsibilities to parents and siblings; these lessons are then carried forward to relations with others outside the family. Thus, children who grow up in loving and supportive families find that their identities are positively shaped by these early and ongoing relationships throughout their lives, and they have reason to feel gratitude for the care they have received (Hourdequin and Wong 2021).

Although gratitude is sometimes conceptualized transactionally, as grounding attitudes and actions that repay a benefactor for what has been received, gratitude in the Confucian tradition is not understood primarily in terms of debt and repayment (Hourdequin and Wong 2021). The care that young children receive from their parents is understood as a basis for gratitude, and for reciprocating care to one's aging parents, as well as to others. However, it would be a mistake to interpret certain Confucian practices – such as an extended mourning period for parents when they die (*Analects* 17.21) – as a kind of repayment for care received (Hourdequin and Wong 2021). The care that loving parents provide for their children cannot be repaid: How can we repay others for giving us life or for enabling us to become the people we are (Ivanhoe 2007, 304)? Instead, from a Confucian perspective, we can think of gratitude as flowing from the recognition of what others have given us, but not as requiring that those gifts flow back to our benefactors in the same degree or form. Gratitude can not only motivate us to care and support those who have supported us, but also to nurture others and support the development of *their* good.

In this sense, Confucian gratitude is linked to the relational conception of the self, and to a sense of broad reciprocity that enables people to see themselves as part of a community in which people care for one another and reciprocate both directly and indirectly (by supporting others in turn) for the care they have received. Kongzi demonstrates this ethos of care when he expresses his central aspirations in *Analects* 5.26: "to bring peace and contentment to the aged, to share relationships of trust and confidence with my friends, and to love and protect the young." Kongzi's aspirations are clearly multigenerational, spanning from the old to the young, and, more generally, Confucian care and gratitude extend beyond presently living persons to encompass respect for ancestors and concern for future generations. This sense of embeddedness in and care for a multi- and transgenerational community is at the heart of Confucian intergenerational ethics.

As we have already seen, Kongzi's efforts toward social renewal draw on moral models from the past, and moral learning also occurs intergenerationally within the family. Respect for elders and ancestors in Confucianism reflects an appreciation for one's own place within a broader community extended through time. Traditions that honor and show reverence for ancestors reinforce this sense of temporally extended community, as does the Confucian idea that one can honor one's parents and ancestors by carrying forward key values and practices (*Analects* 1.11), while also adjusting to new circumstances (*Analects* 9.3). Although Kongzi clearly emphasizes the importance of tradition, the *Analects* also recognizes the need for adaptation and change, suggesting that change can occur in ways that continue to honor insights from the past (Hourdequin 2004). The forward-looking dimensions of Confucianism also include the idea that multigenerational learning is not unidirectional, from elders to the youth: The young can offer important perspectives that extend, fill out, or challenge the perspectives of those in older generations (see, e.g., *Analects* 4.18, 9.23).

What brings together the contributions of young and old, and ancestors and contemporaries, in early Confucianism is a common goal and commitment to the shared human project of restoring and "[broadening] the Way (*dao*)" (*Analects* 15.29), by developing and sustaining harmonious relations within society and in relation to the broader world. This itself is a multigenerational project, which Kongzi recognizes well. Perhaps in part for this reason, Kongzi is devastated by the loss of one of his favorite students, Yan Hui. Throughout the *Analects*, Kongzi praises Yan Hui's insight, his commitment to self-cultivation, and his love of learning (*Analects* 11.7). Yan Hui's death is not only a personal loss for Kongzi, it is also the loss of a valuable, younger partner in work that Kongzi likely expected his student would carry forward (Hourdequin and Wong 2021). Kongzi's efforts, as well as his devastation in the face of Yan Hui's death, can be understood in light of this shared work:

> [I]f persons are understood as persons-in-relation, and if moral personhood involves contributing to the growth and sustenance of others and to the human community as a whole, then Confucius's effort to restore social harmony should not be seen as merely a personal interest or pet project, but as a commitment to a shared *human* project, to which *all* Confucian moral persons are committed. (Hourdequin and Wong 2021)

Confucian ethics invites all persons to contribute to this project. Through self-cultivation, each person sets themselves on a path through which they can develop intrapersonal and interpersonal harmonies, and through which they can contribute to harmony among humans and in relation to the broader universe (Li 2008).

Harmony, or *he*, is arguably a central concept in Chinese thought and in the Confucian tradition in particular (Li 2008; Wong 2012). Chenyang Li argues that harmony emerged as a key ideal prior to Kongzi's own lifetime. For example, Li (2008, 424) explains that in the *Shi Jing* (Book of Odes), "The happy life is one in harmony with other people and with nature." The ideal of harmony is further thematized in the *Analects* (1.12, 13.23), the *Mengzi* (3B1), and the *Xunzi*, where the *li* (rituals/traditions) are seen as particularly important in the development of social harmonies (Li 2008). It is important to note that the Confucian conception of harmony is not harmony through sameness, but rather a harmony that emerges from combining distinct elements into a balanced whole (Li 2008; Wong 2012; Wong 2020). The metaphor of bringing different musical instruments together to produce a beautiful composition, or a variety of ingredients combining to make a flavorful soup, exemplifies the idea of *he* (cf. *Analects* 3.23, 13.23). For individual persons, the work of contributing to dynamic harmonies that incorporate "different elements in creative tension" (Li 2008, 427) can provide meaning in human lives and ground an immanent sense of the life's purpose (Ames 2011, ch. V, see also Rosemont 2006, 10).

Confucianism foregrounds social relations and harmonious human societies, but it also situates human community in relation to Heaven (*tian*) and Earth (*di*). As Xunzi explains: "When Heaven has its proper seasons, Earth has its proper resources, and humankind has its proper order, – this is called being able to form a triad" (see *Xunzi*, chapter 17, "Discourse on Heaven," in Hutton 2014, 175–76). There are, thus, ecological and cosmic dimensions in Confucian ethics, in addition to the intra- and intergenerational human ones. Xunzi and Mengzi, in particular, draw out some basic tenets of sustainability in relation to land, waters, animals, and ecosystems (on Mengzi and the environment, see Wee 2009). For example, Mengzi describes the thoughtful use of natural resources as key to human flourishing in 1A3:

> If you do not interfere with the busy seasons in the fields, then there will be more grain than the people can eat; if you do not allow nets with too fine a mesh to be used in large ponds, then there will be more fish and turtles than they can eat; if hatchets and axes are permitted in the forests on the hills only in the proper seasons, then there will be more timber than they can use. (Lau 2003, 5)

Here, Mengzi suggests that certain kinds of restraint can ensure that resources are sufficiently abundant to support human needs. Xunzi goes further, suggesting that timeliness in relation to natural cycles is key to sustainability:

> When the grasses and trees are flowering and abundant, then axes and hatchets are not to enter the mountains and forests, so as not to cut short their life, and not to break off their growth. When the turtles and crocodiles, fish and eels are pregnant and giving birth, then nets and poisons are not to enter the marshes, so as not to cut short their life, and not to break off their growth. Plow in the spring, weed in the summer, harvest in the fall, and store in the winter. These four activities are not to miss their proper times, and then the five grains will not be depleted, and the common people will have a surplus to eat. Be vigilant in the seasonal prohibitions concerning ponds, rivers, and marshes, and then turtles and fish will be fine and plentiful, and the common people will have a surplus to use. Cutting and nurturing are not to miss their proper times, and then the mountains and forests will not be barren, and the common people will have surplus materials. (Hutton 2014, 77)

Underlying this idea of things having "their proper times" is the suggestion that an awareness of seasonal changes and of the patterns of life and growth in the natural world is key to developing harmonies with the broader environment. Later Confucian thought, particularly Song and Ming dynasty neo-Confucianism, extends the idea of harmony even further, to all elements of the world and to the broader universe or cosmos. In the *Western Inscription*, for example, the Song dynasty philosopher Zhang Zai (who lived from 1020 to 1077 CE) writes: "Heaven is the father; Earth is the mother. And I, this tiny thing, dwell enfolded in Them. Hence, what fills Heaven and Earth is my body, and what rules Heaven and Earth is my nature. The people are my siblings, and all living things are my companions" (Zhang Zai 2014, 135). Building on these and other Confucian ideas, contemporary philosopher Tu Weiming describes a Confucian anthropocosmic vision, "in which the human is embedded in the cosmic order" and contrasts this with "an anthropocentric worldview, in which the human is alienated, either by choice or by default, from the natural world." (Tu 2001, 244). Elsewhere, Tu describes the idea that the Confucian vision extends to encompass the entire world, with a "message of cosmic harmony." (Tu 2012, 79) This vision builds on the idea that the Confucian self-in-relation is constituted not only in relation to other past, present, and future people, but in relation to the Earth and broader universe.

Putting the pieces together, early Confucianism – in conjunction with subsequent developments that elaborate a wider view of community as encompassing the broader world and universe as a whole – provides a basis for an ethic that emphasizes harmonies at multiple scales, extending to include not only human communities, but also the broader natural world, and not only present persons, but also past and future generations. The relational conception of the self, the gratitude that can emerge from the recognition of support we have received from others, and the sense that each person can contribute to a common human project are important elements of this view. Together, they suggest that meaning in life can be found in one's relations with others and in one's contributions to the creative and dynamic harmonies that sustain human societies and the broader world over time.

5 Conclusion

What is distinctive about early Confucian philosophy as compared to dominant contemporary philosophies of sustainability and intergenerational ethics? A key difference lies in the conceptualization of community, and of relations between generations. In discourses of intergenerational ethics that focus on distributive justice across generations, the focus is on each generation getting its due. In rights-based intergenerational ethics, the focus is on what each generation owes to others, and on how potentially conflicting rights should be balanced. Similarly, many conceptions of sustainability following the *Our Common Future* report focused on balancing the needs of distinct groups – present generations and future generations – and these needs were often conceptualized as competing with one another. Although Confucianism, too, recognizes distinctions between the young and old and attends to different generational positions, relations between generations are not generally viewed as agonistic. Prior generations – including those many generations removed – are seen as a source of knowledge and wisdom with continued relevance. Thus, the legacy that prior generations leave for those that follow is not merely a pile of stuff, nor merely a repository of natural resources (though resources are important), but insight into living well together, insight that subsequent generations can build upon and adapt.

Confucian ethics is animated by the shared project of generating and regenerating dynamic harmonies among people, and between people, the earth, and the cosmos as a whole. This again offers a contrast with dominant frameworks, in which humans and nature are often set in opposition. As scientist, professor, and author Robin Wall Kimmerer observes, in many contemporary contexts, people find it difficult to imagine positive relations between humans and nature (2013, 6). Confucianism, in contrast, presupposes the possibility of such positive relations in the idea that humans can form a triad with Heaven and Earth, and in the notion that humans can contribute to – or broaden – the Dao.

Confucianism is not the only philosophical tradition that conceptualizes community intergenerationally, nor the only tradition that envisions the possibility of dynamic harmonies that encompass humans and the broader world. As Kimmerer (2013) points out, many Indigenous philosophies – though diverse – share the view that humans have a constructive role to play in the natural world, as partners who can contribute to the wellbeing of the land through reciprocal relations with it, and many Indigenous traditions take as central the importance of intergenerational relations (Whyte 2018). In addition, within the "Western" tradition, broadly construed, there are communitarian and relational, care-ethical approaches to intergenerational ethics that resonate strongly with key aspects of the Confucian view. Avner de-Shalit, for example, develops a communitarian theory of intergenerational justice in which "[o]ur obligations to future generations derive from a sense of community that stretches and extends over generations and into the future" (1995, 14), and Adam and Groves (2011, 23) suggest that "a care perspective … acknowledges the way in which the present is always involved with the future, in the weaving of a common fate with others." Janna Thompson further emphasizes the importance of shared intergenerational projects in the contemporary world: "In a global society the intergenerational projects of many people are shared with individuals and groups in other countries or depend on their cooperation. There are projects that everyone has good reason to share: for example, to maintain a healthy natural environment to pass on as an inheritance to future generations" (Thompson 2017, p. 324).

Thus, although Confucianism provides a distinctive ethical outlook, Confucianism shares with a variety of other philosophical perspectives the core idea of an extended, intergenerational community, and this conception of community can both motivate and ground intergenerational obligations. In a world beset by individualism, including *generational* individualism – a kind of "each generation for itself" point of view – the sense that each of us can contribute to a shared human project of developing social and ecological harmonies through time has attenuated. Although intergenerational, social, and ecological harmonies are an aspirational ideal, aspirations matter, and institutions, policies, and practices can follow.

Bibliography

Adam, Barbara and Chris Groves. 2011. "Futures Tended: Care and Future-Oriented Responsibility." *Bulletin of Science, Technology & Society* 31, no. 1: 17–27.

Ames, Roger T. 2011. *Confucian Role Ethics: A Vocabulary*. Honolulu, HI: University of Hawaii Press.

Ames, Roger T. and Henry Rosemont Jr. 1998. *The Analects: A Philosophical Translation*. New York, NY: Ballantine Books.

Beckerman, Wilfred and Joanna Pasek. 2001. *Justice, Posterity, and the Environment*. Oxford: Oxford University Press.

De-Shalit, Avner. 1995. *Why Posterity Matters: Environmental Policies and Future Generations*. New York, NY: Routledge.

Fingarette, Henry. 1972. *Confucius: The Secular as Sacred.* New York, NY: Harper Torchbooks.

Hourdequin, Marion. 2004. "Tradition and Morality in the *Analects*: A Reply to Hansen." *Journal of Chinese Philosophy* 31, no.4: 517–533.

Hourdequin, Marion. and David B. Wong. 2021. "Confucianism and Intergenerational ethics." In *The Oxford Handbook of Intergenerational Ethics,* edited by Stephen M. Gardiner. Oxford: Oxford Academic. https://doi.org/10.1093/oxfordhb/9780190881931.013.16.

Hutton, Eric L. 2014. *Xunzi: The Complete Text.* Princeton, NJ: Princeton University Press.

Ihara, Craig K. 2004. "Are Individual Rights Necessary? A Confucian Perspective." In *Confucian Ethics: A Comparative Study of Self, Autonomy, and Community*, edited by Kwong-loi Shun and David B. Wong, 11–30. New York, NY: Cambridge University Press.

Ivanhoe, Philip J. 2007. "Filial Piety as a Virtue." In *Working Virtue: Virtue Ethics and Contemporary Moral Problems*, edited by R. L. Walker and P J. Ivanhoe, 297–312. New York, NY: Oxford University Press.

Kimmerer, Robin W. 2013. *Braiding Sweetgrass: Indigenous Wisdom, Scientific Knowledge, and the Teachings of Plants.* Minneapolis, MN: Milkweed Editions.

Lau, D.C. 2003. *Mencius.* London: Penguin Classics.

Li, Chenyang. 2008. "The Philosophy of Harmony in Classical Confucianism." *Philosophy Compass* 3, no. 3: 423–435.

2014. *The Confucian Philosophy of Harmony.* New York, NY: Routledge.

Meyer, Lukas. 2021. "Intergenerational Justice." In *The Stanford Encyclopedia of Philosophy*, Summer 2021 ed, edited by E. N. Zalta. https://plato.stanford.edu/archives/sum2021/entries/justice-intergenerational/.

Norton, Bryan G. 2005. *Sustainability: A Philosophy of Adaptive Ecosystem Management.* Chicago, IL: University of Chicago Press.

Olberding, Amy. 2019. *The Wrong of Rudeness: Learning Modern Civility from Ancient Chinese Philosophy.* New York, NY: Oxford.

Rosemont Jr., Henry. 1991. "Rights-Bearing Individuals and Role-Bearing Persons." In *Rites, Rituals, and Responsibility*, edited by M. Bockover, 71–101. LaSalle, IL: Opencourt.

2006. "Two Loci of Authority: Autonomous Individuals and Related Persons." In *Confucian Cultures of Authority*, edited by P. D. Hershock and R. T. Ames, 1–20. Albany, NY: SUNY.

Thompson, Janna. 2017. "The Ethics of Intergenerational Relationships." *Canadian Journal of Philosophy* 47 no. 2–3: 313–326.

Tu, Weiming. 2001. "The Ecological Turn in New Confucian Humanism: Implications for China and the World." *Daedalus* 130 no. 4: 243–264.

2012. "Ecological Implications of Confucian Humanism." In *Exploring Synergies between Faith Values and Education for Sustainable Development*, edited by R. Clugston and S. Holt, 78–81. San José, Costa Rica: Earth Charter International and Earth Charter Center for Education for Sustainable Development at UPEACE.

Wee, Cecilia. 2009. "Mencius and the Natural Environment." *Environmental Ethics 31* no. 4: 359–374.

Whyte, Kyle. 2018. "What Do Indigenous Knowledges Do for Indigenous Peoples?" In *Traditional Ecological Knowledge: Learning from Indigenous Practices for Environmental Sustainability*, edited by M. Nelson and D. Shilling, 57–82. Cambridge: Cambridge University Press.

Wong, David. 2020. "Soup, Harmony, and Disagreement." *Journal of the American Philosophical Association* 6 no. 2: 139–155.

Wong, Pak-Hang. 2012. "Dao, Harmony and Personhood: Towards a Confucian Ethics of Technology." *Philosophy of Technology* 25: 67–86.

World Commission on Environment and Development (WCED). 1987. *Our Common Future* [English version]. United Nations. https://digitallibrary.un.org/record/139811?ln=en

Zhang, Zai. (2014). "The Western Inscription," translated by B. W. Van Norden and J. Tiwald. In *Readings in Later Chinese Philosophy: Han Dynasty to the 20th Century*, edited by J. Tiwald and B. W. Van Norden, 134–136. Indianapolis, IN: Hackett.

7

Moral Motivation for Future Generations, Naturally

A Mencian Proposal

Jing Iris Hu

1 Introduction

Hourdequin and Wong have recently offered an important model to explain a central question of intergenerational ethics; namely, why should or do we care about people in the future, especially those who are not related to us in meaningful ways and whose lives will not overlap with ours on this earth (Hourdequin and Wong 2021)? In other words, how does our moral motivation to do good extend to the future beyond our own time? The model Hourdequin and Wong offer is a Confucian-inspired relational construction of human agency and morality. In this model, we appreciate that relationships with others define and shape our moral agency and identity; we acknowledge that we are the product not only of our own devotion and efforts, but also of others' moral influences, gained through both subconscious socialization and purposeful emulation. It is in this spirit that the gratitude and admiration we feel and the moral legacies we receive direct us not to the original individuals who influenced us, but to those who might be influenced by us, no matter whether they are present in our time or in the future. We are motivated by emotions such as gratitude to return the debt we owe the moral exemplars who inspired us; however, the subjects of such repayment are not always those we originally admired, but those who may be inspired by us in similar ways. It is in the same spirit that we owe our gratitude to our moral forebearers and owe our good conduct to future generations, so as to pass on this gift of virtuous moral influence.

The relational understanding of moral agency and moral interaction provides an important platform from which to understand our interpersonal relationships in a spatial and temporal manner. Communal moral influences can reach people both nearby and far away; they can also be passed down so that the influence extends beyond the life of the moral agent.

However, in this chapter, I argue that this model needs to be supplemented with other insights from early Confucians – especially Mencius and Xunzi and their naturalistic understanding of ethics – in order to be more effective in terms of intergenerational ethics. Their invaluable contributions are to treat emotions and some normative beginnings in them as the natural foundation of a moral theory, and to focus on internalizing values through moral education rather than relying solely on incentive/punishment-based policies to best motivate individuals.

In the following, I will first summarize the relational understanding of Confucian morality and its merits in Hourdequin and Wong's account, as well as the challenges it faces. In the second section I will explicate the reasons why I think, despite its enormous promise, it remains incomplete in addressing the question of why we should care about the wellbeing and moral plight of future generations, and will proceed by posing the challenge of "the loss of continuity" of communities and cultures. I argue that only a naturalistic ethics rooted in emotions, such as Mencius's, can be expected to motivate people across time. The commonality based on emotions can provide us with an account that resonates with individuals across different time periods and generations – people can still be properly motivated to care about and attribute moral weight to distant others based on these shared emotions across time, space and culture. On its own, without such a moral foundation, the relational understanding in Confucian ethics cannot reach its goal. Mencius's naturalistic ethics center around the shared common emotional responses with which people across cultures and generations can connect and resonate while, more importantly, allowing enough flexibility as to how people in the future might react and carry out their own actions. This adaptability prevents paternalistic interference and any attempt by current generations to manipulate future generations. The Mencian account shows why such attempts at interference with and manipulation of future persons would inevitably fail.

I should note that my purpose here is to enrich the toolbox in intergenerational ethics from a Confucian-inspired perspective; such tools are by no means exclusive to the Confucian philosophical tradition. A naturalistic understanding of morality, for example, is not limited to the Confucian tradition, nor are moral motivation and education based on it. It is also the case that the Confucian-inspired (specifically Mencian) models I discuss do not claim to present themselves as the only possible interpretations of the diverse early Confucian texts.

2 Relational Perspective on Intergenerational Ethics

Confucian ethics is well-known for its focus on relationships, so much so that some would advocate a role-based or relation-based understanding of Confucian ethics in which the individual's roles and relationships, which help to construct moral identities and provide ethical guidance, are considered essential to their being a moral agent. Some would even argue that the moral guidance one receives from such relationships replaces concepts such as rights and justice (Ames and Rosemont 1999; Rosemont 2016), although this view has attracted criticism, since some version of the idea of justice is clearly present in Confucian ethics and its denial would be at the expense of the accuracy of the texts (Ivanhoe 2008). Other criticisms, from Paul Goldin and Aaron Stalnaker, are also highly relevant. Stalnaker claims that the so-called relational understanding of Confucian agents would lead to the false conclusion that, within such a framework, the person cannot rebel against their roles and relationships if these roles and relationships were the sole source of their moral guidance (Stalnaker 2019). Acts of rebelliousness can be justified on Confucian grounds, as we can see in texts such as *The Mencius* and *The Book of Odes* that contain stories about moral agents and, especially, women's moral struggles against the expectations stemming from their familial roles (Stalnaker 2019). In addition, as Goldin points out, women are frequently placed in impossible moral dilemmas that require them to choose between their moral duties as faithful wives, loyal daughters and devoted mothers – and the Confucian texts give no hope that there could be any theoretical reconciliation when such conflicts arise (Goldin 2016). As a matter of fact, in many of these stories, these women have to commit suicide to demonstrate their moral integrity, and even the celebrated *Confucian Four Books for Women* does not always provide a moral solution to its readers (Goldin 2016; Pang-White 2018). The concern here is that roles-and-relationship-based understandings of moral agency can fail to provide theoretical resources when conflicts between the moral expectations of one's various roles arise; and this concern is particularly relevant in regards to women, whose plight is less frequently discussed in philosophical texts. Stalnaker casts doubt upon the moral emphasis on relationships, worrying that such social and familial relationships may limit, rather than support, one's moral development. While the relational understanding of ethics is considered an essential feature of Confucian value-theory, it may not provide sufficient theoretical resources for people facing struggles against their relationships – for example, people in abusive or oppressive relationships who rebel against their roles and relationships (Goldin 2016; Mattice 2016; Stalnaker 2019).

Wong provides a much more nuanced view that elegantly avoids the criticisms centered around the idea that one may not have a moral sense that is independent of the various demands of one's roles and relationships. He proposes that the relational approach in Confucian ethics ought to be understood in a developmental sense, in which one grows and learns morality while being situated in one's ever-changing roles and relationships (Wong 2004). We co-develop our moral agency with others who influence us in gaining a mature sense of our moral identity that we can, in turn, use to guide our moral conduct and attitudes when navigating relationships. In other words, by introducing the temporal dimension to the understanding of relationality, Wong's view is able to answer the question of how we can expect to rebel against or otherwise navigate relationships with our own moral sense. We should acknowledge that who we are today is the result not only of our own choices, efforts and devotion, but also of the moral influences of others throughout the course of our moral upbringing and learning – which, according to Confucius, should be a life-long process. As the products of such co-development with others around us, we are also a part of their moral co-development. In the same manner that we acknowledge and appreciate the moral influences of others, we are also predisposed to influence others in our own time and in the future.

The parent–child relationship, which is reciprocal but not transactional, is the most important resource for the Confucian insights on the topic of intergenerational relations in Hourdequin and Wong's paper. The reciprocity is realized through socialization, education and ritual practices and is based on the taming of emotions and virtues such as gratitude, filial piety and empathy (Hourdequin and Wong 2021). In addition, due to their admirable characters, a number of moral exemplars – such as the three legendary sage-kings – are held in high regard by the early Confucians (Hourdequin and Wong 2021). Their stories are often cited and used as moral inspirations and arguments for certain moral practices (e.g., sage-king Shun's stories are recited many times in the *Analects* and *Mencius*). People's respect and appreciation for moral traditions, as well as their ongoing efforts to draw moral inspiration and guidance from ancient moral sages, has allowed the legacies of these moral exemplars to live on through generations, with their moral influence extending for thousands of years (this is criticized and mocked by some of the early Confucians' contemporary rivals, such as the legalist Han Feizi). Perhaps what is more important – in addition to the more apparent celebration of parent–child relationships and the quest for moral inspiration and guidance from the ancient moral exemplars – is, as Hourdequin and Wong observe, the early Confucians' focus on the "importance of ongoing human community and sustained, collective work to develop a flourishing society in which multigenerational relationships play a central role" (Hourdequin and Wong 2021, 2). A relational understanding of agency enables us to see the long-lasting influence of the ways in which one interacts with others and conducts oneself; sometimes those influences may not be direct but they are nonetheless significant when situated in the collective endeavor of sustaining a flourishing community.

There are, however, certain reservations about the idea that, by itself, the relational perspective can save the day – that is, can answer the question of how and why one has moral reasons to be motivated to care about the well-being of future generations. One such reservation concerns the problem of the loss of continuity: or, in other words, the question as to whether or not, if a community or a culture were to become extinct, there would be reasons for people within that culture to care about the loss of future people to inherit moral influences from them or from their community? The potential loss of continuity means that reciprocity can no longer be justified or expected, in theory. After all, the future generations could be imagined as people like me, my nephews and nieces, my friends, my students, my community members, my readers, or people who also listen to Beethoven, read the *Monkey King* or watch the World Cup, who represent my influences or those of my communities and cultures. On the other hand, we could also imagine that the future generations of the population have little to do with us or our moral influences. They could adopt entirely different moral practices that are against everything we stand for today. They may reject and be ungrateful for the moral legacy we intend to leave them; or, worse, they may simply ignore and forget our influences entirely, including the moral legacy we intend to pass down and the moral lessons or pitfalls we ourselves faced and that future generations could have learned from. It is possible that, despite the causal relationship that would connect us, our moral and cultural influences would be of little or no consequence to them. And it seems that, taking the relational approach, we would naturally be disposed towards helping those who stand a chance of passing down the torch, so to speak, rather than those with whom we have no shared ties, through blood or cultural relationships. The central issue is that, even though the relational approach can expand our circle of moral concern from ourselves and those we care about over a few generations to large cultural and moral communities that can evolve and flourish over hundreds or thousands of years, it does not solve the problem of the loss of continuity or the fact that, no matter the scope of our moral concern, each unit will eventually face its own death. The relational approach merely delays our own eventual death and that of our community. The assumption that our community will always flourish and continue to exist must be queried, and the question of how to extend our moral concern beyond the end of our relations and communities remains unanswered.

The interruption of positive, moral-influence feedback loops by unthankful actors is another challenge for the relational approach. Many, such as the Legalists (School of Fa) – one of the early Confucians' rival schools – would adamantly deny the importance of carrying on traditions or of aligning ourselves with ancient sages whose teachings, they claim, are simply outdated. Knowing that such views might always exist, and might not be in the minority, can we nonetheless assume a positive outlook and be morally motivated towards future generations and their concerns, despite knowing that they may "betray" us? Han Feizi (unknown — 233 BCE), for example, mocks the Confucians for regarding the ancient sages' teaching as moral guidance:

> In the most ancient times, when men were few and creatures numerous, human beings could not overcome the birds, beasts, insects, and reptiles. Then a sage appeared who fashioned nests of wood to protect men from harm. The people were delighted and made him ruler of the world, calling him the Nest Builder. The people lived on fruits, berriews, mussels, and calms—things rank and evil-smelling that hurt their bellies, so that many of them fell ill. Then a sage appeared who drilled with sticks and produced fire with which to transform the rank and putrid foods. The people were delighted and made him ruler of the world, calling him the Drill Man.
>
> ...
>
> Now if anyone had built wooden nests of drilled for fire in the time of the Xia dynasty, Gun and Yu would have laughted at him... For the sage does not try to practice the ways of antiquity or to abide by a fixed standard, but examines the affairs of the age and take what precautions are necessary. (Han Feizi, 49, Five Vermin, trans. Watson 2003: 97–98)

Han Feizi's states that only a fool would live in a nest on a tree in his time, even though, when the ancient sage invented nests for people to live in (possibly referring to housing structures detached from the ground), it was a great invention at the time that helped people avoid the dangers posed by insects and animals. Equally, only a fool would start fires in Han Feizi's day by drilling wood, as the ancient people did (chapter 49). Such traditions are no longer useful and have run their course – in the same way that our behaviors, whether morally praiseworthy or blameworthy, are only of significance to our own time. We don't owe it to our ancestors to pass down their legacy. Han Feizi goes on to say, "That is the reason why the sage neither seeks to follow the ways of the ancients nor establishes any fixed standard for all times but examines the things of his age and then prepares to deal with them" (*Han Feizi,* Chapter 49, "Five Vermin," translated by Liao 1939).

We might reasonably call people like Han Feizi "morally ungrateful," in the sense that they do not acknowledge that the current generation has received meaningful moral gifts in the form of positive moral influence from the past, nor are they especially concerned that they have special obligations or reasons to set good moral examples for future generations to look up to. The relational view that enables positive moral influences to spread and pass down the line will quickly dissolve when significant individuals are "morally ungrateful." The central problem with the relational account is that it can only prolong and extend one's social influence and concern through one's relational network, but such extension cannot be indefinite. When communities come to an end – whether this is the result of "morally ungrateful" people who refuse to participate in such a view or of the community running its natural course and dying out – the relational approach may not be capable of being stretched any further in a vacuum of relations.

The addition of temporal aspects is undeniably significant for the relational approach because it broadens the scope of our moral concern – not only for those who influence us, but also for those whom we influence throughout history or into the future. However, the problems discussed above, of the loss of continuity through kinship or culture and the problem of morally ungrateful actors, would have to be addressed in this line of thought.[1]

3 Can Empathy Provide Enough Help?

Hourdequin (2012) points out that one potential way to supplement the relational model is to understand how others' needs might be apprehended through emotional mechanisms, such as empathy. Through our natural emotional capacities, such as empathy, we can be motivated by ends that are not our own. In other words, others' well-being, plight and moral ends are sufficient moral reasons for us to act and do not need to be related to our own moral ends. She argues:

> Moral agents, in virtue of their capacities for empathy (understood as a particular kind of attunement and responsiveness to others' emotions) and shared intentionality (understood as a particular kind of attunement and responsiveness to others' goals), are sensitive to reasons that do not directly link up with their

[1] Another issue with Wong and Hourdequin's relational approach, based on parent–child relationships, is that it does not take competing relationships seriously in these models, which is precisely one of the central problems of intergenerational ethics. When different generations' interests come into conflict, how should we best address such issues? While I agree that a relational approach modeled after familial and communal relationships is necessary, it is equally important to consider intergenerational ethics from the lenses of conflicts – especially when the resources we are sharing with the future people are scarce, or at least finite. The relational approach would be significantly strengthened if resources that help to show how intergenerational conflicts could be solved within such a framework can be provided and discussed. On the other hand, when the relational approach is not based on parent–child relationships, but other types of relationships, such as those between friends, we would face a richer set of possibilities that could possibly address competing relationships outside of the family structure. I thank Mario Wenning for this point.

> pre-existing ends. More specifically, they are sensitive to, and hence can be motivated by, reasons grounded in the desires, projects, commitments, concerns, and interests of others. (Hourdequin 2012, 403)

In this model, the moral concerns of future generations can motivate us, so long as we can put ourselves in their shoes and empathize with their plight. By adopting empathy as a useful mechanism we can overcome the problem of loss of continuity, since we can empathize with people who we do not know or who do not belong to the same cultural communities as us. However, despite being a promising approach, it is worth exploring questions about how strong a moral motivation empathy might be, especially when our own interests stand between us and our empathy.

Paul Bloom (2016) and Jesse Prinz (2011a, 2011b), notably, question the usefulness and reliability of empathy as, among other functions, a moral motivator. Prinz defines empathy as a "vicarious emotional response to another's emotions," which is largely consonant with Hourdequin's understanding of empathy (Prinz 2011a, 2011b; Hourdequin 2012). How reliable can empathy be as a moral motivator? The issue Prinz brings forth is straightforward: An emotion we "catch" through empathy from another is normally weaker than the original emotion. If, for example, I am upset as a result of empathizing with my student Jamie, who is upset that his submission to a prestigious philosophy conference was turned down, then, according to Prinz, my "second-hand" state of upset will be a weaker version of Jamie's. How can we expect a weaker version of the emotion to be a reliable motivator and to help the original, stronger emotion?

One response would be to debunk the assumption that a "second-hand" emotion is necessarily weaker than the original one, both in terms of intensity and motivating power. A parent might experience stronger distress when empathizing with their children's distress; By empathizing with a new victim, a previous victim of systemic injustices may have a stronger emotional response than the new victim who has just fallen prey to such systemic injustice and is oblivious to such social patterns. To assert that the result of empathy is, most likely, a weaker version of the original emotion is to demonstrate a lack of understanding of the complexities of human emotional responses.

Further, it is not the case that a more intense emotion in terms of feeling is always linked to a stronger reaction – or motivation. I have argued elsewhere that empathy can bring people to feel the distress of, and be morally motivated to help, people who are far away, non-kin and abstract (Hu 2018). My arguments were based on some of Mencius's texts, such as 1A7, in which Mencius demonstrates that the way to extend King Xuan's empathetic response to a suffering ox to the people of his country is by evoking his emotions

(McRae 2011; Wong 2015a, 2015b). I should note that the term "empathy" in my work is understood to be slightly different than Prinz's and Hourdequin's use of the term. Instead of requiring that one be feeling the same emotion as the empathized, I include the congruent emotional responses one feels as a result of the original emotion as a form of empathy. This choice of terminology echoes that of many empirical studies, such as those by Martin Hoffman, Daniel Batson and Franz de Waal (Hoffman 2001, 2011; Preston and Waal 2002; de Waal 2008; Batson 2011a, b). In my framework, empathizing with someone who is depressed could result in feelings of concern; Prinz would not call this empathy because the resultant emotion and the original emotion are not the same. In my definition, one can retain a level of flexibility when empathizing with another – one can react to the plight of others in the ways that one sees fit.

However, even after debunking the claim that a "second-hand" emotion cannot be as strong as the original emotion and provide the effective help that Prinz puts forth, the question as to empathy's efficacy and reliability still remains: Can we be sufficiently motivated by empathy to care for and act on the plight of future generations? The conclusion seems to be that, through empathy and in the right contexts, it is possible, plausible and practical to care about people in the future with whom one shares no ties, biological or cultural. However, given competing factors, it is not the case that empathy alone can always be a reliable motivator. At least theoretically, the case of empathy shows that we *can* care about future generations and their well-being and moral plight, but it does not provide a strong enough basis for the claim that empathy-motivated moral actions demand us to do so, morally.

I supplement two additional points to advance the idea that a Confucian – specifically the Mencian – view of a naturalistic understanding of moral potentials, would be better suited to help us address questions faced in environmental ethics. In the next section, I argue that Mencian ethics is particularly useful in addressing the problem of our motivation towards the welfare and moral concerns of future generations. While I agree that the relational understanding of personhood and empathy are useful tools in the Confucian philosophy-inspired toolbox, it is only when paired with a Mencian naturalistic framework that they are most effective.

4 Naturalistic Morality

Mencius, a fourth-century BCE thinker, was a follower of Confucius's teaching. Mencius is frequently referred to as the "second sage," who is second only to Confucius himself; and his insights in moral psychology and ethical theory have received long-lasting attention in Chinese philosophy. Many debates center around his claim concerning the goodness of human nature, and many others focus on his contribution to moral education as he employs psychologically sound methods that take into consideration the subtlety of emotions in his attempts at persuasion (e.g., 1A7, 3A5).

In the following, I will argue that a relational approach should be accompanied by a naturalistic understanding of morality so as to be effective in addressing the theoretical challenges facing intergenerational ethics. In order to make this point, I will contrast the Mencian naturalistic ethics, in which normative beginnings reside in moral emotions, with the view of his fellow Confucian philosopher Xunzi, who views basic emotions as entirely natural and harboring no moral values prior to education and socialization. I will demonstrate that the Mencian framework could explain why we have moral motivation for ends beyond our own and for those with whom we have no shared ties in the future – its function in moral education cannot be replaced by a top-down, policy-driven approach.

The Confucians are known as "naturalists" in the sense that their moral theories are frequently based on deeply seated psychological features of humans and human groups. These psychological features are, in turn, woven into a normative framework of ethics and political philosophy. Schools in Confucianism typically focus on people's natural moral potential, as well as their cultivational efforts and the function of social constructions, such as *li* (rituals). Irene Bloom provides the most notable attempt to address the issue – much-debated by contemporary scholars – as to whether human nature, which is seen as the moral foundation and beginning by both Mencius and Xunzi, should be seen as a descriptive or normative concept (Bloom 1997). Her answer is that human nature is both descriptive and normative. Bloom argues that Mencius answers the question "what [do] people share and what causes them to differ" (Bloom 1997, 23). In other words, any theory of moral origin or foundation must first address this question.

This idea is particularly relevant to our inquiry into intergenerational ethics, since what people share in the past, present and future could eventually serve as the common basis upon which to bring their concerns into our moral deliberation.

4.1 Mencian Ethics

Since Mencius starts his arguments about human nature with something as basic as one's reaction to seeing an endangered child (2A6), many are puzzled by the biological and normative components in his theory, and, more specifically, by the question of how they relate and connect to one another. As a matter of fact, the normative aspects of Mencian ethics are carefully woven into its seemingly biological description of certain human psychological features. Many observe the close relationship between the normative and the biological features, and some go so far as to claim that Mencius is advocating for an ethic in which "biology implies ethics" (Virág 2017). Although this claim is controversial, and some would argue it is the other way around, it nonetheless highlights the importance of biological features and their close relationship with the normative aspects of the ethical framework.

Mencius employs a famous botanical metaphor to illustrate his notion of the goodness of human nature. He states that all human beings have four sprouts (or beginnings): the sprout of *ceyin* (compassion-like emotion), *xiuwu* (shame-like feelings), *cirang* (deference) and *shifei* (right and wrong). They have the potential to mature into four virtues, namely, *ren* (benevolence, humaneness), *yi* (righteousness), *li* (propriety, observance of rites) and *zhi* (wisdom). This means that every human being is innately predisposed towards these ethical ideals. Mencius stresses that these innate qualities must be strengthened and guided so as to achieve ethical ends; thus, the focus of Mencian ethics consists of the innate disposition towards goodness and proper ethical cultivation.

In the next subsection, I aim to address the question of how the naturalistic interpretation of Mencian ethics connects with the normative aspects of Mencian ethics. I point out that the seemingly naturalistic aspects of Mencian ethics that are sometimes its celebrated characteristics furnish merely one aspect of his philosophy, and that the normative aspects are skillfully merged with the naturalistic side. My goal is to investigate and identify the origins of the normative claim and how it manifests itself in natural human biological functions.

4.2 Mencian "Natural" Normativity

Mencian ethics can be understood as a naturalistic philosophy, meaning that it draws insights from seemingly biological and psychological features of the human being, such as the basic emotion of sympathy or empathy, care for our young and our kin, our natural aversion towards certain situations and so on. The four sprouts, which are arguably the most representative and the foundation of Mencian ethics, represent four types of universal emotional responses.

There are a few places where the normative aspect is carefully woven into Mencius's seemingly biological description of general human conditions. We all care for our young, for example, and have some innate altruistic impulses. As one example, in the famous 2A6 case, he describes a situation in which a child is about to fall into mortal danger – a deep well – and everyone in that situation, according to Mencius, would have a robust sympathetic feeling and an urge to help (2A6). Now, what Mencius described here is descriptively true, as this thought experiment resonates with many of us across different cultures and time periods. It may not seem as if there is any normative twist in the story until he turns our attention to the rest of the four sprouts.

It is interesting to note that to which Mencius leads our philosophical attention and that which he leaves out of his discussion of human nature and outside of our understanding. Because, not only the part he focuses on, but also, perhaps more importantly, the part he intentionally omits, are where the normativity of Mencian ethics kicks in. Mencius acknowledges that we have *yu* (desires). These desire-based motivations lack the ethical potential – that is, the inclination towards goodness – that the four sprouts have. Insofar as your desires are not oriented towards ethical ends, they can be regarded as morally neutral. Regarding his views upon desires, Mencius is actually in agreement with Xunzi that there exist interest-driven desires and other neutral desires in humans. Unlike Xunzi, who would later proclaim that human nature is selfish and profit-driven, Mencius simply draws attention to the selected four sprouts (from all the other natural emotions) and claims that those are what we should be focusing on when thinking of our nature and our natural endowment for moral propensity. A moralistic attempt was made in the selection process.

On the other hand, moral inclination, defined as the tendencies of the four sprouts to grow and develop, is another area where the normativity of Mencian ethics comes into play. Mencius uses two notable metaphors to describe the four beginnings: the botanic metaphor, in which the four beginnings are likened to, and referred to as, sprouts (2A6); and the idea that our moral potentials will develop towards ethical ends, just as water will flow downward (6A2). These two dynamic metaphors – one biological and one physical, as noted by Wong – showcase that, in Mencius's view, moral potential and the four sprouts are dynamic in nature and have certain tendencies towards ethical ends that, even though they may be temporarily obscured, will nonetheless retain their resilience (Wong 2015b). It is telling that Mencius chose the botanical and water metaphors to describe our natural moral tendencies, as they are both dynamic in nature. The inclinations to become morally better are embedded in his theory in such a way that even though, like Mencius, we do acknowledge that the moral sprouts may not grow to maturity due to environmental issues, such as those in the Ox Mountain passage (6A8) or personal problems (lack of consistency or devotion in moral cultivation in 1A7, poor professional choice in 2A7), we are led to focus on the inclination towards moral betterment. This is perhaps one of the biggest theoretical differences between Mencius and Xunzi, aside from their definitions and understandings of what is and what should be considered human nature: Mencius thinks there is a moral inclination in us to be good, whereas Xunzi does not think that we hold any such proclivity. That is why, to the Xunzi, moral cultivation relies on human efforts (*wei*), and normativity resides in human efforts instead of natural endowment.

In this section, we have discussed Mencius building the beginnings of normativity into our understanding of "human nature," and the ways in which these beginnings can become connected to an increasingly sophisticated cultural and moral system focused on self-cultivation and ritual practices. In his understanding, every human being is innately predisposed towards the ethical ideals embedded in the four sprouts, which, given the proper conditions, will blossom. The very exciting possibility that Mencian ethics brings to contemporary ethics is that of a framework wherein our basic emotions and capacities carry the potential for complex moral systems which would eventually allow moral ideals to flourish and relationships to grow.

4.3 Mencian Ethics and People in Power

Mencius frequently engages in discussion with people in power. In the famous 1A7 passage, Mencius tries to urge his interlocutor, King Xuan of Qi – who confesses that he is only interested in strengthening his military strength and expanding his territory – also to take into consideration the hardships facing the people (1A7). The tribulations of the people may be physically and psychologically remote from the king's daily life and ethical and political reasoning: They may exist merely as concepts or ideas that lack the emotional charge Mencius tries to arouse in the king. Mencius's attempt to bring the king to feel for his people's suffering and align the king's emotions with those of his people is consistent with his political philosophy; namely, that a reign has legitimacy only when the ruler has the people's approval in some form, and that a successful ruler would always "rejoice with the people" (*yu min tong le*). There are some similarities between, on the one hand, the problem Mencius faces in mobilizing concern for the plight of the people on the part of the king; and, on the other hand, the problem of how to motivate the current generation to consider the plight of future people: In both instances, the people facing potential suffering are remote and have little power with which to bargain. It is difficult or impossible to make their voices heard. In the same way that a commoner would have a hard time communicating the tragedy of suffering caused by constant wars, military drafts and high taxation to the king, whose actions can change their plight for better or worse, it is impossible for the future generations to voice their concerns or protest their unfair treatment to people in our time, whose actions can change the fate of future people. This power asymmetry, among others, is described in the famous metaphor of the "perfect storm" by Stephen Gardiner (2006, 2011) to illustrate the difficulties in motivating current generations to take action for the sake of future generations, especially when their interests may be in conflict with ours.

The fact that many of the conversations in which Mencius emphasized the importance of *ceyin zhi xin* (the heart/mind of sympathy or the sprout of benevolence) were held with a powerful and influential figure such as a king (as we see in 1A7, 6A2, etc.) is quite telling. It seems that Mencius is really trying to make *ceyin zhi xin* work for those kings or dukes in high, but potentially isolating, positions – in order that they can empathize and emotionally connect with their people. The terms *wang* (king) and *min* (people, subjects or citizens) appear together many times when emotional connection is discussed in *Mencius*. More importantly, while Mencius frequently refers to King Wen and King Wu as moral exemplars due to their virtuous deeds, he also praises them as role models for all rulers to follow because of their emotional connection with their people. Not only do they feel and understand their people's struggle and delight, but the people, in turn, also delight in the king's delight and worry about the king's worries.

Mencius also emphasises, in conversations with powerful rulers, the importance of sharing emotions with their people. After a conversation, he makes King Xuan realise that delighting in common music rather than classic or ancient music is fine; what matters most is who he is enjoying the music with. Mencius asks, "Is it more delightful to delight in music with a few people or to delight in music with a multitude of people?" King Xuan answers, "It's more delightful with a multitude of people than with a few people" (1B1). Similarly, when King Hui of Liang asks if wise princes would find pleasure in the beauty of a scene of large geese and deer walking by a pond, Mencius responds by saying that only the wise and good princes can enjoy them because they know their people will also delight in them. Unkind rulers, on the other hand, cannot enjoy the beauty of such a scene even if they possess it, knowing that their people would only wish them ill (1A2).

Further, using King Wen as an example, Mencius states that:

> King Wen used the strength of the people to make his tower and his pond, and yet the people rejoiced to do the work, calling the tower "the marvelous tower,"

> calling the pond "the marvelous pond," and rejoicing that he had his large deer, his fishes, and turtles. The ancients caused the people to have pleasure as well as themselves, and therefore they could enjoy it. (Mencius 1A2)[2]

In another passage, Mencius emphasizes the importance of sharing one's delight in music with one's people, concluding that rejoicing with people is the key to successful ruling (1B1) and proclaiming that "If a ruler rejoices with his people, he can be called the true king" (1B1). In fact, many conversations between Mencius and the kings and dukes stress the idea of "rejoicing with the people" as a political ideal. Meanwhile, as we have seen in the quotes above, rejoicing with the people is not uni-directional: In the ideal state, not only would the king resonate with his people's happiness and worries, but the people would also share the king's delights and worries. In other words, this is a reciprocal, or at least bi-directional, idea. In fact, this very basic idea runs through Mencian thought, emphasizing the moral and political importance of what the people feel and desire and the question of whether or not the king possesses the ability to resonate with his own people's feelings and desires. Of course, "rejoicing with the people" involves more than listening to the same music or admiring beautiful wild animals together; rather, it requires the rulers to take the commoners' concerns and worries to heart and to avoid letting their power isolate them from the people. However, to be able to do this while making political decisions, the king must have a deep emotional connection with his people. The above passages can be understood as an attempt to strengthen this connection so that the king can act upon the concerns of the people, or at least take them into consideration, even when making difficult decisions, and the people, in turn, will then have trust in their ruler.

Emotional connection is, according to Mencius, the hallmark of successful and benevolent state rule. However, it is made possible not only by the efforts of the ruler, but also by the naturalistic ethical framework that Mencius has carefully laid out. It is precisely because rulers also have the basic emotional responses that they can be expected to have shared emotional experiences with their people, who are far away and sometimes described as an "abstract group." But it is also because of the fact that within these emotions reside normative beginnings; the shared emotional experience is meaningful and morally significant, and can later be connected to moral values, such as benevolent rule, that affect both the rulers and the people.

[2] Translation from the Chinese Text Project https://ctext.org/ens which adopts the sections of *Mencius* from "The Works of Mencius" (Legge 1861).

Returning, then, to similar issues that arise in intergenerational ethics, the insights from Mencian ethics – a framework that is naturalistic in nature and normative in its construction of certain emotions – tell us that, through the emotions, one is able to have meaningful connection with people in the future with whom we may have no biological or cultural ties, and who we are unable to identify as specific individuals with personal preferences. We can, nonetheless, based on our shared emotions, delight in their delights and worry about their worries. Such emotional sharing demands of us that we develop the relevant moral beginnings in order that they may be extended to the people in the future who might share our emotions.

One may think of empathy and wonder what difference there is between the empathy-based approach that Hourdequin discusses and the Mencian naturalistic framework outlined above. It may seem that both approaches rely on some emotional mechanism to connect people. The fundamental difference between these two approaches is that, in the Mencian view, the emotional sharing process carries ethical and normative demands based on emotional connectedness. The origins of this normative inclination and its demands are to be found in the ethical beginnings Mencius attributes to the basic emotions when he selects compassion-like emotion, shame-like feelings, deference and a sense of right and wrong as the four moral sprouts. We may not be able to gather enough normative and motivational force to take distant future people's needs into our hearts solely on the basis of empathy, especially when empathy is understood as a psychological response that mirrors another's emotional state.

5 Alternatives: Xunzian Naturalistic Ethics and Its Shortcomings

In this section, I would like to compare Mencius's naturalistic ethics with Xunzi's, who has a slightly different outlook on the role of normative values in his understanding of morality. I do so to demonstrate that, in dealing with intergenerational issues, there is an evident superiority to a Mencian-like framework in which normative beginnings are planted in basic emotions rather than, as Xunzi believes, in socialization and purposeful learning. This section is not an attack on Xunzi's philosophy, but rather an attempt to demonstrate that – to the extent that they ground all normative components in socialization or nurturing – ethical frameworks such as his do not fare well when confronted with the problems raised by intergenerational ethics. This comparison is significant, because many ethical theories have a Xunzian-like view and see no normative components in our basic biological and psychological functions.

My argument in this section will show how and why such ethical theories suffer setbacks when addressing intergenerational ethical issues.

When discussing our natural emotions, Xunzi thinks that humans are selfish and profit driven, and that there is no normative value in the natural form of their emotions or desires. This is one of the reasons why he claims that human nature is self-interested and profit-seeking. In Xunzi's mind, the emotions are raw materials that may be transformed by socialization and cultivation, such as ritual practices, but lack any moral values or beginning in themselves prior to socialization and moral cultivation. In other words, raw, natural emotions hold no normative values even though they can be cultivated so as to become as versions of emotions that are intertwined with ethical values.

For example, Xunzi makes the distinction between "ethical honour and shame" (*yi rong* and *yi ru*), that come from one's inner moral dispositions, and "natural honour and shame" (*shi rong* and *shi ru*), that come from the external situation one is in. In his opinion, it is not a moral issue to feel the kind of shame that arises when confronted with public humiliation, as, for example, when receiving corporal punishment in public; the shame and disgrace one feels is due to the circumstances, not the person. Therefore, this type of shame does not necessarily indicate moral shortcomings or psychological weakness. It is simply how this type of natural shame works. In other words, according to the cultural scripts and the emotional script, it is appropriate to feel shame here, even though it may not be morally justified or have ethical significance (D'Arm and Jacobson 2000). The same is true for honor derived from circumstance, which is merely a natural reaction people would have when, for example, being praised in public by people of authority or as a result of fame. Honor that comes from within, on the other hand, would have ethical significance because it reflects a person's assessment of their own behavior in relation to their moral values. For example, Xunzi claims that:

> When one is perverse and corrupt, when one goes against what has been allotted and disrupts and proper order, when one is arrogantly violent and greedy for profit, this is a case where [shame] derives from within. This is called [shame] from what is *yi* [*yi ru*, or shame coming "from one's inner disposition;" Zhao 2018]. When one is cursed at or insulted, when one is dragged by the hair or pummeled, when one is caned or has one's feet cut off, when one is decapitated or drawn and quartered, or when one's family records are destroyed or one's descendants are eradicated, this is a case where [shame] comes from outside. This is called [shame] in terms of one's circumstances… And so, it is possible for a gentleman [that is, an exemplary person; JH notes] to suffer [shame] in terms of their circumstances, but it is not possible for him to suffer [shame] from what is *yi* [or from his inner disposition; Zhao 2018]. (Zhenglun Chapter, Xunzi; modified from Hutton 2014, Ch. 10: 517–526)

In this passage, Xunzi claims that there are two types of shame one could experience: one that comes from the circumstances and is external to one, and one that comes from one's inner disposition and is internal to one. The former has no moral values, even though we are all vulnerable to it, including the morally cultivated. After all, who can remain intact when facing public insults or public corporal punishments, such as being "dragged by the hair or pummeled," "caned" or "having one's feet cut off," that are designed to evoke shame and ruin one's public image and reputation (Zhenglun Chapter, *Xunzi*; modified from Hutton 2014, Ch. 10: 517–526)?

Xunzi acknowledges that there is a natural and amoral type of honor and shame that is not governed by his ethical theory. These natural and primitive forms of amoral shame can become morally potent only through ritual cultivation and value internalization. However, the rituals or other measures of moral education in any particular time period, such as Xunzi's, will eventually be of limited relevance to a society in the future, which means that the ethical values and practices associated with emotions will also evolve. Thus, it is likely that our current moral theories and moral education would provide little direct guidance to us in addressing the concerns of future people; similarly, the social contexts and rituals in Xunzi's time provided very limited guidance to his contemporaries in terms of envisioning the difficulties we now face in the twenty-first century. I am not claiming that either Xunzi's ethical theory or all of our popular moral practices today will be completely useless in addressing a problem in the distant future, or that we should be discouraged by the possibility of our morality becoming outdated and irrelevant in regards to the problems of future generations; rather, I am highlighting a problem that theories such as Xunzi's must address. I point out the realistic concern that moral theories and practices will become less relevant and will be based only on shared natural emotions with the people of the future. We would have to invest more to account for why and how we would still care for the concerns of future generations when it is unclear whether or not our current understanding will be useful or relevant.

In contrast, for Mencius, a sense of shame is the root of morality and contains an ethical inclination to align oneself with good behaviors and distance oneself from those that are problematic. According to Mencius, normativity starts at the beginning of the most natural form of emotion that we share with people in the future; whereas, for Xunzi, it starts with human interventions in cultivation. A sense of shame, in Mencius, is one of the four moral beginnings or sprouts. The heart of *xiuwu* exists to help us distinguish between the morally pleasing and the morally repugnant in ourselves and others. The heart of *xiuwu,* when cultivated, can then guide us in our moral decisions and conduct so that we carry ourselves in a way that lives up to our moral values.

The clever strategy in Mencius' theory is that the normative components are hidden in plain sight in the emotions that people share across time and culture, so much so that – if you can motivate others to share their emotional experience or "rejoice" with each other – one would gain a pivot point that is of ethical significance. And, from this emotional pivot, more sophisticated arguments can be developed. In other words, if you share my feelings, you are likely to share my moral inclinations and feel them as meaningful moral concerns. This, of course, does not guarantee that you would always act in my best interest or treat my concerns as priorities in your moral reasoning. The inability of the emotional pivot point to assume priority in the moral reasoning of others, or to dictate their behaviors, is not a theoretical flaw but an advantage: People who open themselves to being emotionally moved and connected should have their own autonomous deliberative process instead of one that is vulnerable to being hijacked or manipulated by others. The advantage of this Mencian approach is not only that we stand a better chance at persuasion and moral education when emotions are shared, but also that it leaves open a rich set of possibilities for the ways in which the person on the receiving end might formulate their thoughts and carry out their actions. This theoretical flexibility is important, because it sometimes marks the difference between paternalistic manipulation and persuasion in good faith. This is especially important in the context of intergenerational ethics, where we can only hope that future generations – who are likely to have moral and cultural frameworks that differ from our own and will be confronted with ever-changing circumstances – will devise their own solutions. Over-prescribing what they should or should not do would inevitably be futile and arrogant, and project an "egocentric" framework based on the current generations' understanding of the world.

6 Conclusion

In this chapter, I have argued that a naturalistic ethical framework that roots normative components in basic human functions, such as emotions, would stand at significant theoretical advantage in addressing questions in intergenerational ethics. I used Mencius's ethical framework, in which the normative beginnings are woven into his understanding of human nature and the basic human emotions, as an example with which to demonstrate how, through establishing emotional pivot points, we can take the concerns and worries of others into our own hearts and moral deliberation, regardless of how remote they are from us, physically or temporally. Such emotional sharing points enable us to treat the concerns of others as meaningful moral factors in our moral deliberations.

I have argued, using the example of Xunzi, that an ethical framework that posits normative values not as natural endowments, but as the products of socialization and ritualized moral cultivation, would fare less well, especially considering that the social contexts and rituals we have now will almost certainly not survive changes in time. In fact, given that Xunzi has, as some would argue, a far better argumentative style in his texts, many attribute Mencius's lasting legacy to the flexibility and openness of his ethics and not to his sophisticated arguments (Hansen 1992). Mencius's philosophy experienced a great revival in the so-called Neo-Confucian school of thought that spanned from the eleventh to the sixteenth century, during which time many Mencian concepts, such as the four sprouts and the heart/mind (*xin*), were developed and re-interpreted to address challenges posed by the new metaphysical questions imported by the foreign Buddhist philosophers and local Neo-Daoist thinkers. The fact that Mencian ethics was re-developed more than a thousand years later serves as evidence that its philosophical framework has the merit of possessing the flexibility and adaptability to connect people from the past to the present and from the present to the future, in ways that are both emotionally and ethically significant.

Bibliography

Ames, Roger T. and Henry Rosemont. 1999. *The Analects of Confucius: A Philosophical Translation*. New York, NY: Ballantine Books.

Batson, Charles Daniel. 2011a. "These Things Called Empathy: Eight Related but Distinct Phenomona." In *The Social Neuroscience of Empathy*, edited by Jean Decety and William Ickes, 3–15. Cambridge, MA: MIT Press.

2011b. *Altruism in Humans*. New York, NY: Oxford University Press.

Bloom, Irene. 1997. "Human Nature and Biological Nature in Mencius." *Philosophy East and West* 47, no. 1: 21–32.

D'Arms, Justin and Daniel Jacobson. 2000. "The Moralistic Fallacy: On the 'Appropriateness' of Emotions." *Philosophy and Phenomenological Research* 61, no. 1: 65.

Gardiner, Stephen M. 2006. "A Perfect Moral Storm: Climate Change, Intergenerational Ethics and the Problem of Moral Corruption." *Environmental Values* 15, no. 3: 397–413.

2011. *A Perfect Moral Storm: The Ethical Tragedy of Climate Change*. New York, NY: Oxford University Press.

Goldin, Paul R. 2016. "Women and Moral Dilemmas in Early Chinese Narrative." In *The Bloomsbury Research Handbook of Chinese Philosophy and Gender*, edited by Ann Pang-White, 25–36. London: Bloomsbury.

Hansen, Chad. 1992. *A Daoist Theory of Chinese Thought: A Philosophical Interpretation*. New York, NY: Oxford University Press.

Hoffman, Martin L. 2001. *Empathy and Moral Development: Implications for Caring and Justice*. Cambridge: Cambridge University Press.

2011. "Empathy, Justice, and the Law." In *Empathy: Philosophical and Psychological Perspectives*, edited by Amy Coplan and Peter Goldie, 230–54. New York, NY: Oxford University Press.

Hourdequin, Marion. 2012. "Empathy, Shared Intentionality, and Motivation by Moral Reasons." *Ethical Theory and Moral Practice* 15: 403–419.

Hourdequin, Marion and David B. Wong. 2021. "Confucianism and Intergenerational Ethics." In *The Oxford Handbook of Intergenerational Ethics*, edited by Stephen M. Gardiner, 1st ed. New York, NY: Oxford University Press.

Hu, Jing. 2018. "Empathy for Non-Kin, the Faraway, the Unfamiliar, and the Abstract? An Interdisciplinary Study on Mencian Moral Cultivation and a Response to Prinz." *Dao: A Journal of Comparative Philosophy* 17, no. 3: 349–62.

Hutton, Eric L. 2014. *Xunzi: The Complete Text*. Princeton, NJ: Princeton University Press.

Ivanhoe, Philip J. 2008. "The Shade of Confucius: Social Roles, Ethical Theory, and the Self." In *Polishing the Chinese Mirror: Essays in Honor of Henry Rosemont, Jr*, edited by Marthe Chandler and Ronnie Littlejohn, 34–49. New York, NY: Global Scholarly Publications.

Legge, James. 1861. *The Works of Mencius*. London: Clarendon.

Liao, W. K. 1939. *The Complete Works of Han Fei Tzu*. London: A. Probsthain.

Mattice, Sarah A. 2016. "Confucian Role Ethics in the 21st Century: Domestic Violence, Same-sex Marriage, and Christian Family Values." In *Feminist Encounters with Confucius*, edited by Mathew Foust and Sor-Hoon Tan, 198–225. Leiden: Brill.

McRae, Emily. 2011. "The Cultivation of Moral Feelings and Mengzi's Method of Extension." *Philosophy East and West* 61, no. 4: 587–608.

Pang-White, A. 2018. *The Confucian Four Books for Women: A New Translation of The Nü Sishu and The Commentary of Wang Xiang*. New York, NY: Oxford University Press.

Preston, Stephanie D. and Frans BM De Waal. 2002. "Empathy: Its Ultimate and Proximate Bases." *Behavioral and Brain Sciences* 25, no. 1: 1–20.

Prinz, Jesse. 2011a. "Against Empathy." *The Southern Journal of Philosophy* 49 no. s1: 214–233.

2011b. "Is Empathy Necessary for Morality?" In *Empathy: Philosophical and Psychological Perspectives*, edited by Amy Coplan and Peter Goldie. 211–239. New York, NY: Oxford University Press.

Rosemont, Henry. 2016. "Rights-Bearing Individuals and Role-Bearing Persons." In *Confucian Role Ethics: A Moral Vision for the 21st Century*, edited by Roger Ames and Henry Rosemont, 33–57. Taiwan: V&R Academic National Taiwan University Press.

Stalnaker, Aaron. 2019. "Roles and Virtues: Early Confucians on Social Order and the Different Aspects of Ethics." In *Perspectives in Role Ethics Virtues, Reasons, and Obligation*, edited by Tim Dare and Christine Swanton, 120–148. New York, NY: Routledge.

Virág, Curie. 2017. *The Emotions in Early Chinese Philosophy*. Oxford: Oxford University Press.

Waal, Frans BM De. 2008. "Putting the Altruism Back into Altruism: The Evolution of Empathy." *Annual Review of Psychology* 59: 279–300.

Wong, David B. 2015a. "Early Confucian Philosophy and the Development of Compassion." *Dao: A Journal of Comparative Philosophy* 14, no. 2: 157–94.

2015b. "Growing Virtue: The Theory and Science of Developing Compassion from a Mencian Perspective." In *The Philosophical Challenge from China*, edited by Brian Bruya, 23–58. Cambridge, MA: MIT Press.

Zhao, Jingyi Jenny. 2018. "Shame and Moral Education in Aristotle and Xunzi." In *Ancient Greece and China Compared, by Qiaosheng Dong*, 1st edn., edited by G. E. R. Lloyd and Jingyi Jenny Zhao, 110–130. Cambridge: Cambridge University Press.

8

Transience, Responsible Transformation, and Deep Time in Daoist Thought

James Miller

1 Introduction

Daoism is often described as a cosmological philosophy and, later, a religion that aims to link human beings with the processes of change and transformation that occur all around us. Indeed, the concept of Dao, or "path," links space and time together, understanding the cosmos not simply as a static place or an order that is given to us, but, rather, as a dynamic process that is always on the move from one place to another. The nature of Dao, according to the *Daode Jing*, is to give birth to the myriad things (*wanwu* 万物) that constitute the world around us, in a process of constant transformation (*bianhua* 变化) that, optimally, leads to their full flourishing (*fanrong* 繁荣). The universe is a space for things, and it also has a time in which things arise, transform, and decay. Dao is the mysterious source from which the myriad things arise and, hence, constitute the universe of space and time that we inhabit. We human beings are no different from the things that constitute the world around us. We too are subject to the same process of transformation, flourishing, and decay as the myriad things.

This unity of space and time is also revealed in the Chinese term *yuzhou* 宇宙, which means universe, but is more accurately translated as "spacetime." The word is comprised of two characters, *yu* 宇, which refers to the four cardinal points plus up and down, and *zhou* 宙, which refers to the duration of time from past to present and to future (Wang 2021, 103). One consequence of this orientation to the universe as a "spacetime" process is that research into the specifically temporal aspects of the universe has not been extensive in Chinese thought. Rather, time and space have been studied together as elements of the spacetime process, and a greater emphasis has been placed in both Confucian and Daoist thought on the relationship between the individual and the cosmological patterns that we can observe all around us in the cycles of time. Temporal and spatial aspects of the cosmos are usually correlated with each other: The morning is correlated with the sun's rising in the east; the winter with the north, and so on. An integrated spacetime cosmology means that time has not frequently been considered an independent variable, but rather as something always correlated with spatial processes.

The cyclical nature of time does not preclude a sense of progress or evolution. The *Daodejing* (ch. 42) famously understands the creation of the universe as a process of "birthing" where the Dao gives birth to one, two, three – and eventually the myriad – things or processes that we find in the cosmos. But, unlike modern Western understandings of temporal progress, the evolutionary aspect of time is not always viewed by Daoists in a positive way. Daoist alchemy often seeks to "reverse" or "revert" temporal processes, and many Daoist texts call for humans to "return" to the Dao, advocating that which is simple or pure over what is complex or ornamental.

Recently, there has been some considerable research into the concept of time in Daoist thought, stimulated by a conference on *Daoism and Time* in Los Angeles in 2019, which took place next to the seventeenth triennial conference of the *International Society for the Study of Time*. This society was established about fifty years ago by J. T. Fraser (1923–2010), who conducted a major study of the concept of time, in which he distinguishes six different "chronotypes" or frames of time which mediate human experience of time. The contiguity of the two conferences has meant that Fraser's thought has had something of an impact on the study of time in Daoist thought, and in the volume of essays that arose from the conference (Kohn 2021). The essays in that volume make a powerful case that time has been a neglected topic in the study of Daoism, and that, especially in relation to the experience of time in the body, the concept of transformation, and alchemical processes to "reverse" time, the Daoist experience has paid close attention to time as a foundational element of the human condition.

If we consider time as an independent concept in Chinese thought, then, Joseph Needham (1954) notes, there are two concepts in addition to that of the more complex "spacetime" (*yuzhou*). The first is *shi* 时, the common word for time, but which also has an important secondary connotation of "timeliness" or "seasonality"; the second is *jiu* 久 which refers to "duration" or "permanence." The first concept, timeliness, refers to the importance of acting in accordance with time or at the right time. Thus, foods must be eaten in the correct season, medicines must be adjusted according to the time of day or time of year, and in politics, interventions must be made at the right time, not too early or too late, if they are to be successful. In this regard, Chinese thought about time bears a close resemblance to what Wole Soyinka (1995 [1976], 10) refers to as "traditional thinking" which "creates a cyclical reality, not a linear timeline." This "cyclical reality" can be seen in that the traditional Chinese calendar is not a linear calendar in which years accumulate in an infinite linear series from a conventionally designated starting point.

The traditional Chinese calendar gives names to years based on a combination of the five elements and the twelve animals, which resets itself every sixty years: 2023, for example is the "water rabbit" year. In the Chinese calendar, 2083 will be the same "water rabbit" year as 2023. The only way, traditionally, to differentiate times that are sixty years apart is by reference to the reign title of the emperor and the name of the dynasty. Thus, 1580 is the "metal dragon" year of the Wanli emperor of the Ming dynasty. But there is no explicit sense that this date is chronologically later than (let alone morally or ethically superior to) the "metal dragon" year of the Zhengde emperor, which occurred in 1520. The year 1580 is simply a different (not a better, or more progressive) political reality than the year 1520. Time is denominated politically rather than enumerated mathematically. A powerful effect of this denomination of time is to diminish the sense of time as a teleological, linear accumulation, something akin to the modern Western concept of "progress." Indeed, this concept of progress is precisely what gives a normative orientation to the modern sense of time, a sense that what is newer must be better than what is older, and that we have a moral obligation to make progress and improve things step by step. This normative orientation is absent in the cyclical concept of time. Rather, cyclical time has the normative orientation of "seasonality": of doing things that are in the correct time or at the appropriate moment. To do things out of season or at the wrong time is to go against the normativity that is embedded in the cyclical concept of seasonality.

The second Chinese concept of time that Needham refers to is *jiu*, which we can understand more as "duration" or as "a stretch of time." This also carries a normative sense to it in that the ability to "last" in the face of the constant changing of times is considered to be a moral ideal. An excellent example of this "staying power" can be found in the famous story of Zhuangzi (ch. 4) called "the useless tree." In this story, a carpenter complains that a gnarled and knotted tree is useless because it cannot easily be turned into a useful source of wood. On the contrary, says Zhuangzi, the tree has perdured precisely because of its uselessness to the carpenter. For this reason, the tree becomes, paradoxically, a moral exemplar in Zhuangzi's universe: an element of nature that has withstood the ravages not only of time, but of human intervention. The word Zhuangzi uses here to refer to the tree's perduration is *shou* 寿, usually translated as "longevity" or even "immortality." Where *jiu* refers abstractly to a "stretch of time," *shou* refers more concretely to the successful "living out" of one of the myriad things (including human beings) across a long period. It too is a temporal ideal in Daoist thought and contributes to the quest for immortality and transcendence in Daoism. The paradox here is that the tree becomes a moral exemplar by managing to eschew any "intent" to become an example of anything. Unlike the deliberate quest of Confucians to attain sagehood as a state of moral and spiritual transcendence, the tree becomes so effortlessly.

At this point a question arises: How can Daoist thought prize both cyclicality and longevity? Do these normative ideals not contradict each other? Should Daoists accept the transformation of things within the cycles of time, or should they seek to transcend those cycles and achieve something supra-natural or "beyond time?" To address this question, it is necessary to investigate further the concept of time as transformation (*bianhua*).

2 Transience and Transformation

A common understanding is that time is associated with change, and change fundamentally means decay or loss. Time means the transformation of something – that is, into something that it is not – and this is often perceived as a loss of identity. Jing Liu (2021, 70) notes that, in Chinese, this sense of time is understood through the concept of "passing" (*shi* 逝) in the sense of "passing away," which is a homophone of the word for time itself (*shi* 时). Whatever the original thing was, through the process of time, it has become what it was not. She writes:

> The transience of time, … originates from a sense of loss. It is in the sense of loss that the passage of time is most clearly, even painfully felt. All present and future is inevitably coming past, everything that is gained in time will eventually be lost; moments are given, then gone; life is given to us, running toward death every minute. All beings have already, are becoming, or will become nonbeing. (70)

The difference in the Daoist context is that this transition is also viewed positively. While the passage of time can be "painfully felt" and Daoists can rightfully lament the conditions of war and devastation that they see around them, this lament does not define the whole of the Daoist's attitude to time. If we think about Dao as the wellspring for cosmic transformation, the path of spacetime, what we see is that the passage of time, alternation, transience, and things becoming what they are not, is precisely the source of life. That is to say, change is what enables life to take place. Biologically, we know that the process of evolution could not take place without the deaths of individual animals. Indeed it is death that enables life, growth, and evolution to take place. Rather than viewing transience with a sense of loss or regret, Daoists tend to celebrate the transitory nature of life as intrinsic to vitality. To move, to change, to alter is to be alive. To remain the same, unaltered is indeed a horrifying prospect.

A further story from Zhuangzi (ch. 6) can serve to illustrate this idea. This is the extreme, even absurd, story of Master Yu who becomes disabled and eventually dies. The first stage of his illness causes him to be hunched over so that his "back sticks up like a hunchback and my vital organs are on top of me." This process of transformation, however, causes him no distress, rather the opposite:

> If the process continues, perhaps in time he'll transform my left arm into a rooster. In that case I'll keep watch on the night. Or perhaps in time he'll transform my right arm into a crossbow pellet and I'll shoot down an owl for roasting. Or perhaps in time he'll transform my buttocks into cartwheels. Then, with my spirit for a horse, I'll climb up and go for a ride. What need will I ever have for a carriage again? (trans. Watson 1968, 80)

Just before Master Yu's death, Master Li approaches him with the following insight: "How marvelous the Creator is! What is he going to make of you next? Where is he going to send you? Will he make you into a rat's liver? Will he make you into a bug's arm?" (trans. Watson 1968, 81). The sense here is that human beings have the capacity to experience transience not only as loss, but also as cause for celebration. The loss of form and the loss of identity that occurs through disease, disability, and death are not chiefly to be resented, but to be celebrated as the processes by which life occurs. Far from exhibiting the calm, stoic acceptance of the inevitability of change and decay, the masters in this story exhibit a kind of giddy, childish delight.

This emphasis on delight in transformation lies at the heart of the Daoist response to the sense of time as passing, or passing away. It also helps to resolve the contradiction between the normative values of "seasonality" and "longevity." Here, longevity or immortality do not mean the perduration of a thing in a specific form for an infinite period of time, or even liberation from the changes that take place through time but, rather, entering a state of "extended transience." That is to say, it is not permanence that is supremely valued but rather a "positive transience," a transience that is not viewed negatively as a "passing away" but as the condition for the possibility of transformation itself.

The high value placed on transience in Daoist thought is also connected, in the *Daodejing*, to a preference for the "soft and weak" over the "hard and strong." The *locus classicus* for this way of thinking can be found in *Daodejing* 76:

Humans are born soft and weak.
They die stiff and strong.
The ten thousand plants and trees
Are born soft tender,
And die withered and sere.
The stiff and strong
Are Death's companions
The soft and weak
Are Life's companions.
Therefore the strongest armies do not conquer,
The greatest trees are cut down.
The strong and great sink down.
The soft and weak rise up.

(trans. Addiss and Lombardo 1993)

It is precisely because of the softness, pliability, or "weakness" of natural things that they are able to change and grow. Only dead things are hard and cannot change. This realization produces a reversal in the normal concept of agency. In Indo-European languages, agency and passivity are linguistically embedded in the active and passive moods of verbs. In order for a verb to be used in a sentence, there must be a declaration of whether the verb is in the active mood or the passive mood. While there are occasional quirks to this rule, such as deponent and semi-deponent verbs, in general, one must always indicate whether a verb is being used in the active or passive mood. This linguistic rule reflects the semantic importance attached to knowing whether a subject is acting on an object or vice versa, and a preference for subjects to demonstrate their agency over objects. But in Daoist thought, it is precisely the passivity of subjects, our ability to be constituted rather than to constitute, that gives rise to our vitality. If we understand agency as the projection of penetrating force that has the ability to deform a passive object without it itself being deformed, then this is nothing less than the mistaken exaltation of death over life. Indeed, the repudiation of destructive military power is one of the most consistent ethical themes in the *Daodejing*.

To be alive is not to be a subject with sufficient agency to bring death or destruction to others, but to be a subject with sufficient passivity to allow oneself to be constituted and even penetrated by the Dao's life-sustaining powers. The gendered aspect of this way of thinking goes without saying, and can be seen in Daoism's preference for the *yin* (feminine) over the *yang* (masculine). Ontologically, it can be seen in the priority given to nonbeing (*wu* 无) over being (*you* 有). Praxiologically, it can be seen in the priority given to non-assertive action (*wuwei* 无为) over assertive action (*wei*为). The Daoist preference for the soft, passive, pliant, and even penetrable, constitutes a major repudiation of the phallogocentrism embedded in Indo-European languages.

Generally, Indo-European languages require sentences to be articulated with verbs in the active or the passive voice. A subject does something to an object. While some languages have middle, deponent, or semi-deponent voices that complicate this picture, the default function of a verb is to denote the action of a subject towards an object. When the male gender is associated with activity and the female gender is associated with passivity, a gendered aspect of the linguistic construction of reality inevitably arises. Men are, naturally, presumed to be the actors and women the objects of action. Chinese, as a non-inflected language, does not have this particular linguistic problem.

3 Deep Time

There has been a strong movement in the past decades to place human history within a much longer or deeper timeline than that of recorded human history. Thanks to the development of evolutionary science, astrobiology, and cosmology, we can now begin to place the story of human life within that of the 4.5 billion-year history of the earth, or even the 13.8 billion-year history of the universe. Although the concept of the Anthropocene has become a keyword of modern thought, it is intriguing to put this recent event of human–planetary relations into a much larger cosmic perspective. One example of this has been the work of Brian Swimme and Mary Evelyn Tucker, whose *Journey of the Universe* film and book (Swimme and Tucker 2011) seeks not only to place human life within a cosmic timescale, but also to evoke intimate connections between human life and the lives of animals, planets, and even stars. They rely here on the Confucian concept of principle or pattern (*li* 理) according to which it is possible to evoke a connection between human life and "heavenly" or "natural" life. The common Chinese phrase here is "the harmony of humanity and nature" (*tianren heyi* 天人合一). (Note that the Chinese term heaven (*tian* 天) can also mean nature or environment). Swimme and Tucker evoke this concept visually in the film through images of swirling galaxies that fade into images of whirlpools, suggesting a "patterning" that cuts across the many dimensions, and epochs, of cosmic life.

The part of the film that has always resonated most with my students is where Swimme intones "The stars are our ancestors," evoking a deeply filial connection between anthropogenesis and cosmogenesis. The phrase also brings to mind the first line of the famous *Western Inscription* (a text placed on the west wall of the scholar's study in his home in Hengqu, Shaanxi) by the Confucian philosopher Zhang Zai (1020–1077): "Heaven is my father and Earth is my mother, and even such a small creature as I finds an intimate place in their midst" (trans. Chan 1963, 497). Zhang Zai makes the argument that all of us are brothers and sisters because we are all descended from heaven and earth (*yang* and *yin*), the two primordial ontogenetic principles out of which the myriad things emerge. Modern cosmology tells us that these are not just symbolic affiliations but rather deep time affiliations. Just as we gaze into outer space, we gaze into the deep past, so also when we evoke macrocosm–microcosm correspondences between humans and stars, we are also tracing a connection that threads back billions of years.

The Daoist religious tradition conceptualized the relationship between humans and the stars in terms of the relationship between the outer space of heavenly bodies and the inner space of the subtle Qi-body of human beings. Gods were seen to descend from the stars and enter one's vital organs by Daoist practitioners of visualization meditation. The correspondence here is not simply between an inner landscape and an outer landscape, but between deep cosmic time and human time. The grandeur of deep space and deep time is also experienced as a moment of subtle intimacy, the outer space and deep time of the stars and the planets conjoined with the inner space and shallow time of the human body (see Miller 2017).

But deep time, in the human perspective, flows not only from the past, but long into the future. David Farrier has written about the importance of thinking about the long-term, deep-time effects of contemporary human life. In his article published in *The Atlantic*, Farrier (2016) notes two particular misnamings that are central to our present worldview. The first is that "plastic" is anything but plastic, and indeed far more persistent than its human creators. He writes:

> Plastics, which began being mass-produced in the middle of the 20th century, give us back the world as the West has been taught to see it – pliable, immediately available, and smoothed to our advantage. Yet almost every piece of plastic ever made remains in existence in some form, and their chemical traces are increasingly present in our bodies. … Single-use plastic might seem to disappear when I dispose of it, but it (and therefore I) will nonetheless continue to act on the environments in which it persists for millennia.

Here, we see the deep time effects of a deadly linguistic inversion. By misunderstanding plastic as something "soft" and ephemeral, we have blinded ourselves to its deep impact not only on the environment today, but far into the future.

The second misnaming he cites is "the cloud." The cloud implies something ephemeral, immaterial, or heavenly, invisible data occupying no space or time. But the reverse is the case. He writes: "Despite the appealing connotations of 'the cloud', this data has to go somewhere. Greenpeace estimates that the power consumption of just one of Apple's immense data centers is equivalent to the annual supply for 250,000 European homes. Traces of this seemingly ephemeral data will persist into the deep time of the future, as rising concentrations of carbon warm the atmosphere." Farrier's critique of our misapprehension of these two key elements of modern life echoes Daoist arguments about our mistaken predilection for the permanent and the hard over the transient and the soft. The things that we think of as transient, *yin*, or soft (plastics or cloud data) are in fact instances of material persistence, *yang*, or hard, whose effects will be felt well into the future, and which cannot easily be undone. From a Daoist point of view, such deep time "persistences" do not contribute to the overall vitality of the cosmos because, in effect, they refuse to die.

4 The "Invironment"

Farrier's work recalls the arguments made by Zhuangzi and others that our "normal" view of the world is not only mistaken but actually upside down, causing us to mistake one thing for its opposite. I would like to connect this false inversion of transience and persistence to another false inversion that I first explored in my book *China's Green Religion; Daoism and the Quest for a Sustainable Future* (Miller 2017). In that book, I developed the argument that the received wisdom that humans are somehow supposed to "save the environment" is misguided, because it preserves the notion that the environment is a thing that exists in space outside our bodies. So long as we think of the "environment" as something that is separate from us in any important respect, it will be impossible to transition to a way of thinking that starts from the mutual intertwining of human life and planetary life. My study of Daoist thought about the identification of the microcosm of the body and the macrocosm of the word around us suggests that we should not think of the environment as something that exists outside the hermetically sealed walls of our bodies. Indeed, Daoist art is famous for its depiction of the body as a landscape, using images of mountains, clouds, stars, and gods to show the Daoist experience of vital energy flowing through the meridians of the body. This leads me to conclude that we should not imagine the "environment" as something that "exists" beyond our bodies, but more like an "invironment": something that "insists" deeply within our bodies.

This way of thinking leads to two related conclusions. Firstly, human life is not to be understood as a form of "existence" but as a form of "insistence," the coming together of all the various vital forces into a particular form that allows us to be. Secondly, the environment is not a backdrop on which human actions take place; rather, it informs, insists, and indwells our bodies, enabling us to have life. These two conclusions, moreover, can be further extended to the concept of time as well as space. If, from a Daoist perspective, the world indwells the body just as much as the body indwells the world, so also deep time inscribes itself in human history just as much as human history inscribes itself within cosmic time. We do not "exist" in deep time; rather, deep time "insists" in us.

The result of this spatial inversion of body and world, and this temporal inversion of human history and deep time, does not, from a Daoist perspective demean or diminish what it means to be human. The contrary is the case. To think through spacetime is not to imagine human life as a transitory flash within a majestic unfolding of the evolution of the cosmos over 13.8 billion years but, rather, to see our transience and the transience of the cosmos itself as the glorious, complex, and as-yet undetermined outworking of spacetime creative powers. Inasmuch as human actions enable that transitory, creative process to continue, they are to be celebrated. Inasmuch as they inhibit the flourishing of the world through ossification, they are to be deprecated. Our error comes when we mistake one for the other, when we treat plastics as disposable, and data clouds as immaterial and ephemeral.

5 Responsibility

Finally I would like to move to consider the question of responsibility. There has been a lot of research on Daoism and ecology over the past twenty years, but largely focused on nature, rather than time. Indeed, I've previously written that one way to think about the relationship between Confucianism and Daoism in Chinese thought is to think of Confucianism as taking care of time, and Daoism as taking care of space (Miller 2017, 74). Confucianism is concerned with patriarchal genetics, anchored in the concept of filial piety. Filial piety, which is the foundation of Confucian ethics, means the obligation of the person to their genetic creator. If that is one's ethical foundation, then it is principally the responsibility of younger generations to take care of older generations and not the other way around. Confucianism is founded on intergenerational ethics, but it is ordered the wrong way around from the perspective of long-term responsibility for the future. It is not in the DNA of Confucians to worry about seven generations into the future (see Chapter 2 by Matthias Fritsch and Chapter 7 by Jing Iris Hu). Rather the reverse: Descendants have the obligation to take care of their ancestors seven generations into the past.

Can Daoism help remedy this defect in Chinese philosophy? Firstly, I think that the Daoist diagnosis of the human condition as misreading soft and hard, and misvaluing permanence and transience is a step in the right direction. This perhaps points to the role that philosophy can play in general, identifying truths about things and critiquing misperceptions about things. But as the *Daodejing* notes, simply understanding the problem does not mean that it is easy to fix it.

Secondly, however, if we think of the Daoist attempt to dissolve the boundaries between "inner space" and "outer space" via the concept of the porosity of the body, not simply in terms of landscape or spaces, then we can begin to construct an ethic of responsibility to one's past and one's future, one that aims to conserve or even increase the "soft" over the "hard." Daoists have not, however, been deeply concerned with imagining the futures of their children, yet alone their children's children, but rather have sought to cultivate ways of living in the world that maximize the flourishing in transformation processes. This ethic of care, or responsible transformation, can only be realized in the context of a porous body. We live and breathe because we ingest and excrete, not because we isolate our minds and bodies from the planetary context that enables us to draw breath in the first place. Inasmuch as that planetary context is not simply a "place" but a "process" and a transformation, then Daoists will always advocate agility and suppleness, an ethic of plasticity in the true sense of the word.

Bibliography

Addiss, Stephen and Stanley Lombardo. 1993. *Tao Te Ching*. Bloomington, IN: Hackett.

Chan, Wing-Tsit. 1963. *A Source Book in Chinese Philosophy*. Princeton, NJ: Princeton University Press.

Farrier, David. 2016. "How the Concept of Deep Time Is Changing." *The Atlantic*, www.theatlantic.com/science/archive/2016/10/aeon-deep-time/505922/.

Kohn, Livia, ed. 2021. *Dao and Time: Classical Philosophy*. St Petersburg, FL: Three Pines Press.

Liu, Jing. 2021. "Permanence and Transcendence: Time in the *Daode Jing*." In *Dao and Time: Classical Philosophy*, edited by Livia Kohn, 68–84. St Petersburg, FL: Three Pines Press.

Miller, James. 2017. *China's Green Religion: Daoism and the Quest for a Sustainable Future*. New York, NY: Columbia University Press.

Needham, Joseph. 1954. *Science and Civilisation in China*. Vol. 3 of *Mathematics and the Sciences of the Heavens and the Earth*. Cambridge: Cambridge University Press.

Soyinka, Wole. 1995 [1976]. *Myth, literature and the African world*. Cambridge: Cambridge University Press.

Swimme, Brian Thomas and Mary Evelyn Tucker. 2011. *Journey of the Universe*. New Haven, CT: Yale University Press.

Wang, Shuwen. 2021. "Time and Self in the Zhuangzi." In *Dao and Time: Classical Philosophy*, edited by Livia Kohn, 102–118. St Petersburg, FL: Three Pines Press.

Watson, Burton. 2013. *The Complete Works of Chuang Tzu*. New York, NY: Columbia University Press.

PART III

Humanity Facing the Near Environmental Future

9

Double Intergenerational Responsibility

From a Western-Eastern View

Hiroshi Abe

1 Introduction

I would like to begin this chapter by clarifying its objective. In my view, environmental problems are difficult to solve primarily because they will inevitably and greatly affect much more than one generation, and yet, each generation tends only to its own interests in its own time regardless of the potential interests of those who will live later. What is the root of such a self-centred and temporally insular attitude? I maintain that it is the idea of self-responsibility, according to which, as the subject of responsibility, each generation should be responsible *for* itself as well as *to* itself. Here, the notion of 'responsibility *for*' points to the object of our responsibility; whereas, following the German philosopher Georg Picht, I understand that as 'an authority which gives orders underlying the responsibility' (Picht 1969, 319) the notion of our 'responsibility to' something is an assignation that requires us to take charge of that object and to account for our performance in the discharge of our responsibility.

Needless to say, it is characteristic of self-responsibility that the subject, the object and the authority of this responsibility are identical and must be located at the same time and place. In other words, insofar as the self is the subject, the object and the authority of responsibility, it is always existent 'here' and 'now', where and when the self is related to itself. This implies that self-responsibility is essentially present-oriented. Consequently, the above-mentioned 'selfish' attitude of each generation within its own time can be interpreted in terms of the concept of a present-oriented responsibility.

If this is indeed the case, environmental philosophy might contribute to the solution of environmental problems through the critique of this present-oriented responsibility and by striving to replace it with a new type of responsibility: one that would find each generation – and, above all, us, the current people – owing a duty to the generations that follow. The present chapter aims to consider what such an alternative intergenerational responsibility should be.

For this purpose, I try to show the following two points: first, future-oriented responsibility essentially requires past-oriented responsibility and vice versa (I call the former the 'foreseeing-care-prevention' type, and the latter the 'letting-the-dead-be' type); hence, second, intergenerational responsibility is composed of these two different and interdependent types of responsibility.

2 A Philosophical Confrontation with Parfit's 'Non-Identity Problem'

However, some people might oppose my idea of burdening us, the present people, with intergenerational responsibility, insisting that we have long been driven by such an enormous and inevitable drift of industrial-technological civilization triggered by the second industrial revolution that, strictly speaking, we ourselves are neither in a position to halt our activities causing environmental destruction nor accountable for them. I think in a different way than they do.

In order to explain this, let me refer to Victor Hugo's famous novel *Les Misérables*. The protagonist of this novel, Jean Valjean, once stole a loaf of bread, because he was under pressure to do so: though he was extremely poor, he had to care for his widowed sister and her seven children. Despite this difficult situation, in my view, it was not necessarily impossible for him to observe the laws. This is because he could also have chosen not to steal, albeit at the cost, in the worst case, of his family's death by starvation. Naturally, whether he should have prioritised observance of the law over his family's life is a different question. But the point is that, having made the decision to steal, he has to explain why he chose to steal, rather than chose not to. Similarly, from my point of view, in spite of the compulsive and trans-individual pressures of industrialization that we face today, we are responsible for the lives of future people: lives which could be worse than miserable. In other words, we, the present generation, would have to account for the lack of foresight in our actions if, a hundred years from now, our 'victims' (or indeed other generations as third and neutral parties) have reason to blame us for what we did or did not do.

Nevertheless, another objection might be raised against my position: it is still doubtful whether the present generation is to blame for future people's misery if we take into consideration, for example, the case of 'the 14-year-old girl' discussed by Derek Parfit. As is well known, in *Reasons and Persons*, he introduces this case as follows:

> *The 14-Year-Old Girl.* This girl chooses to have a child. Because she is so young, she gives her child a bad start in life. Though this will have bad effects throughout this child's life, his life will, predictably, be worth living. If this girl had waited for several years, she would have had a different child, to whom she would have given a better start in life. […] She had a child when she was 14, and, as we predicted, she gave him a bad start in life. Were we right to claim that her decision was worse for her child? If she had waited, this particular child would never have existed. And, despite its bad start, his life is worth living. (Parfit 1984, 358–59)

Let us now accept this thought experiment by Parfit and apply it to the relationship between today's people and future generations. Then potential objectors would claim: even if the actions of the current generation cause more harm to future people than those of any other generation, they are not to blame and there are two reasons for this. First, whether directly or indirectly, it is to all activities of today's generation that future people necessarily owe the very existence and identity unique to them as a whole. Hence, it is impossible to insist from an objective viewpoint (e.g., a third-party generation's disinterested viewpoint) that a person in the future would have been better off had the present generation acted otherwise: that person who would come to exist as a result of such different actions by the people of today is someone other than *this* particular person. This is because the present generation's choice of action can easily affect the identities of future people. As is well known, Parfit calls the dependence of potential people's identities on the behaviour of the current generation the 'non-identity problem', which can be formulated thus: 'In the different outcomes, different people would exist' (Parfit 1984, 378). Second, even if the life of a future person is damaged by the careless actions of the current generation, her life can be affirmed from her own viewpoint: as Parfit's thought experiment assumes, her life is 'worth living' for her, 'despite its bad start'. In this sense, she herself has no subjective reason to blame the present generation.

As shown in the discussion so far, Parfit's case of 'the 14-year-old girl' can be read as suggesting that, whether from a subjective or an objective point of view, even the most harmful choice of action by us, the current generation, would never be bad for those who live later. Hence, their (allegedly) 'miserable' life cannot be imputed to us. I would like to call this the 'non-imputability claim'.

If, indeed, this is the case, does it follow from the non-imputability claim that the present generation is free from any kind of future-oriented responsibility? Distinguishing 'being bad *for someone*' from 'having a bad effect [on someone]', Parfit seems to answer this question in the negative. In his view, any specific choice made by those of us living today can have a bad effect in the future, even if this choice will not be bad for anyone. He, thus, contends that 'we can deserve to be blamed for harming others, even when this is not worse for them' (Parfit 1984, 372). However, this contention lacks theoretical grounding in as much as *Reasons and Persons*, as Parfit himself admits, ends up being a 'failure' (Parfit 1984, 443) in the attempt to propound 'Theory X': a theory capable of solving the non-identity problem.[1] And thus, if the question of future-oriented responsibility is to be pursued further and more satisfactorily, we are confronted with the need to try an altogether different approach to that pursued by Parfit.

Like Parfit, we answer 'no' to the question of whether the present generation is free from any kind of responsibility toward the future. However, our reason for this reply differentiates our approach from his. We accept the non-imputability claim and admit that future people (say, in 2123) are in no position to ascribe their own 'bad' existence to the present generation's activities in 2023, insofar as they try to do so retrospectively from a factual-causal point of view. Nevertheless, we would like to insist that it is plausible for them to imagine looking forward from 2023 and *foreseeing* counterfactually that someone (in 2123) would have had a more desirable life were her ancestors (in 2023) to have taken care of her in advance. To motivate and clarify the notion of a point of view grounded in contrafactual foresight, let me quote a significant passage from Parfit's commentary on the aforementioned case of the 14-year-old girl.

> I [= Parfit] believe that, if *I* was the actual child of this girl, I could accept (3) [= that it would have been better if the child who existed had not been her actual child]. (3) does not imply that my existence is *bad*, or intrinsically morally undesirable. The claim is merely that, since a child born later would probably have had a better life than mine, it would have been better if my mother had waited, and had a child later. This claim need not imply that I ought rationally to regret that my mother had *me*, or that she ought rationally to regret this. (Parfit 1984, 360)

As Parfit himself suggests here, I would like to emphasize that, due to its contrafactuality, the supposition of any such foresight does not imply that the lives of future people in 2123 are 'bad'. And, in my view, if this is indeed the case, then, without ceasing to affirm their own lives, future people can also ask

[1] What is 'Theory X'? Since the present chapter lacks the space in which to address Parfit's later work *On What Matters*, let us be content to sketch out his idea of Theory X in *Reasons and Persons* only as far as the idea concerns the non-identity problem. In this book, Parfit argues that what might be able to solve the non-identity problem is 'same-number quality claim', in other words, the claim that 'if in either of two possible outcomes the same number of people would ever live, it would be worse if those who live are worse off, or have a lower quality of life, than those who would have lived' (Parfit 1984, 360). However, this claim does not yet cover 'different number choices', that is, cases where, 'in the different outcomes, different numbers would ever live' (Parfit 1984, 361). Theory X is an unknown comprehensive theory that he expects to solve the non-identity problem, even in the different number choices scenario.

whether the initial conditions of their existence, which are beyond their control, are good or bad. It is clear that any such care grounded in foreseeing or anticipating coming generations – a 'foreseeing care' – can be accomplished not only by future people themselves, but also by the third party or the present generation in 2023, on whose activities the lives of future people are dependent. It can, thus, be said that because we, the people of today, are able to influence future generations, we must expose ourselves to, and reply to, the following critical question that can be posed not only by us, but also by those who may be affected by us later and by the third party: why do you choose to act in this way, rather than another, toward future people?

The suggestion seems to be that the foreseeing care for future generations – from which we, the present generation, are not exempted – counts as a kind of responsibility. If this is so, then we need to ask: what kind of responsibility is this prospective care?

3 The 'Foreseeing-Care-Prevention' Type of Responsibility

Because the foreseeing care for future people is, as Hans Jonas points out, not concerned with 'the ex post facto account for what has been done, but the forward determination of what is to be done', (Jonas 1984, 92) it is the type of responsibility that does not focus on the negative results of acts done in the past, but on positive and desirable states for its own objects (e.g., coming generations) in the future. In other words, such care is the type of responsibility that seeks to prevent its objects from possible harm in advance rather than imputing their actual damage retrospectively to those who did them harm. Let us call this a 'foreseeing-care-prevention' type of responsibility.

It is true that this type of responsibility is especially important today, insofar as we are living, as Günther Anders insists, in 'the final times so far (*Endzeit*)': times which, given the magnitude of the destructive power of technological civilization, hold the unrelenting and catastrophic possibility of becoming 'the end of all times (*Zeitenende*)' (Anders 2011, 67). Hans Jonas, thus, thinks of the foreseeing-care-prevention type of responsibility as being 'as *novel* as the eventualities which it must meet' (Jonas 1984, 18; emphasis added). Nevertheless, and to the contrary, I would like to insist that such prospective-preventive responsibility toward coming generations has been altogether familiar to us from the very beginning of human history (notwithstanding that, prior to modern industrialization, its temporal-spatial scope had long been rather shorter than today); and, indeed, we find some such suggestion in Jonas' discussion of the two 'eminent paradigms' (Jonas 1984, 98) of responsibility to future people: one being the responsibility of politicians toward their nation, the other being the responsibility of parents to their children, which, in addition, serves as 'the archetype of all responsibility' (Jonas 1984, 101). Needless to say, however, neither of these kinds of responsibility, the parental or the political, are by any means 'novel'.

Importantly, these two examples illustrate how better to understand the foreseeing-care-prevention type of responsibility for future generations. In order to simplify the present discussion, however, let us now focus solely on parental responsibility. On the one hand, as parental care for a small child ought not to be partial and temporary but should exercise continuous responsibility for her total being – the needs of which range from feeding and proper hygiene to bodily communication to physical, emotional, moral and intellectual education – this type of responsibility requires us, the current generation, to prepare and ensure the integrity of the (potential) whole being of future people. And, for this purpose, it also demands that our action can and should be controlled in advance by our forecast of how (or to what extent or how probable it is that) we thereby affect those who live later. Thus, in Jonas' words, '[such anticipative] knowledge must be commensurate with the causal scale of our action'. (Jonas 1984, 7f.) Let us call this 'commensurability claim'.

On the other hand, as the goal of child-rearing is the independence of the grown-up child from this very nurturing, the foreseeing-care-prevention type of responsibility prompts us to respect and keep 'the spontaneity or freedom' (Jonas 1984, 107) of future generations. However, this is unpredictable, since such an unconstrained overflow of human freedom counts as 'the greatest of all unknowns' (Jonas 1984, 107). This being the case, it turns out that the commensurability claim can no longer work. In other words, it is actually difficult, and perhaps (almost) impossible, to render our anticipative knowledge commensurate with the causal effects of our power on those who live spontaneously in future. Furthermore, such commensuration is all the more improbable for the increasing causal complexity brought about by temporal distance and the technological power of action – uncontrollably self-accelerating – which even the most penetrating powers of prediction cannot encompass. Hence, the foreseeing-care-prevention type of responsibility encourages us to confront 'the gap between the ability to foretell and the power to act' (Jonas 1984, 8), and to adopt the precautionary principle in the sense of the imperative of emphasizing 'the prophecy of doom' (Jonas 1984, 31) or possible worst-case scenarios and taking pre-emptive measures to avoid them, whether they are probable or not.

Why, however, are such worst-case scenarios worthy of special attention? Because they show us the most fearful potentialities in a thematic way and simultaneously, thereby, help us to discover – albeit in an un-thematic or (in Edmund Husserl's terms) 'appresentative' manner – something that we could not see without such terrible fear, that is, something for the sake of which we are in fear. According to my interpretation, this is what Jonas means when he explains his idea of the 'heuristics of fear' as follows: 'Just as we should not know the value of truth without being aware of lies, nor of freedom without the lack of it [...], we need the [potential] threats to the image of the Human [...] to assure ourselves of her true image by the very recoil from these threats' (Jonas 1984, 26f.; alteration added). If this is the case, the foreseeing-care-prevention type of responsibility is essentially accompanied and guided by the 'image of the Human', which Jonas understands to be 'the normative conception of human beings' (Jonas 1984, 26; alteration added). What, however, does such an abstract conception mean? Obviously, we need to give it a concrete interpretation. For this purpose, I would like to refer to the Japanese philosopher Tetsurô Watsuji.

Watsuji emphasizes that a human being is 'a community itself and an individual in the community at the same time' (Watsuji 1962, 20). This means the following: on the one hand, we are particular individual persons and compose a certain community by acting in certain respective capacities. On the other hand, it is this very communal 'betweenness' (*aidagara* 間柄) that prescribes and distributes such specific roles to us and, accordingly, determines the existence of each person in advance. Interestingly, Watsuji calls this communal aspect 'the wholeness of human beings' and argues that it is characterized not only by inter-personality but also by inter-generationality or historicity. Taking the family as a common example that represents the wholeness of human beings, he claims:

> According to ancient Japanese custom, every household must have a Buddhist shrine at which one's ancestors are worshipped, and each year on the date of one's parent death, the family as a whole must observe this event by means of religious abstinence. [...] Therefore, we can no longer say that the head of a house is still the absolute head. Indeed, he cannot decide his family's destiny by his own self-will, for he is also under the control of his ancestors: all that he does is to preserve the 'house' he inherited from his ancestors. His obligation is to hand it on to his descendants without having damaged it. (Watsuji 1996, 88)

With this in mind, it can be said that the foreseeing-care-prevention type of responsibility obliges us, as the current generation, to prevent future people from possible harm in advance under the guidance of the historical wholeness of human beings, which finds us responsible to the authority of ancestors.

4 The 'Letting-the-Dead-Be' Type of Responsibility

Obviously, the foreseeing-care-prevention type of responsibility toward the future comprises an obligation that we have to the past. What does such a past-oriented obligation imply? In this context, the *Book of Rites* (*Li-ji* 禮記), one of the 'Five Classics' (*wu-jing* 五経) of Confucianism, merits attention. Here, we find that what we call 'rites' consist in promoting 'the return [...] to the beginning' (Legge 1968, 219).[2] Furthermore, for the purpose of going back to the beginning, one may not 'forget those to whom she owes her life' (Legge 1968, 222; alteration added).[3] Thus, rites represent a duty that we owe to our ancestors. Importantly, the *Book of Rites* teaches that we have two different ways to realize our connection with the preceding generations:

> Where the starting-point is affection, one way begins from the father [who is the most familiar with us]. Going up from him by degrees it reaches to the (high) ancestor [who is the most unfamiliar with us], and is said to 'diminish' [our affection as we draw to the ancestor]. Where the starting-point is the consideration of what is right, the other way begins with the ancestor [who is the most awe-inspiring and authoritative]. Coming down by natural degrees from him, it reaches to the father [who is less awe-inspiring and authoritative than anyone else in the ancestry], and is said to 'increase' [our respect as we draw again to the ancestor]. (Legge 1968, 64; alteration added)[4]

More importantly, the *Book of Rites* provides the following remarkable comment concerning the ways in which we actualize our ancestral connections: 'The course of humanity is all comprehended in the love for kindred. From the affection for parents comes the honouring of ancestors' (Legge 1968, 66; alteration added).[5] I would like to read this passage as proposing that we prioritize the first way that is mentioned in the quotation that precedes it, namely the way of 'diminishment' that extends from our parents back to our earliest ancestors. In other words, just as Hans Jonas suggests that the object of our 'parental' responsibility is expandable so as to enfold future generations far beyond our own children, so Confucianism teaches that our 'filial' responsibility is applicable to past generations long before our own parents.

How, then, can we grasp the responsibility toward ancestors that begins with affection for parents or relatives? Let me introduce here a 'strange' linguistic phenomenon in the Japanese language. In Japanese, there are some *intransitive*

[2] Cf. 『禮記』祭義第二十四：「天下之禮、到反始也。」(Takeuchi 1977, 711).
[3] Cf. 『禮記』祭義第二十四：「君子反古復始、不忘其所由生也。」(Takeuchi 1977, 714).
[4] Cf. 『禮記』大伝第十六：「自仁率親、等而上之至于祖、名曰軽。自義率祖、順而下之至于禰、名曰重。」(Takeuchi 1977, 518).
[5] Cf. 『禮記』大伝第十六：「是故人道親親也。親親故尊祖。」(Takeuchi 1977, 521).

verbs that are very frequently made *passive*. For example, the Japanese word *furu* (to fall; to rain) has its passive form *furareru* (literally: to *be fallen*; to *be rained*) though it is an intransitive verb. Hence, the Japanese sentence '*ame ga futta*' (it rained) can be turned around into '*ame ni furareta*' (we got rained on; or literally: we *were rained*.)

Similarly, I can say in Japanese, for example: *Oji ni shinaremashita*. (I was bereaved of my uncles. Or literally: I *was died* by my uncles.) What does this passive intransitive verb '*shinareru*' (to *be died*) truly imply?

On the one hand, it is true that 'to die' is intransitive and my death is, as Martin Heidegger claims, 'essentially in each case mine (je meines)' (Heidegger 1986, 240). Each person must undertake her own death and finally leave this world alone. On the other hand, however, I think that 'to die' is, in reality, *transitive* and, hence, a person who has passed away has *affected* someone that was bereaved by the very death of this person. In this meaning, I would like to say against Heidegger that my death is, essentially, in each case *ours* and, hence, can make someone bereaved.

To every action there is a corresponding reaction. If this is the case, what is the reaction of the bereaved that correlates with the death (or 'to die' in the transitive meaning) of the dead? In order to answer this question, I would like to refer to Tamiki Hara, a Japanese novelist who was one of the survivors of the atomic bombing of Hiroshima. In his short novel *Requiem* (*Chinkonka* 鎮魂歌), which he wrote just two years before he committed suicide, he describes poetically how to communicate with his family who were taken away from him.

> In the depth of life … I find myself in the depth of life and carry the weight of the death on my back … […] How sublime the space appears from this depth of life! There exist visions. […] My father, you are – on the armchair on the veranda. My mother, you are – under the pomegranate tree in the garden. My elder sister, you are – in the dew-drenched grape arbor. And my wife, you are – everywhere as far as I see, whether in the nearest or in the furthest place, as if you were my sincerest prayer itself. The dead, the dead, you sink me into the depth of life … Oh, how calm you are, when I look up to you from this depth of life! (Hara 1973, 138)

According to my interpretation, this passage shows that the protagonist who 'was died by' his parents, his elder sister and his wife, and who can be obviously identified as Hara himself, reactively *lets* them *be* – naturally not as the living, like himself, but as they are, that is, as the dead. To put it another way, once they have passed away, they *are* qua the dead, as long as he correspondingly reacts – as long as he lets them be.

In my view, it is this reaction of the living to the dead that is meant by the afore-mentioned notion of past-oriented responsibility. Let us call this the 'letting-the-dead-be' type of responsibility: we bear responsibility toward past generations so that they stay with us, still 'alive' in a certain sense.

5 Conclusion

To summarize: in this chapter, we have discussed two different types of responsibility. One is the future-oriented 'foreseeing-care-prevention' type and the other is the past-oriented 'letting-the-dead-be' type. However, we need to ask how the two are related to each other. In my view, without the former, the latter would be impossible. Why? As is well known, the ancient Chinese philosopher of Confucianism, Mencius, argues: 'there are three things which are un-filial. The most serious of them is to have no posterity' (Kobayashi 1972, 55).[6] According to Zhao Qi (趙岐)'s traditional commentary, the phrase 'to have no posterity' implies that 'nobody will worship ancestors anymore' (「絶先祖祀」) (Kobayashi 1972, 55). In this sense, the foreseeing-care-prevention type of responsibility is pre-supposed and requested by the letting-the-dead-be type.

On the other hand, it can be also said that the former needs the latter. As we have seen, the foreseeing-care-prevention type of responsibility is to be accompanied and guided by what Jonas calls the 'image of the Human', which we have connected with Watsuji, Confucianism and Hara and, thereby, interpreted to denote the letting-the-dead-be type of responsibility. To put it simply, this means that we are responsible *for* future people as long as we are responsible *to* past generations, who are in a position to prevent us from our present-oriented and 'selfish' tendency.

If this is the case, a new kind of responsibility that we can expect to overcome today's paradigmatic idea of self-responsibility consists of these types of responsibility: the two types of intergenerational responsibility which are tightly interconnected and can restrain the present-oriented responsibility, so to speak, on both 'past-oriented' and 'future-oriented' flanks.

Bibliography

Anders, Günther. 2011. *Die Zerstörung unserer Zukunft. Ein Lesebuch*. Zürich: Diogenes.

Hara, Tamiki. 1973. *Natsu-no-hana / Chinkonka [Summer Flowers / Requiem]*. Tokyo: Kôdansha.

Heidegger, Martin. 1986. *Sein und Zeit*. Tübingen: Max Niemeyer.

[6] Cf. 『孟子』離婁章句上：「孟子曰、不孝有三、無後爲大。」.

Jonas, Hans. 1984. *The Imperative of Responsibility. In Search of an Ethics for the Technological Age*. Chicago: The University of Chicago Press.
Kobayashi, Katsundo, trans. 1972. *Moushi [Mencius]*. Vol. 2. Tokyo: Iwanami.
Legge, James, trans. 1968. *The Sacred Books of China. The Texts of Confuciansm*. Part 2163 of *The LI KI, XI-XL*VI. Delhi: Motilal Banarsidass.
Parfit, Derek. 1984. *Reasons and Persons*. Oxford: Oxford University Press.
Picht, Georg. 1969. *Wahrheit – Vernunft – Verantwortung. Philosophische Studien [Truth – Reason – Responsibility. Philosophical Studies]*. Stuttgart: Klett-Cotta.
Takeuchi, Teruo, trans. 1977. *Raiki [The Book of Rites]*. Vol. 2. Tokyo: Meiji-Shoin.
Watsuji, Tetsurô. 1962. *Watsuji Tetsurô Zenshû [Collected Works of Tetsurô Watsuji]*, Vol. 9. Tokyo: Iwanami.
1996. *Watsuji Tetsurô's Rinrigaku. Ethics in Japan*. Translated by Seisaku Yamamoto and Robert E. Carter. Albany, NY: State University of New York Press.

10

Guidelines for a Global Constitutional Convention for Future Generations

Stephen M. Gardiner

1 Institutional Denial

Humanity faces a serious problem of institutional design. Existing institutions have a dangerous blind spot when it comes to protecting the future. This leaves the young and other future generations especially vulnerable to decisions biased against their concerns. While the threat is quite general, it is particularly severe for paradigmatically global and ecological challenges. One such problem – climate change – already poses extreme risks not only to vulnerable populations, but also to societies as we know them, and potentially to the survival of the species itself. The rapid pace of human expansion suggests that similar intergenerational challenges may not be far behind. Sadly, the current institutional architecture is poorly placed to cope, globally and nationally. Indeed, it appears both actively to encourage many of the drivers of 'dangerous anthropogenic interference' with Earth systems, and to resist efforts to prevent, mitigate, adapt, cope, and endure. As a result, humanity's design problem is now on the brink of becoming a full-blown planetary crisis.

Initially, such claims may seem radical. So, it is worth underlining why they are plausible. Consider the climate situation. More than thirty years have passed since the first IPCC report (1990) explained the emerging threat, and the countries of the world adopted the United Nations Framework Convention on Climate Change (UNFCCC) at the Rio Earth Summit (1992). The central aim of the UNFCCC is to protect current and future generations of humankind by preventing 'dangerous anthropogenic interference' with the climate system.

Components of this paper were included in presentations at Lehigh University, Oxford University, the University of Edinburgh, the University of Newcastle, the University of Washington, and the conference *Justice Between Generations: Asian, African, Indigenous and Western Perspectives* in Montreal. I thank those audiences, and especially Liz Cripps, Blake Francis, Matthias Fritsch, Jing Iris Hu, Marion Hourdequin, Bernhard Malkmus, Romy Opperman, and César Palacios-González. I am also grateful to Lukas Meyer and Mario Wenning.

In 2015, the Paris Agreement defined this objective in terms of holding the average global temperature rise below 2°C, and pursuing efforts to get closer to 1.5°C.

There are good reasons for such targets. For instance, a rise in the global average of 4–5°C is comparable to an ice age shift but happening over a few decades. Such a shift threatens fundamental human support systems, such as global agriculture. Thus, among scientists, we are told, 'there is a widespread view that a 4°C future is incompatible with any reasonable characterisation of an organised, equitable and civilised global community' (Anderson 2012, 29). Even a lesser increase of around 3°C threatens catastrophe on a broad scale. For instance, millions will likely die from factors such as sea level rise, drought, and extreme heat; under such pressure, some communities may experience social collapse, with severe negative consequences both for their own citizens and for the wider international community.

Unfortunately, the international effort is in serious trouble. Annual emissions of greenhouse gases have risen by more than 60 per cent (in terms of carbon dioxide equivalent) since the early nineties. The UN has described the period from 2009 to 2019 as a 'lost decade', with emissions in 2019 'almost exactly at the level of emissions projected for 2020 under the business-as-usual, or no-policy, scenarios [in 2009]', because the 'effects of climate policies have been too small to offset the impact of key drivers of emissions such as economic growth and population growth' (UNEP 2019, 4). Moreover, global emissions continue to increase: 2022 was another record year, with emissions 1.2 per cent higher than in 2021.

Such news is disturbing. It becomes more so when put into context. Mainstream projections stress that, despite recent progress, 'real world action based on current policies' implies a rise in the global average temperature of 2.7°C by 2100, with an uncertainty range of 2.2–3.4°C (Climate Action Tracker 2022). This is bad enough. Nevertheless, the conventional approach tends to understate the depth of humanity's predicament, since the mainstream projections are conservative in ways that make focusing on them alone seem *unduly complacent* from the ethical point of view (Gardiner 2023a). Consider three examples.[1]

First, being 'on track' for reaching a particular temperature – such as 1.5°C, 2.0°C, or 2.7°C – is typically understood in terms of a 50–66 per cent chance of

[1] In addition, the conventional focus on 2100 appears to downplay the longer-term risks to future generations. For example, climate science projects a rise in average global temperature in intermediate emissions scenarios of 2.1–3.5°C for 2100 and 2.3–4.6°C for 2200; in a very high emission scenario it projects 3.3–5.7°C by 2100 and 6.6–14.1°C by 2200 (IPCC 2022). Under both scenarios, the numbers for 2200 are notably higher than for 2100 (e.g., in the intermediate scenario, the high end goes from 3.5°C in 2100 to 4.6°C in 2200, and in the high scenario, the low end goes from 3.3°C to 6.6°C).

staying below the given temperature. (For example, Climate Action Tracker's 2.7°C is based on 50 per cent.[2]) Yet this approach is morally disturbing. Most notably, in thinking about the Paris targets we should not say that we are 'on track' to avoid dangerous climate change if there is still a 50 per cent chance of exceeding 2°C or 1.5°C. Surely, we are morally required to provide a greater degree of protection for the future than that.

Second, mainstream projections typically assume a mid-range climate sensitivity. By contrast, some models suggest that a high climate sensitivity would imply that the carbon budget for 1.5°C had already been breached by 2021, while others project that a high sensitivity, high emission scenario would result in a stunning global temperature rise of around 4.5–7°C by 2100 (Forster et al. 2020). These numbers are truly alarming. They imply catastrophic threats on multiple scales, including death and suffering for millions (or billions), through to social collapse, and even onto human extinction. In other words, there is a realistic threat that human activity may 'erode the fundamental preconditions of human life and society' (e.g., Gardiner 2011a, 159).[3]

Third, mainstream projections *assume* that much of the burden of limiting climate change this century will be taken up by a massive deployment of carbon removal technologies, yet these technologies are currently expensive and unproven at scale (e.g., Anderson and Peters 2016). Thus, what counts as 'being on track' already embeds pronounced optimism about the future. This seems deeply ethically problematic.

Given all this, it seems clear that conventional institutions have failed to address the climate problem in a reasonable and timely manner. The spectre of institutional failure is occasionally raised even by leading figures in the political establishment. Consider three examples, commenting on different periods of international climate politics. First, reflecting on the period 1992–2008, Mary Robinson, former President of Ireland, United Nations Human Rights Commissioner, and United Nations Secretary-General's Special Envoy on Climate Change, once wrote: 'The scope of these problems – and of the action required to treat them – *reach beyond previous human challenges*. Yet in the sixteen years since the UNFCCC was signed, global negotiations have proceeded at a glacial pace. *We have collectively failed to grasp the scale and urgency of the problem. Climate change shows*

[2] 'The temperatures on the CAT thermometer are "median" warming estimates in 2100. This means that there is a 50 per cent chance that the calculated temperature would be exceeded if the given emissions pathway is followed' (Climate Action Tracker 2022).

[3] As one source puts it, under such scenarios 'within eight decades, the warming has a 50 per cent probability of subjecting the global population to catastrophic (>3°C) to unknown risks (>5°C) and a 5 per cent probability of being fully in the unknown risk category, which also includes existential threats for everyone' (Xu and Ramanathen 2017).

up countless weaknesses in our current institutional architecture' (Robinson 2008, xix; emphasis added).

Second, in 2009, looking forward to the Copenhagen climate meeting which was, even then, regarded as critical in addressing the climate crisis, Connie Hedegaard, the Danish Minister for Climate and Energy, and subsequently EU commissioner on climate action, said: 'If the whole world comes to Copenhagen and leaves without making the needed political agreement, then I think it's a failure that is not just about climate. Then it's the whole global democratic system not being able to deliver results in one of the defining challenges of our century. And that ... *should not be a possibility*' (Von Bulow 2009; emphasis added). Hedegaard's worry was apt. Copenhagen did fail, with the result that really substantive improvements in global climate action were indeed stalled (see the above quote from UNEP 2019).

Third, and perhaps most strikingly, in 2015 an architect of the most recent initiative – the Paris Agreement – stated: 'This is a success for the high ambition coalition ... *This was the last chance* [for the UN process] and we have taken it' (United Nations 2015; emphasis added). In making this claim, Miguel Arias Cañete, EU climate commissioner, was explicitly acknowledging past institutional failures, and implicitly recognizing the implications should Paris fail. Yet, as it turns out, seven years later, Paris is failing. Currently, it is not achieving high ambition, and time is fast running out. Moreover, this failure was quite predictable, given the basic flaws baked into the institutional design (Gardiner 2022a; also 2004, 2011a, 2014; Dimitrov et al. 2019). In short, at the time of writing it seems highly plausible that, to put the point bluntly, conventional institutions have indeed blown their 'last chance'.

By now it should be clear that there is an urgent need for something different. The time is ripe – indeed well beyond ripe – for a new approach. Yet strikingly, despite the history and urgency of the climate crisis, conventional public discussion rarely highlights humanity's institutional design problem. Instead, it is as if we are collectively in the grip of a *deep institutional denial*. Most public discourse continues to proceed as if the only real obstacles to robust climate action are bad actors, lack of genuine political leadership, and persistent resistance to basic science by some politicians, corporations, and sections of the public. Much of the mainstream literature in policy and academia tends to encourage the same vision. Even many of those who accept that 'business as usual' economic development is untenable, typically implicitly advocate '*business-as-usual*' *institutionalism*.[4]

[4] One major exception is anti-capitalist writers, and some progressive politicians and activists. Still, to my knowledge none advocate for a global constitutional convention.

In my view, these attitudes are highly complacent, and likely to be self-defeating. Indeed, institutional denial may be even more dangerous than the ongoing denial of basic climate science. Humanity needs to wake up to the fact that we lack effective structures for dealing with paradigmatically global, intergenerational, and ecological challenges. We should also recognize that this institutional vacuum helps to fuel the more visible failures. For instance, it is partly because we have defective institutions that we lack effective leaders (e.g., since the way current institutions are set up actively encourages the emergence of some kinds of leaders and not others). Thus, better institutions have a role to play there too. Overcoming institutional denialism is central to addressing threats to fundamental values, including global security, justice, freedom, rights, community, and individual wellbeing.

Over more than two decades, I have been offering a more specific diagnosis of humanity's institutional problem and exploring a positive strategy for resolving it. The diagnosis is that climate change constitutes a perfect moral storm, one central aspect of which is that humanity faces a basic standing threat involving intergenerational relations, and a dangerous governance gap in confronting that threat.[5] My proposed strategy to deal with this aspect of the problem is to call for a global constitutional convention (GCC) focused on future generations. This deliberative body would confront the serious 'governance gap' that currently exists for concern for future generations by considering the extent to which that gap requires structural solutions, and especially substantial institutional reform.

One reason for the call for a GCC is the threat of severe and potentially catastrophic climate change. Still, in my view, climate change is just one instantiation of a wider phenomenon. The future is in peril from numerous sources. Some are already recognized (e.g., nuclear weapons; nuclear waste). Others are less familiar (e.g., the threat to the food supply posed by modern agricultural methods), speculative (e.g., a geoengineering arms race),[6] or have yet to be imagined. In any case, the possibility of major global and intergenerational challenges looms large over the next century or so (Bostrom and Milan Cirkovic 2008; Ord 2021). Consequently, the central issue I am raising is much more general: the call for a GCC responds to a *basic standing threat* to humanity and to nonhuman nature, one to which we have a strong duty to respond.

The call for a GCC, like all substantial proposals for reform, faces serious initial obstacles, most obviously those of profound scepticism and cynicism. Elsewhere, I motivate the call by offering a natural argument for the GCC that

[5] Note that this is only one central aspect of the climate problem, not the whole story.
[6] Gardiner 2011a, 2013.

is difficult to resist and then addressing some common objections (Gardiner 2019). In this chapter, I set such concerns aside and propose some early guidelines for how we might go about thinking about the GCC itself. Guidelines are needed, in part, because existing institutions have failed to protect the future. Given this, I suggest that we should not approach the task of developing new institutions by being too strongly influenced by those we already have. Although there are lessons to be learned from their successes, we must also highlight both their failures and the distinctiveness of the challenge ahead. Intergenerational institutions aim to protect the future, including from the present. They must be designed with that purpose in mind.

2 The Perfect Moral Storm

My diagnosis of the climate problem is that it is a perfect moral storm (Gardiner 2011a). A perfect moral storm involves the convergence of a number of factors that challenge the ability of agents to behave ethically. Consequently, it 'throws down the gauntlet' to us as ethical agents, including to our moral theories and to our political systems.

In the climate case, the converging factors or 'storms' are that the climate problem (first) is genuinely global, (second) is profoundly intergenerational, (third) crosses species boundaries, and (fourth) occurs in a setting where our theories and institutions are weak. Each storm invites temptations for unethical action, and when they converge, they are mutually reinforcing. Thus, the perfect moral storm seriously compromises the prospects for ethically responsible behaviour. Now, a full description of the perfect moral storm is well beyond the scope of this paper. Still, to get a sense of it, let us briefly highlight three dimensions. Strong temptations exist to deflect the burdens of our behaviour to others (or 'pass the buck') across space, time, and species.

The global storm focuses on the spatial dimension. Here, deflection typically involves agents seeking to push burdens onto different countries, classes, races, castes, genders, and so on. Many of these factors, especially race and class, are highlighted by traditional environmental justice movements. Typically, they reflect the ongoing influence of background injustices that are sadly familiar, such as colonialism, feudalism, sexism, and institutional racism. These are central aspects of the global storm.

The intergenerational storm focuses on the temporal dimension. This is prominent in the climate case. For instance, many of the effects of climate change set in motion by the current generation of decision-makers, are likely only to be fully realized decades, centuries, or even millennia into the future.

(Examples include the collapse of the West Antarctic Ice Sheet, a massive release of methane from the deep ocean, or the crossing of a major tipping point in the global system around 2150.) Given this, similar temptations to pass the buck play out over time as over space, especially by imposing burdens on the young and other future generations. For instance, the generation of decision-makers over 50 will be tempted to take comparatively modest benefits from high emissions now, even when doing so inflicts risks of severe harm onto people alive later this century and beyond.

Intergenerational buck-passing by one generation is a form of intergenerational tyranny and, in severe cases, typically constitutes a fundamental injustice in its own right. It is even more striking when a number of generations in a generational sequence succumb to temptation and, thereby, impose accelerating burdens on the future. In general, taking the intergenerational storm seriously reveals a fundamental collective action problem, the *tyranny of the contemporary* ('TYKE'), which constitutes a basic standing threat in human affairs. Worryingly, there are reasons to believe that the TYKE is being played out in the climate case, possibly even to the extent of provoking an *intergenerational arms race* (Gardiner 2011a).

To be clear, in highlighting intergenerational tyranny I am not saying that other dimensions of injustice are not relevant. For instance, many temporal injustices will, no doubt, amplify the more familiar threats mentioned above, such as those associated with race, class, gender, and xenophobia. Still, it is worth recognizing that sometimes aspects of injustice pull against each other. So, for instance, one live possibility is that of *unholy alliances against the future*. One example would be if the current generation of a poor population were willing to accept short-term benefits for itself in exchange for cooperating in a tyranny of the contemporary against future generations. Thus, some apparently 'pro-poor' policies may risk exacerbating intergenerational injustice in the longer term, including against future generations of the global poor or other marginalized populations.

The ecological storm emphasizes buck passing across species (Gardiner and Weisbach 2016, 32–37; Gardiner 2011a, 43–44). Faced with negative impacts, human communities are likely to deflect burdens from themselves onto nonhumans, including populations, species, and ecosystems. This is the ecological storm. So, for example, one may see a 'kick the dog' scenario emerging. Recall the terrible old nursery rhyme, where the farmer kicks his wife, the wife kicks the child, and the child then lashes out at the dog. Similarly, we may see a chain reaction where the rich divert harms onto the poor, who then pass them onto the nonhuman world. In short, there are high risks of a *tyranny of humanity* ('TMAN') over the rest of nature.

One notable upshot of the convergence involved in the perfect moral storm is that it encourages a lurking problem of moral corruption. Given the various storms, bad ethical behaviour will be tempting for the current generation of decision-makers, and especially for richer and more powerful groups within it. Thus, those who can influence the levers of power are likely to find enticing ways of thinking and talking about climate change that obscure what is going on. After all, distorted framings of the situation can conceal injustice and facilitate self-deception. Elsewhere, I argue that this is common with climate change. Among the most obvious examples is undue scepticism about the state of climate science. A less obvious instance is the dominance of the idea that climate change is a traditional tragedy of the commons played out between nation states, where each country is implicitly assumed to be an *effective intergenerational steward* that can be relied upon to protect the interests of its own people indefinitely into the future, across hundreds or thousands of years.

3 Guidelines

One response to the perfect moral storm, and in particular to its intergenerational dimension, is to call for a GCC focused on future generations (Gardiner 2014, 2019). The GCC would be a deliberative body put in place to confront the serious 'governance gap' that currently exists for concern for future generations by considering the extent to which that gap requires structural solutions, and especially substantial institutional reform.

In practice, a GCC may take various forms. Moreover, it seems likely that the precise form chosen will influence the eventual outcome in significant ways. Given that, I propose a set of ten initial guidelines for how to go about constituting an actual GCC.[7] These guidelines help to mark out the way ahead and also serve as benchmarks (e.g., parameters and constraints) against which more substantial proposals can be judged or assessed. Notably, the guidelines are not intended to be comprehensive, exhaustive, or the final word. Instead, the idea is to set out the beginnings of a working list which we (the community as a group) might add to and amend.

In one way, the arguments for the guidelines are intended in the spirit of the 'baby steps' approach I have pursued elsewhere (Gardiner 2019). Each guideline is intended as a modest development of the general argument for the GCC, since each emerges through small, natural steps from what has come

[7] The account here builds on a brief introduction of the guidelines in Gardiner 2014. Two are discussed in more detail in Gardiner 2022b.

before in that argument. Nevertheless, in another way each step moves us in a radical direction relative to the status quo. As in earlier parts of the baby steps argument, it soon becomes clear that these comparatively small and largely analytical moves take us in directions that are deeply unfamiliar in mainstream debate, and in stark contrast to prevailing discussions.

Despite the radical implications, I maintain that my guidelines ought to be the focus of any serious discussion of intergenerational institutional reform, especially for global and ecological problems. One reason is that they impose a significant burden of proof. This burden exerts itself against rival, less ambitious approaches to climate change and other intergenerational problems. It also places substantial demands on the concrete proposals to be considered within the GCC later in the process.

Another reason that the guidelines should be our focus is that they have status independently of the bare proposal for a GCC and more concrete instantiations of it. Thus, even those rejecting my whole methodology have reason to take the guidelines seriously. They ought to be able to explain how their rival approaches respond to the guidelines and justify any deviations from them. Not to do so risks consigning their alternatives to inadequacy. Ultimately, it may also signal a failure to give intergenerational problems their due. One reason this might matter is that such a failure may indicate an abdication of responsibility, and perhaps even an encouragement, facilitation, or direct manifestation of moral corruption. If we are to defend our efforts on behalf of the future to the young and other future generations, then it is wise to keep these concerns in mind.

I shall now set out the ten guidelines. They fall into natural groupings. They also happen to come roughly in order of increasing controversy.

3.1 Relational Characteristics

My first set of guidelines concern the *status* of the global constitutional convention for future generations within humanity's social systems, as understood through the relationship of the GCC to other institutions.

The first guideline concerns relative independence:

> (GL1) *Autonomy*: the global constitutional convention for future generations should have considerable autonomy from other institutions, and especially from those dominated by factors that generate or facilitate the tyranny of the contemporary and perfect moral storm more generally.

The word autonomy means self-rule and signals a kind of independence. The idea of the autonomy guideline is that the GCC must be able to operate to a considerable extent without influence from other institutions. Here it is good to remember that the whole point of the GCC is (temporarily) to represent humanity in its *fundamental* relations on a particular dimension, that of intergenerational concern.[8] Therefore, we (those developing the GCC, humanity at large) want a GCC that does this job well. We want it to be an effective voice of the people in its appropriate domain. We do not want a GCC that is unduly influenced by, dominated by, or risks being hijacked by, other concerns. This includes those concerns best registered by other institutions, even acknowledging that many of those other concerns and institutions are legitimate.

This last caveat is worth emphasizing. Importantly, the autonomy guideline holds even when one grants that some other institutions also represent fundamental relations. The background thought is that there is more than one domain of human concern, including fundamental concern. The point of the autonomy guideline is then that intergenerational concern is *one* example of a primary kind of concern, a concern that should be addressed at a fundamental level. It is not a secondary matter, derived from other concerns and to be treated underneath other institutions created for different purposes.

This rationale could perhaps be expressed more modestly as a presumption in favour of institutional autonomy: it should not be assumed at the outset that intergenerational concern can or will be *absorbed* by institutions with other fundamental purposes. One piece of evidence against the absorption model is the ongoing failure of existing social systems to address the tyranny of the contemporary in the case of climate. This means that there is a (strong) presumption in favour of institutional autonomy, at least at this stage. Perhaps the GCC could be formed and then decide that the status quo is best. However, this seems seriously unlikely and, given what we have seen in the earlier sections, would require substantial explanation and defence.

Notably, autonomy for the GCC is especially needed from those current institutions that are a primary source of the tyranny of the contemporary, such as those dominated by short-term, narrowly economic factors. So, for example, we would not want a GCC constituted by the finance ministers of the largest industrialized nations, or the CEOs of the world's biggest corporations, or their functional equivalents. The point is not that there is necessarily anything wrong with those roles or the people who occupy them. Instead, it is that, given

[8] The term 'represent' is controversial in the literature. One reason is that it can be used in broad or narrow ways. Some of the narrow ways (often tied to specific accounts of democracy) cast doubt on whether "representation" is possible for future people. For simplicity, in this paper I set such disputes aside. Thus, I intend only a very broad sense of 'represent' that can cover a wide range of views about how to understand the appropriate relationships between (for example) those who attend the GCC, future people, current people, and humanity as such.

their roles, the experience they have, the pressures they are under, the kind of training they typically receive, and so on, such people are likely to be poor delegates to the GCC. Most obviously, being strongly influenced by the short-term and narrowly economic, they are likely to prejudice the GCC towards the tyranny of the contemporary rather than away from it.

Other sources of implicit bias may be less obvious. For example, some years ago a friend recounted to me the fate of a special session at an international meeting that had been set aside to discuss concern for future generations. Within a few minutes, that session quickly dissolved into a debate about the pressing concern of the day, a humanitarian crisis in a war-torn region. Notably, this discussion was initiated and largely sustained by pressure from NGOs (not national governments, corporations, or any of the other usual suspects). The upshot was that that the opportunity to discuss future generations was lost. Instead, discussion was given over to the sort of issue that is always on the table in venues of this kind.

There is no reason to think that this loss was caused by any animosity on the part of the NGOs or the rest of the assembly towards future generations.[9] Nevertheless, concern for the future fell victim to how other priorities are already built into how many people think about the world and its problems. The structural biases incorporated within the NGOs and existing international institutions – including the strong focus on the present and especially on the crises of the day – effectively dominated concern for future generations, and just as strongly as if there were active discrimination against them.

By contrast, the idea behind the autonomy guideline is that attempts must be made to *insulate* the GCC from these predictable kinds of bias, which distract from its central purpose. The guidelines suggests that the design of the GCC should pay particular attention to resisting or limiting influences from short-term, narrowly economic forces.

The second guideline is, in some ways, the flipside of the first, as it concerns limits to the independence of the GCC:

> (GL2) *Mutual accountability*: the global constitutional convention for future generations should be to some extent accountable to other major institutions, and they should be accountable to it.

This guideline reminds us that, although the GCC should have considerable autonomy, we should not think of it as the *sole* site of legitimate authority within a global institutional architecture, any more than the Presidency, or the Supreme Court, or the Congress are the sole sites of political authority

[9] That said, one must always be mindful of the risk of 'unholy alliances against the future' (Gardiner 2022a, 2022c).

within the US political system. The GCC represents society in one fundamental aspect, but not in all. It deserves respect from other institutions because of its standing, but they also deserve some respect from it. This is especially true for those that also represent society in (different) fundamental aspects.

Importantly, this is so in both directions. Thus, for example, while the GCC should not be able to decide unilaterally that national institutions should be radically supplanted, it is also not appropriate for conventional national governments to have a simple veto on the recommendations of the GCC concerning institutions for future generations, including those that would result in sharp limits to the current powers of national governments themselves. Each has appropriate authority in its own sphere. How that is to be understood in practice – and who gets to decide where the limits are – are important issues that should be discussed under the second guideline. Notably, one specific challenge is that conventional national governments should not be permitted to overreach beyond their realms of competence and legitimacy. If they do act against legitimate intergenerational institutions, it is they who are the usurpers.[10]

The third guideline concerns adequacy:

> (GL3) *Functional adequacy*: the global constitutional convention for future generations should be constructed in such a way that it is highly likely to produce recommendations that are functionally adequate to the task.

This guideline reflects the fact that the GCC, like other aspects of the social system, has a role to play, that playing this role effectively is its central task, and that the GCC will ultimately be judged by how effectively it carries out that task, in terms both of procedures and outcomes.

One might think that this guideline is so obvious as to barely be worth stating. Unfortunately, it is vital to be explicit since this guideline is one most likely to be violated by mainstream proposals. For instance, the need for functional adequacy implies that the tasks of the GCC should not be assigned to any currently existing body whose design and authority is unsuitable. Yet, in my view the venues most usually suggested are grossly inadequate, including those sometimes proposed by other august bodies.

Consider three examples. First, in 2009, the UK's Royal Society suggested that solar geoengineering should be taken up by the UN's Commission for Sustainable Development (Shepherd et. Al. 2009; Gardiner 2011b, 165). Unfortunately, as things stand, this body is only a minor venue in the global

[10] Some doubt the coherency of the very idea of intergenerational legitimacy (e.g., Gosseries 2023). I leave that issue for another occasion.

system and has almost no powers. Moreover, it operates within an institution which, itself, has limited influence on global affairs.

Second, in 2013, the UN Secretary General proposed addressing concern for the future by creating a new UN High Commissioner for Future Generations, on a par with the High Commissioner for Human Rights.[11] Again, this is a minor role in the global system with very limited powers. (Indeed, it seems inadequate for human rights too.) Similar things might be said about various proposals for an ombudsman for the future at the domestic level that have been discussed in some countries and occasionally implemented.

Third, in 2018, an expert group investigating geoengineering governance called for a high-level citizen assembly to provide advice to the international community. While this proposal bears a limited resemblance to the GCC – it is, after all, a global and deliberative international body – it lacks the basic political status of the GCC and serves more as a 'focus group' to advise the powers that be (in this case, likely, national governments).

In my opinion, each of these proposals is inadequate – I would say woefully inadequate – to the task. In saying this, I do not mean to denigrate those who made the effort, or to claim that the proposals have no merit for any purposes whatever. (For example, perhaps each could prove useful as pragmatic, incremental moves that highlight the importance of intergenerational issues.) Instead, my central point is that these proposals (and others like them) are much too modest to reflect the gravity of the threats posed by climate change in particular and the tyranny of the contemporary more generally. Notably, assigning concern for future generations to such venues is *strikingly unambitious* given what is at stake. They lack the basic, foundational status of the GCC. For instance, they lack the appropriate standing and authority with respect to other institutions and the public. In short, they are *much too peripheral, shallow, and weak* to do what needs to be done. By contrast, with the GCC, humanity would be seeking to ground its intergenerational institutions in ways that make them *central, deep, and strong*. The third guideline serves to bring this demand to the fore. If the GCC is to fulfil its basic function, it must take seriously the nature of its task.

In summary, in this section we considered three initial guidelines: autonomy, mutual accountability, and functional adequacy. These guidelines may initially appear fairly obvious and unobjectionable. They follow on as 'baby steps' from the basic idea of the GCC itself. Nevertheless, each baby step provides a strong challenge to conventional ways of thinking in climate change governance, and in global politics in general.

[11] United Nations Secretary-General, *Intergenerational Solidarity and the Needs of Future Generations*, 2013. Notably, this report cites Gardiner 2011a.

One way to illustrate this is to highlight the contrast between the three guidelines and the way conventional climate politics is actually carried out. There, the focal point is the UNFCCC. This is an *ad hoc* body run by national governments which has a *limited remit*. It has major meetings *only once a year*, and ones of deep consequence only about *once a decade* (e.g., 1997, 2009, 2015). In general, it can be accused of being a relatively shallow, peripheral, and weak institution. It is certainly not central, deep, or strong. More specifically, it violates the three initial guidelines. It has no meaningful autonomy from national governments or the short-term forces that typically move them. Accountability runs in only one direction – the UNFCCC is accountable to national institutions, but they are not accountable to it. More generally, it is not functionally adequate or 'fit for purpose'. For instance, plausible institutions would not rely merely on voluntary, self-imposed climate targets considered in splendid isolation from the rest of global affairs. Instead, they would involve meaningful integration with central international issues, such as trade and security.

Given all of this, the failure of the conventional approach was predictable, especially in light of the tyranny of the contemporary, the problem of moral corruption, and the wider challenge of the perfect moral storm. Indeed, some of us did predict failure, and continue to do so (e.g., Gardiner 2004, 2011a, 2022a; Spash 2016). This is not to denigrate the valiant efforts of some of those involved in the UNFCCC process. Nevertheless, we cannot continue to hide behind the dangerous illusion that it is up to the task. The risks are too high, including of various kinds of catastrophe, ranging from death and suffering for many millions, to social collapse, to human extinction. In short, the fate of humanity itself may lie in the balance. It is in this spirit that we move on to the next set of guidelines.

3.2 Aims

My second set of guidelines reflects the basic *remit* of the GCC. They are:

> (GL4) *Comprehensiveness*: the global constitutional convention for future generations should be under a mandate to consider and respond to a very broad range of global intergenerational issues, to address such issues at a foundational level, and to recommend institutional reform accordingly.

> (GL5) *Standing authority*: while the global constitutional convention for future generations may recommend the establishment of some temporary and issue-specific bodies, its central focus should be on the establishment of institutions with standing authority over the long-term.

In my view, it is natural (again, a baby step) to infer this second set of guidelines from the GCC and its status. In particular, the GCC must respond to the tyranny of the contemporary. Yet the TYKE has a very broad range, being manifest in numerous forms over different time-periods, with different generational groupings, and different spatial scales. One implication is that the tyranny of the contemporary is not a temporary, episodic, or peripheral concern, but constitutes a *basic standing threat* to social systems and to humanity as such. To say that it is a *standing* threat is to say that it is persistent, ongoing or permanent in a way that is built into the fabric of human life. To say that is it a *basic* threat is to say that it strikes at the foundations of social systems, undermining them at their roots.[12] If the tyranny of the contemporary is a basic standing threat, it is natural to infer that we need permanent, established institutions to address it that make future generations salient and are empowered to bring concerns of intergenerational ethics to the fore.[13]

Again, our guidelines stand in marked contrast to the usual approaches to governing global and intergenerational issues in both the national and international spheres. In these realms, temporary and issue-specific bodies are very much the norm. In the case of climate change, the UNFCCC and the IPCC are prime examples. We see similar institutions for other global, intergenerational problems, such as nuclear proliferation, ozone depletion, deforestation, and so on.

Whatever the successes and failures of particular bodies, this piecemeal (*ad hoc*, issue-specific) approach has notable defects from the point of view of addressing the TYKE as a basic standing threat.[14] The first defect is that it tends to make global affairs *highly reactive*. The focus is on responding to problems that are already known to be developing, where awareness has risen to a significant level, and to political salience, for independent reasons. By contrast, a much more *proactive* approach seems appropriate. In proposing new institutions, the GCC will want them to have a mandate not just to address active and known threats (such as climate change, nuclear proliferation, and large asteroid detection), but also to identify further sources of global, intergenerational

[12] There is a parallel between the tyranny of the contemporary and other basic standing threats. For instance, the tyranny of the majority is a basic standing threat within democratic institutions, and despotism is a basic standing threat in systems of government more generally.

[13] Notably, other institutions are often blind to the tyranny of the contemporary, or in effect hinder the manifestation of intergenerational concern, or even actively encourage the emergence of intergenerational tyranny and block attempts at solutions. Moreover, the contexts in which the TYKE manifests itself are rarely neutral. Typically, there are considerable risks of moral corruption, where the very terms in which social questions are discussed are skewed such as to steer us away from taking the TYKE seriously, including by failing to identify it and underplaying the threat.

[14] The Montreal Protocol is often said to be highly successful in its domain. Still, in encouraging the piecemeal approach it may turn out, retrospectively, to be the most dangerously successful agreement in human history.

threats, making sure that these are investigated, monitoring their progress, and devising responses when needed.

The second defect of the piecemeal approach is to *disperse* concern for the future across many venues ('climate change here, nuclear proliferation there, asteroid detection over there'). Notably, under the status quo, the energies of advocates for the future are spread across many issue-specific bodies for different global issues, and this dilutes their effectiveness. This tends to weaken the impact of intergenerational concern on the overall system and undermine the prospects for a coordinated approach. One upshot is that the piecemeal approach tends to function so as to keep intergenerational concerns sharply constrained in their influence, much less visible (indeed, largely out of sight), and under the thumb of conventional institutions. For example, as noted above, the major meetings of the UNFCCC take place only once a year, and truly momentous ones only about once a decade or so. Thus, such institutions are far from central to normal political processes in the global system. Among other things, this is a significant threat to functional adequacy (GL3). By contrast, a notable virtue of the GCC approach is that it provides a venue for addressing intergenerational relations that concentrates intergenerational concern and befits its fundamental status.

In summary, again we see that although the guidelines on the remit of the GCC are, in one respect, baby steps from identifying the tyranny of the contemporary as a basic standing threat, they are radical in their implications with respect to the status quo. To make intergenerational concerns effective, institutions need to be central, deep and strong. The guidelines for comprehensiveness and standing authority facilitate that. The conventional, ad hoc, and issue-specific approach does not. Rather, it encourages the dilution of intergenerational concern by making it too reactive and dispersing it across multiple weak venues.

3.3 Composition

My third set of guidelines centre on the basic *internal character* of the GCC as a body. At this point, our analysis suggests guidelines that are perhaps initially more surprising. One involves how members of the GCC should understand their roles:

> (GL 6) *Generational representation*: within the global constitutional convention for future generations those expected to live during different time-periods, as members of different birth cohorts, should receive distinct representation.[15]

[15] As indicated in an earlier footnote, here I use the term 'representation' only in a loose, generic sense, rather than a technical sense, so as to cover multiple understandings of the more precise roles that those involved might play, their relationship to future generations, and so on. I hope to address the underlying issues further in future work.

Another relates to the *reach* of representation:

> (GL 7) *Indefinite time-horizon*: within the global constitutional convention for future generations, representatives should be provided for a suitably long time-horizon of at least centuries, and probably millennia. Special provision should also be made for longer-term representation for issues that merit it.

As with earlier guidelines, each of these emerges directly from the concern with the tyranny of the contemporary. Representatives are to be put in place to try to block many different kinds of intergenerational buck-passing, covering a range of salient generational units.[16]

The sixth guideline – generational representation – aims to encourage appropriate representation to occur. It *directly* confronts the complaint that conventional institutions fail in this regard. For instance, the average age of decision-makers in government (and elsewhere) is typically so high that it does not reflect the perspective of those most likely to be future victims of current choices. In the climate case, the political leadership (including presidents, prime ministers, and law-makers) in most countries is largely drawn from those over fifty, whereas many climate impacts will be disproportionately suffered by younger people and other future generations.[17] *Indirectly*, the generational representation guideline also partially addresses a predictable bias in how representatives are selected – towards those with more experience, community recognition, and so on – which tends to skew selection towards the older generations, and so embed and give extra status to their concerns.

Generational representation (GL6) is a substantial departure from the more common norms of representation. Typically, delegates are chosen to represent those residing in particular geographical areas, so the focus in on spatial dispersion. By contrast, generational representation explicitly divides delegates on temporal grounds, to reflect different generations. This directly follows from the intent to block intergenerational buck-passing. Notably, temporal representation is *primary* in the GCC. Although there may also be a case for some spatial representation at the GCC, when this occurs it is for secondary, often derivative reasons.

[16] See my account of the salience of 'generations' (Gardiner 2011a, chapter 5; cf. Gardiner 2004).

[17] One example comes from a recent study that examined lifetime exposure to extreme events under current climate policy pledges. It claims that 'changes in extreme event frequencies have relatively little effect on lifetime exposure for cohorts above age 55 in 2020, but this rapidly changes for younger cohorts as they experience increasing extreme events in the coming years and decades' and 'people younger than 10 years in 2020 will experience about a fourfold increase in extreme events if global warming is limited to 1.5°C, an increase that older cohorts will never experience, even if a scenario towards 3.5°C warming is followed .... Under a 3°C global warming pathway, children under 8 years will face an almost fivefold increase in extreme event exposure' (Thiery et al. 2021, 158–159).

The seventh – indefinite time-horizon – guideline also reflects the nature of the tyranny of the contemporary. Since the TYKE can operate over varying timescales, including the very long-term, to the extent possible the GCC must seek to cover *all* these timescales. This implies that its remit goes far into the future. In principle, this may be as far as the relevance of human agency, or perhaps of agency itself if humans end up being surpassed by other forms of agency. In practice, it is likely to be limited to some extent by the ability of humans to understand their influence. Still, the radical ambition to cover the indefinite future is a *guiding aspiration* of the GCC.

Notably, this aspiration reflects the centrality of the TYKE, which does not regard preventing intergenerational buck-passing as any less ethically important just because its victims are in the far future. To the extent possible, the plundering of the future is to be confronted at whatever scale. So, for instance, the GCC should be equally concerned with buck-passing that occurs between generational groups that are comparatively close by (e.g., separated by a few decades), or between those much further apart (e.g., separated by a thousand years); and between those of shorter duration (e.g., a thirty-year cohort) and those of longer duration (e.g., a 3,000-year cohort). Notice, for example, that from the point of view of the GCC, setting in motion a massive release of methane from the deep ocean that would likely destroy humanity (the "Big Burp Apocalypse") is among the central outcomes to be prevented, even if it would take a thousand years for the impacts to come about.

The eighth guideline concerns the *units* of representation:

> (GL8) *Regionalism*: within the global constitutional convention for future generations, representation should be designed to reflect large-scale ecological realities, especially those at a supranational level.

This guideline suggests that representation should be designed to reflect large-scale ecological realities. The aim is to prioritize units that are more appropriate – a better fit – for the distinctively global and intergenerational challenges the GCC is meant to address. This is likely to mean that the GCC should focus on levels beyond the traditional nation state.

To some extent, this guideline can be read as a concession to practicality, through making the GCC itself more functional, by positing a manageable number of delegates. Presumably, one ends up with less delegates if one focuses on the supranational level than on smaller units. This concern for practicality also arises when designing other institutions. For instance, national institutions do not typically seek distinct representatives for each household or street, but for larger units. Similarly, at the global level, one wants a group of manageable size for deliberation, while still maintaining sufficient numbers and diversity of composition to carry authority.

Still, the primary reasons for adopting regionalism are deeper. To some extent the guideline emerges from a negative thesis, and a positive proposal that reacts to that thesis. The *negative thesis* is that, ideally, delegates to the convention ought *not* to be representatives of nation states. Instead, as far as possible, the units of representation should be designed so as to cross national borders and encourage regional perspectives. A number of reasons stand behind the negative thesis. Let me mention two that suggest their general flavour.

The first is that the GCC should not simply replicate at a higher level the concerns made manifest in existing institutions, partly because these concerns are already represented in other ways by those institutions, partly because those institutions are (and have shown themselves to be) inadequate to address the TYKE, and partly because they also tend to inhibit and crowd out intergenerational concern.

The second, even more important, reason is that existing institutions (such as the nation state and economic markets) do not, in any case, tend to track facts that are likely to be deeply relevant over the relevant timeframe of problems like climate change, namely centuries and millennia. In particular, over long periods of time, the importance of current national arrangements and their geographical boundaries is likely to fade dramatically given global development, migration, and other factors. Let us call this, the fading hypothesis.

To see the appeal of the fading hypothesis, we have only to look to the past. Take my own case. I am a citizen of three countries. A few hundred years ago, two of them, the United States and New Zealand, did not even exist. Going back a little more than a thousand years, neither did England, let alone the United Kingdom. As a result, someone aiming to build intergenerational institutions over such long periods would likely have been deeply misled by a purely nationalist approach indexed to a particular time.

Consider a simple illustration. If some of my likely ancestors had begun building very long-term intergenerational versions of their own institutions in 850–900 AD, they may have been aiming to establish effective intergenerational institutions for Wincester or Yorvik or Elmet, for Wessex or Mercia or Northumbria, for the Angles or the Vikings or the Ancient Britons, or (who knows) for Rome or Tuscany or Constantinople. Moreover, if any of these groups had convened an assembly to address such matters, they would likely have regarded their aims as seriously at odds with those of the other groups, and so the choice of, say, an Intergenerational Witan for Wessex, rather than similar institutions for Mercia or Northumbria or elsewhere, as fundamental.

Yet, as it has turned out, they would have been mistaken. The world a thousand years hence makes the tribal infighting of a thousand years ago largely irrelevant to the central interests of the current generation. It is a world where few (if any) really care whether one is of the Angles, the Saxons, the Danes, the Picts, and so on. Partly, this is because for most people of broadly English ancestry there is probably no fact of the matter – one is all these, and more besides. Partly, it is because even for the few for whom there may be a fact of the matter, this is unknowable. Mostly, it is because the import of any fact of the matter is likely to be dwarfed by other, more central concerns, including because these origins play an increasingly minor, arguably negligible, role even in national identity itself.

All of this suggests that genuine intergenerational concern, even over as limited a period of human history as a thousand years or so, requires a much broader frame of reference than is provided by current institutions, including that fairly recent phenomenon, the nation state. The need for a broader frame was there, even in the past. With increased mobility, it is likely to be more so, perhaps dramatically more so, in the future. Just as (say) 1200 years ago it would have been unwise to project Wessex and its rivalry with the Danes into 2020, so we should be careful about wanting to project particular political units of today too far, including by imposing them on the GCC. Perhaps in 3400 CE, any remaining rivalries between the USA, China, Russia, and Europe will look as quaint as those of Wessex and Danelaw do now.

In light of such concerns, my *positive proposal* is that delegates should be selected as representatives of larger units which (ideally) are rooted in ecological facts with likely long-term salience. Often, these would probably *cross* national boundaries and do so in ways that do not simply duplicate current (generational) geopolitical realities or even narrow identities (regional, national). For instance, one might assign representatives for ecologically similar regions (such as the Arctic or large bioregions), or perhaps (to generate a smaller and more manageable total number of delegates) from continents or ecozones. Over time, of course, one might expect these zones to expand as humanity sets out across the solar system and beyond. Hence, the GCC should also give some consideration to how to cope with human expansion beyond the Earth itself.

All of that being said, in concluding I want to emphasize that temporal representation is primary in the GCC and spatial representation secondary. The core aim is to protect against intergenerational tyranny, and the composition of the GCC should be guided by this aim. To the extent that proposals for representation threaten that, they should be revised or rejected. For example, it is possible that both regionalism and generational representation might evolve so as to encourage some forms of intergenerational tyranny or more conventional injustices. Naturally, the GCC should take such concerns seriously and either incorporate safeguards or find better guidelines.

3.4 Domains

My final set of guidelines concerns the appropriate domains to be considered by the global constitutional convention for future generations. The ninth guideline highlights the role of ethical norms:

> (GL9) *Ethical norms*: the global constitutional convention for future generations should consider: (a) how best to identify, protect, and promote intergenerational ethical norms and principles in its recommendations, both within the institutions it proposes and in their relations with other institutions; and (b) how to integrate respect for other ethical norms and principles insofar as they are relevant to its remit (e.g., norms of global justice and community).

This guideline emphasizes that the role of intergenerational institutions is ethical. One reason is that a core function of the GCC is to confront the threat posed by the tyranny of the contemporary, which is essentially one of violating central ethical norms. Another, more general reason is that the whole enterprise of protecting the future and promoting intergenerational concerns is infused with ethics. A specific guideline helps to remind the GCC that these are basic parameters of its task.

Developing the GCC in light of the ninth guideline will raise many questions, especially in respect of relations with other legitimate institutions. This is not the place to pursue that conversation. Instead, I will simply note two early complications.

The first complication is the risk of creating imbalance in the global system. Here, there are concerns on both sides. Consider one example. On the one hand, there is the worry that, once the ninth set of guidelines is introduced, the GCC will seek to take too much control from or of other institutions. This may create new risks, such as those associated with a large concentration of global power, or a new dominance of intergenerational concerns over those of current generations. On the other hand, there is the fear that opening the door even slightly to issues of current injustice will lead to the GCC becoming overwhelmed by those concerns, at the expense of addressing intergenerational ethics. This may both doom the project and impose further risks. So, for instance, it would be all too easy for a GCC to become dominated by concerns about current injustices in such a way that it ultimately evolved into a (perhaps unwitting) accomplice in facilitating unholy alliances against the future.

The second complication flows naturally from the first. Inevitably, there will be a need for a division of labour. The GCC is not the only institution whose remit raises issues of (say) justice and community. Yet exactly what the division of labour between institutions should look like is difficult to ascertain in advance. One reason for this difficulty is that many central issues of (say) global injustice are quite centrally implicated in intergenerational affairs. So, for example, when it comes to climate change, there are strong intersections with challenges such as severe poverty, persistent violations of human rights, and extreme inequalities in wealth and power. Moreover, these factors are themselves often subject to the ongoing influence of wider background injustices, such as colonialism, feudalism, sexism, and institutional racism.

Another reason for the difficulty is that existing institutions appear seriously flawed when it comes to addressing the concerns that might be said to fall more appropriately under their remit. Thus, the global constitutional convention for future generations risks wading into the much broader task of reforming other national and international institutions. Indeed, one might wonder whether it has any hope of addressing its central tasks if it does not.

This thought leads to a more general worry. At the extreme, perhaps existing institutions are so flawed that what is truly needed is fundamental reform of the entire global system as such, at all levels. Then, we might see arguments for an all-encompassing, *universal constitutional convention* ('UCC'), rather than a global constitutional convention focused on future generations. Moreover, it is possible that the GCC itself might ultimately recommend such a strategy if the obstacles to intergenerational reform appear too deep rooted and insurmountable.

The general worry deserves discussion, but I will not pursue it here. Instead, I simply make two points. First, note that proposing a universal constitutional convention goes far beyond the GCC's initial intended purpose and raises broader questions of institutional design. Notably, not only would reforming the entire system at all levels be a much taller order than neutralizing the tyranny of the contemporary, it would likely invite different parameters, constraints, and guidelines. Second, we should be wary of dismissing the GCC itself too quickly. Again, the risk of moral corruption looms large.

My tenth guideline for the GCC addresses the *place* of humanity in its broader ecological and cosmological context:

> (GL10) *The place of humanity*: the global constitutional convention for future generations should make recommendations on how best to direct and contain human activities and influence (including those of intergenerational institutions) in light of wider concerns (a) for the nonhuman world and (b) about how best to understand humanity and its wider role in the universe.

A central motivation for the tenth guideline is that intergenerational institutions should not crowd out either concern for the nonhuman, nor consideration of humanity's wider role in the universe.

Let us begin with (a), the nonhuman world. Under 'the nonhuman', I mean to cover the obvious cases of nonhuman animals, and the more contentious cases of plants, species and ecosystems, together with our relations to particular places and entities (such as rivers, mountains, etc.) that are explicitly valued by some communities and traditions.[18] Naturally, there will be some controversy about whether, why, how, and to what extent each should be included. Nevertheless, it may also be possible to achieve substantial political consensus on more concrete proposals for conservation, protection, and care for the nonhuman, given how deeply it is intertwined with human life. In any case, these are matters to be discussed within the convention.

One question is whether the GCC should make recommendations about how concerns for nonhuman nature are to be accommodated through new institutions. One approach would be to seek direct representation, perhaps in the form of delegates charged with representing those concerns. So, we might consider delegates for particular populations, species, ecosystems, places, and so on.[19] Another approach would be to explore how the remits of human institutions should be *restricted* so as to accommodate appropriate domains for nonhuman nature (e.g., the Half-Earth proposal, cf. Wilson 2016). Such efforts are especially important given the ecological storm and the threat of a tyranny of humanity.

The issue of the nonhuman is a complex and fundamental one, so the development of guidelines here is especially important. Nevertheless, in the spirit of preserving some initial level of modesty in the guidelines, my proposed guideline takes no particular position other than that the questions should be considered. One reason for this modesty is that, strictly speaking, these challenges are not the exclusive domain of the GCC for future generations, since (i) they are not central to its mandate, and (ii) other institutions – such as national or local institutions – also have a legitimate role to play. Nevertheless, the ecological storm and the tyranny of humanity are particularly salient to the GCC given its role of considering the long-term trajectory of humanity. So, one might expect successful intergenerational institutions to play a leading role in humanity's response to these matters, even if other institutions should also play a part. Indeed, there is some reason to think that perhaps the GCC should consider whether and how the new, intergenerational institutions it proposes ought to take on a coordinating function in managing the response of all institutions to the human relationship to nature.

Let us turn now to (b), how best to understand humanity and its wider role in the universe. Many interpretations of the above guidelines will draw, explicitly or implicitly, on an understanding of the place of humanity, not just in relation to the nonhuman, but also through some conception of humanity itself,

[18] See, for example, Watene 2016, Watene in press, and Whyte in press.
[19] For example, Donaldson and Kymlicka 2011.

including its wider role in the universe. Notably, much of the appeal of the GCC is based on the idea that there is such a thing as 'humanity', that it is a normatively relevant category, and that concern for humanity is a fundamental feature of our political lives and responsibilities. Therefore, the GCC will probably need to take some view on what the appropriate form and limits of this idea are at a constitutional level, since this background will shape the general institutions and specific structures that emerge.

Here, as with many questions of foundational political relations, there is a delicate balance to be drawn between, on the one hand, being explicit about the fundamental groundings of association and, on the other hand, avoiding overreaching in a way that prejudices the overall endeavour too far in the direction of specific and contentious positions. For instance, a concern for the survival of humanity, at least in the short-to medium-term, seems appropriate. The claim that the role of the GCC is to bring about God's kingdom on Earth, whether Heaven, Valhalla, Nirvana, or something else, is clearly not acceptable as a starting point. In future work, I will offer some proposals of how to think about developing actual GCCs in response to this guideline. For now, and again in the spirit of preserving some modesty in the guidelines themselves – and the methodology of baby steps – I have merely stated the guideline in minimal terms.

4 Conclusion

Humanity is currently in the grip of a deep institutional denial concerning the adequacy of its institutions for dealing with serious intergenerational challenges such as global climate change. In response, I have called for a GCC focused on developing new institutions to protect future generations and further their interests. In this chapter, I present some initial guidelines concerning how to construct such a GCC. Although each follows as a fairly modest and natural inference (a 'baby step') from the purposes of the convention itself, the implications stand in sharp contrast to the status quo and to most conventional discussions of reform. The GCC is, thus, both modest and radical. Perhaps that makes it just the kind of realistic utopia we need.

Bibliography

Anderson, Kevin. 2012. "Going beyond Dangerous." *Development Dialogue* 61: 16–40.

Anderson, Kevin and Glen Peters. 2016. "The Trouble with Negative Emissions." *Science* 354, no. 6309: 182–183.

Bostrom, Nick and Milan M. Ćirković, eds. 2008. *Global Catastrophic Risks*. New York, NY: Oxford University Press.

Climate Action Tracker. 2022. November update. https://climateactiontracker.org/

Dimitrov, Radoslav, Jon Hovi, Detlef F. Sprinz, Håkon Sælen, and Arild Underdal. 2019. "Institutional and Environmental Effectiveness: Will the Paris Agreement Work?" *WIREs Climate Change* 10: e583.

Donaldson, Sue. and Will Kymlicka. 2011. *Zoopolis: A Political Theory of Animal Rights*. New York, NY: Oxford University Press.

Forster, Piers M., Amanda C. Maycock, Christine M. McKenna and Christopher J. Smith. 2020. "Latest Climate Models Confirm Need for Urgent Mitigation." *Nature Climate Change* 10: 2–10.

Gardiner, Stephen M. 2004. "The Global Warming Tragedy and the Dangerous Illusion of the Kyoto Protocol." *Ethics & International Affairs* 18, no. 1: 23–39.

2011a. *A Perfect Moral Storm: The Ethical Challenge of Climate Change*. New York, NY: Oxford University Press.

2011b. "Some Early Ethics of Geoengineering." *Environmental Values* 20: 163–188.

2013. "The Desperation Argument for Geoengineering." *Political Science & Politics* 46, no. 1: 28–33.

2014. "A Call for a Global Constitutional Convention Focused on Future Generations." *Ethics & International Affairs* 28, no. 3: 299–315.

2019. "Motivating (or Baby-Stepping Toward) A Global Constitutional Convention for Future Generations." *Environmental Ethics* 41: 199–220.

2022a. "Is the Paris Climate Agreement Another Dangerous Illusion?" In *Norwegian Academy of Science and Letters Yearbook 2021*, 157–174. Oslo: Novus.

2022b. "On the Scope of Institutions for Future Generations." *Ethics and International Affairs* 36, no. 2: 157–178.

2022c. "Environmentalizing Bioethics: Planetary Health in a Perfect Moral Storm." *Perspectives in Biology and Medicine* 65, no. 4: 569–585.

2023a. "The Ethics of Climate Targets: Extinction Rebellion vs. the Climate Establishment." In *The Routledge Handbook on Applied Climate Ethics*, ed. by Donald Brown and Katy Gwiazdon, 38–51. London: Routledge.

2023b. "Climate Targets and Moral Corruption." *American Philosophical Association Public Philosophy Blog*.

Gardiner, Stephen M. and David A. Weisbach. 2016. *Debating Climate Ethics*. New York, NY: Oxford University Press.

Gosseries, Axel. 2023. *What Is Intergenerational Justice?* London: Polity Press.

Ord, Toby. 2021. *The Precipice. Existential Risk and the Future of Humanity*. New York, NY: Hachette Books.

Robinson, Mary. 2008. "Foreword." In *Climate Change and Human Rights: A Rough Guide*. Versoix: International Council on Human Rights, pp. iii–iv.

Shepherd, John et al. 2009. *Geoengineering the Climate: Science, Governance and Uncertainty*. London: Royal Society.

Spash, Clive. 2016. "This Changes Nothing: The Paris Agreement to Ignore Reality." *Globalizations* 13, no. 6: 928–933.

Thiery, Wim, Stefan Lange, Joeri Rogelj, et al. 2021. "Intergenerational Inequities in Exposure to Climate Extremes." *Science* 374, no. 6564: 158–160.

United Nations. 2015. "Historic Paris Agreement on Climate Change: 195 Nations Set Path to Keep Temperature Rise Well Below 2 Degrees Celsius." *UN News*. https://unfccc.int/news/finale-cop21.

United Nations Environment Program (UNEP). 2019. *Emissions Gap Report 2019*. www.unep.org/resources/emissions-gap-report-2019.

United Nations Secretary-General. 2013. *Intergenerational Solidarity and the Needs of Future Generations*. United Nations. https://digitallibrary.un.org/record/756820#record-files-collapse-header

Von Bulow, Michael. 2009. "Failure in Copenhagen is Not an Option." *COP Website*. http://en.cop15.dk/news/view+news?newsid=2257 [no longer available].

Watene, Krushil. 2016. "Valuing Nature: Māori Philosophy and the Capability Approach." *Oxford Development Studies* 44, no. 3: 287–296.

In press. "Kaitiakitanga: Toward an Intergenerational Philosophy." In *Oxford Handbook of Intergenerational Ethics*, ed. by Stephen M. Gardiner. New York, NY: Oxford University Press.

Whyte, Kyle Powys. In press. "Ancestry and Crisis: Intergenerational Ethics and Ecocentrism." In *Oxford Handbook of Intergenerational Ethics*, ed. by Stephen M. Gardiner. New York, NY: Oxford University Press.

Xu, Yangyang and Veerabhadran Ramanathen. 2017. "Well Below 2°C: Mitigation Strategies for Avoiding Dangerous to Catastrophic Climate Changes." *Proceedings of the National Academy of Sciences: Earth, Atmospheric and Planetary Sciences* 114, no. 39: 10315–10323.

11

Philosophy for an Ending World

Tim Mulgan

1 A Bleak Thought Experiment

I begin with a bleak thought experiment.[1]

The ending world: Scientists are agreed on the following grim facts. A cataclysmic event for a distant corner of the galaxy, caused by hitherto unknown physical processes, has produced cosmic rays that are spreading throughout the galaxy. These rays will pass through our solar system two hundred years from now. Fortunately, cosmic rays travel slower than the speed of light, so we can observe their impact on other star systems. Unfortunately, that impact is very negative. Cosmic rays destroy everything in their path. When cosmic rays hit, in two centuries' time, life on earth will be extinguished. There is no way to avoid this, nor can we hope to outrun the cosmic rays. (Although they travel slower than light, they travel much faster than any feasible mode of human interstellar travel.)

Humanity, thus, faces an extinction that is unavoidable and imminent, but not immediate.

I explore the philosophy of this slowly ending world at length in my recent monograph *Philosophy for an Ending World* (Mulgan 2024). In this paper, my principal goal is to motivate interest in my new thought experiment, before briefly sketching some of the lessons I hope to draw from it. I argue that my slowly ending world is both a provocative thought experiment and a challenging possible future. To get the most out of this thought experiment, we should explore it from within – adopting the perspective of philosophers living in the ending world. We should then take a step back and ask what

[1] This paper is based on a presentation to a conference of Future Generations held at Concordia University in October 2021. I am grateful to the conference organisers (Hiroshi Abe, Matthias Fritsch, and Mario Wenning) for their invitation to participate, and to conference participants for helpful comments.

we owe to future people who might inhabit such a world, and how we might justify ourselves to them. One central question is whether we could equip our descendants to flourish in an ending world, even if we cannot imagine flourishing there ourselves.

2 Why Think about Imminent, Unavoidable, Non-immediate Human Extinction?

In my ending world scenario, humanity faces an extinction that is unavoidable and imminent, but not immediate. This raises three immediate questions.

1. Why human extinction?
2. Why imminent-but-not-immediate extinction? (Why the two-hundred-year delay?)
3. Why unavoidable extinction?

In this section, I defend each of these three distinctive features of my *slowly* ending world. After briefly explaining the significance of human extinction per se, I turn to the significance of imminent extinction. I argue that focusing on imminent-but-not-immediate extinction clarifies our intuitions about human extinction (Section 2.1); expands our thinking about possible human futures (Section 2.2); and focuses our attention on what we owe to future people who might face either imminent or immediate extinction (Section 2.3). Finally, in Section 2.4, I demonstrate the value of thinking about *unavoidable* extinction.

2.1 Clarifying our Intuitions

Our philosophical thinking is often influenced by contingent claims that we take for granted, but which could, in principle, turn out to be false. Good thought experiments highlight the role of implicit empirical assumptions, and prise apart things that typically go together. Consider two examples: Robert Nozick's famous experience machine thought experiment asks whether pleasure is sufficient for well-being when it is completely isolated from its usual effects (Nozick 1974, 42–45) and Derek Parfit's non-identity scenarios ask whether person-affecting harm is necessary for wrongdoing when significant losses of impersonal value harm no identifiable individual (Parfit 1984, 351–379). Similarly, in our everyday lives, we take it for granted that humanity faces an indefinite future. What difference would it make if we suddenly discovered that it did not? What might we learn about our own present values by imagining away the human future?

Two existing philosophical literatures already engage with human extinction. On one side, a growing interdisciplinary discussion asks how we should think about risks of human extinction – and especially how much we should be prepared to sacrifice to reduce those risks.[2] This literature on 'existential risks' explicitly addresses possible futures, not just imaginary thought experiments. Indeed, it has a clear real-world agenda – arguing that a greater share of present resources (time, intellectual attention, research funding, political capital, philanthropic spending) should be devoted to thinking about how to prevent human extinction.

A second philosophical literature asks *why* human extinction would be bad. In two recent books, Samuel Scheffler (2013, 2018) explores a doomsday scenario where the world will be destroyed thirty days after my death, and an infertility scenario where everyone on earth becomes infertile and the present generation know they will be the last.[3] Scheffler conjectures 'that most of us would find the prospect of humanity's imminent extinction unbearably depressing' (Scheffler 2018, 42). He argues that this 'afterlife conjecture' reveals the importance, for our everyday projects and lives, of the assumption 'that others will continue to live after I have died' (Scheffler 2013, 15).

Avoidable and immediate extinction are already on the philosophical agenda. I depart from the existential risk literature by making extinction unavoidable; and I depart from Scheffler by moving extinction from the immediate future into the near future. I return to avoidability in Section 2.4. I first address my departure from Scheffler. Why add my thought experiment to Scheffler's? Why talk about a *slowly* ending world? What does the extra two hundred years *add*?

My first reply is that the shift to a *slowly* ending world helps to clarify our intuitive reactions to human extinction. Immediate extinction is bad in too many, too obvious ways. Scheffler highlights the significance of the implicit assumption that there will be *some* future generations: some future people whose culture, traditions, values, and projects are connected to, and descended from, our own. It is not hard to see why the denial of this assumption – the removal of any cultural descendants – might be very de-stabilising. In my *slowly* ending world, by contrast, the disruption to present projects is much less obvious. Two hundred years is quite a long time. How many of our present activities will leave any discernible trace in two centuries' time? We

[2] On the importance of existential risks, see, for example, Bostrom 2013; Bostrom and Cirkovic 2008; Ord 2020. For a more sceptical view, see Schuster and Woods 2021.

[3] *Death and the Afterlife* by Samuel Scheffler (2013) also includes commentaries from Susan Wolf, Harry Frankfurt, Seana Shiffrin, and Niko Kolodny.

don't think about distant future people in our daily lives. So why should their absence matter to us?

The slowly ending world, thus, offers a more compelling test case for Scheffler's claims about the importance of future generations, precisely because self-interested prudential reasons are *less* prominent. We *could* simply ignore the prospect of human extinction in two centuries. (Arguably, most present people *do* ignore this possibility!) And yet it seems – at least to me, and to many other people with whom I have discussed this thought experiment – that the removal of the more distant human future would be very destabilising in its own right. If so, how can we explain this?

2.2 A Credible and Worrying Possible Future

A well as being a provocative thought experiment, my slowly ending world is also a credible human future. Scheffler's primary philosophical interest is the role that future generations play in our present actual evaluative lives. His doomsday and infertility scenarios highlight the importance *to us* of future generations. For Scheffler, the plausibility or likelihood of his scenarios is largely irrelevant. Conceivability is sufficient for his purposes. Scheffler does not claim that any future generation is likely to encounter such scenarios. So it is no objection to Scheffler's project that his doomsday scenario – in particular – is quite implausible. (How could I possibly know that, whenever I die, the world will end thirty days after my death?)

By contrast, adding the two-century timeframe gap before inevitable human extinction renders my scenario a more plausible possible future. My slowly ending world is a place where future people might actually live. Something like this might happen. Humanity might well face a genuine extinction threat at some point in the next two hundred years. Our descendants might face real threats of imminent-but-not-immediate extinction.

Thinking about the slowly ending world thus contributes to a broader project that imagines how people might live in a variety of possible futures, and then asks (1) how we should equip those people to best inhabit those futures, and (2) how we could answer to them if we do not.[4]

Why should we think about possible futures? In particular, why should we care what future people might think? Even if you agree that the ending world is a possible future, and even if you accept all my speculations about the ethical and/or philosophical beliefs of its inhabitants, why should you care? What

[4] I explore possible futures in Mulgan 2011, 2014, 2015, 2017, 2018a, 2018b, 2019, and 2020a.

impact should future people's beliefs have on our current ethical or philosophical thinking?

We can explore these questions by drawing comparisons with other interesting possible futures, such as futures broken by climate change (or other catastrophes) where our affluent way of life is no longer available; post-scarcity futures where resource constraints are removed; and virtual or digital futures where people escape a harsh or unpalatable 'real world' by escaping into experience machines or uploading themselves into computers (Mulgan 2014, 2017, 2019).

In my book *Ethics for a Broken World* and elsewhere, I have previously explored the outlook of philosophers inhabiting a future broken by climate change, where a chaotic climate makes life precarious, each generation is worse-off than the last, it is no longer possible to meet everyone's basic needs, and our affluent way of life is no longer an option (Mulgan 2011).

This broken future is credible. No-one can reasonably be confident it won't happen. It involves no outlandish claims, scientific impossibilities, or implausible expectations about human behaviour. Climate change – or some other disaster – might produce a broken future. We do not know exactly what harms climate change will cause. But we do know it may very well cause significant and lasting harm. And climate change is not the only route to a broken world. (Other routes include technological catastrophe, financial collapse, or a global pandemic.)

The credibility of the broken future undermines three common, complacent presumptions of contemporary future ethics: optimism, similarity, and convergence.[5] In a broken future, people are (by definition) worse-off than ourselves; their moral challenges differ from our own; and both the likelihood and the severity of the broken future may depend on *present* choices. In particular, we might be able to mitigate *future* brokenness by making significant *present* sacrifices. Present and future interests, thus, conflict – and one key task for future ethics is to balance these competing interests.

One reason why my (slowly) *ending* future is worth exploring is that it has much in common with this broken future. Scheffler argues that the loss of an indefinite human future itself makes future people worse-off, destabilising their evaluative lives. And if people did lose faith in existing values, this would also disrupt social and economic arrangements, leading to further reductions in well-being and security. In an ending world, as in a broken world, we need new sources of moral motivation. What could motivate people to do the right thing in the face of imminent extinction?

[5] Cf. Mulgan 2020a.

People living in an ending future, thus, face new challenges of inter-generational conflict – and declining well-being and meaningfulness – as humanity nears its end. Furthermore, the ability of the *last* human generation (in particular) to truly flourish without any successors of their own will depend, in large part, on the social, ethical, philosophical, and imaginary resources that we bequeath to them.

The ending world, therefore, has much in common with a broken future. On the other hand, the ending world might instead be a post-scarcity paradise.[6] Freed from the need to worry about the more distant future, the last human generation might enjoy morally unproblematic affluence. Presumably it *is* acceptable to squander resources as if there were no tomorrow when there *is* no tomorrow! If we devote our energies to making their lives as good as possible, then future people may be better-off than us.

The ending world, thus, resembles two opposing possible futures: it might be very good or very bad. This scenario is particularly ethically interesting because it could go either way – and because whether it is a good future or a bad one depends largely on how its inhabitants regard it. In other broken futures, it is an objective fact that resources are scarce relative to basic human needs. By contrast, the badness (or goodness) of the ending world is primarily subjective. It will be very bad if people think it is meaningless – but if people think it is meaningful, then it could be very good.

2.3 Obligations to Future People

In Scheffler's two scenarios, by definition, there are no future people. People mourn the loss of the human future, but they do not otherwise think about inter-generational ethics. By contrast, if we imagine life at the start of the ending world, when humanity still has two hundred years to run, then we imagine a world where present people still have obligations to future people – namely, people who will live closer to humanity's end and, especially, those living in the last human generation.

One urgent question for anyone living at the start of my slowly ending world is whether there will be future people. These people must (collectively) decide whether human extinction will be imminent or immediate. They must decide whether or not there will (or should) *be* future generations. Could we permissibly create new people if we knew they would inherit an ending world, and that their prospects for a human future would be even more constrained than our own? Can early generations in an ending world ensure that life is

[6] I explore the ethics of post-scarcity paradises in Mulgan 2017.

meaningful for their own descendants and, especially, for the last human generation who must handle immediate human extinction? Could they hope to build a just society, or to rectify historical or environmental injustice, in two hundred years?

These questions are most interesting, and most challenging, if we agree with Scheffler that, for us, meaning, well-being, and making sense of our projects and traditions all require future generations who will continue those projects and traditions. One vital question within the ending world is, then, whether our dependence on future generations is an essential feature of the human condition or merely a contingent feature of the way we have been raised or acculturated.

Unlike Scheffler's doomsday and infertility scenarios, the slowly ending world, thus, opens the door to a position I call multi-generationalism – which insists that the best way to find meaning in the ending world is to embark on projects spanning several generations that only come to fruition long after the present generation are gone. I return to multi-generationalism in Section 5, and to procreative ethics more broadly in Section 4.

Imagining possible futures inevitably leads to reflection on our obligations to future people. Reflecting on possible futures in the abstract highlights the urgency of future ethics. Imagining the reactions of future people adds something more. Asking how future people, and especially future philosophers, might evaluate our moral legacy to them gives our future ethics a second-personal dimension.[7] The idea of justifying ourselves to future people is common in everyday language. (We often pause to ask what our descendants will think of us.) Future-directed second-personalism gives our obligations to distant future people the same felt moral urgency as our obligations to our contemporaries, enabling future interests to compete with present interests when the two conflict. Without future-directed second-personalism, the abstractly described future is too easily trumped by the directly encountered present. One sign that we have balanced competing intra- and inter-generational obligations fairly is that we are confident that we could justify ourselves equally well to both present and future people.

Any plausible future ethic includes obligations regarding future people's well-being, flourishing, and quality of life. Other things being equal, we should strive to leave future people as well-off as possible. And perhaps we are obliged to leave them reasonably well-off and/or no worse-off than ourselves. We should also strive to enable future people to live meaningful and morally decent lives. If our descendants must choose between individual flourishing

[7] Cf. Darwall 2009; Mulgan 2018a.

and inter-generational injustice, then we have failed them – even if they end up 'flourishing' (in some non-moral sense) in immoral ways. In my slowly ending world, the relevant question here is: can people living at the start of the ending world ensure that their descendants at humanity's end enjoy morally worthwhile, meaningful lives?

We naturally judge any new possible future against our own present values, priorities, and accounts of well-being. We ask whether we would like to live there ourselves. But what if future people themselves would reasonably have different values, or even a different ethical outlook altogether? We cannot simply assume that what is good, important, or meaningful for us would work equally well for future people. More specifically, we cannot determine what is valuable for future people without knowing what they will value. Some theories of well-being, of course, identify what is good for anyone with whatever they value (or desire, or would desire under ideal conditions, or…). But our reason to imagine future ethical outlooks is not contingent on such extreme subjectivism. Not even the most thoroughgoing objectivist will deny that, as a matter of fact, whether or not someone flourishes is partly dependent on whether they value what they get.

Our legacy to future people includes not only the physical infrastructure, cultural capital, and environmental conditions we leave behind, but also the moral outlook(s) we teach directly to our immediate descendants and, thereby, indirectly bequeath to later generations. This is arguably our most important legacy to the future. Our present choices influence not only the future that people will inhabit, but how they will regard and evaluate that future. We must develop and bequeath a moral outlook that will enable future people to flourish. We must, therefore, ask how competing moral outlooks would actually work for them.

Our ultimate goal is to bequeath a temporally robust moral philosophy: one that provides the inhabitants of a broad range of credible futures with the conceptual resources they need to recognise, confront, and hopefully avoid the particular threats that are most salient to them. At the very least, we must not bequeath an ethic that leaves future people unable to recognise the most worrying threats, prevents them from addressing them, or leads them into avoidable despair.

I have argued elsewhere that broken futures are particularly disturbing because our current moral outlook is not fit for purpose there (Mulgan 2011, 2015). If we allow future people to inherit a broken future, and then bequeath our own unrealistic and unattainable affluent morality, then we will have done them a double disservice. My (slowly) *ending* future is disturbing in exactly the same way. Indeed, as I argued in Section 2.2, the ending world is even more disturbing – because its value (or disvalue) depends so much on what its inhabitants themselves value. Insofar as our current moral outlook attaches significance to the indefinite human future – making present meaning contingent on our connection to future generations – then bequeathing that outlook is simply a recipe for despair and disappointment in an ending world. Can we do better? Are there moral outlooks that would enable future people to flourish in an ending world?

Reflecting on possible futures has a broader impact on contemporary ethics, beyond our obligations to future people. Whenever we encounter another group whose ethical outlook differs from our own, we naturally ask what, if anything, *we* should borrow from that alternative outlook. Imagining the future of ethics promises a similar source of ethical enrichment.

Imaginary thought experiments highlight the *conceptual* contingency of our current ethical beliefs. Imagining possible *futures* highlights their *historical* contingency. Reimagining contemporary philosophy from the point of view of future philosophers promises the same benefits of distance and perspective that we gain from studying past philosophers in their historical and social context. In both cases, we learn to see our own ethical worldview from the outside. The fact that actual past people did, or actual future people might, see the world very differently may make us less confident that we have got things right.

The connection between historical contingency and conceptual contingency raises another intriguing possibility – one that I hope to explore further elsewhere. The ending world may be closer, in some respects, to earlier, less affluent, less settled, less predictable times, than to our affluent present. Perhaps the post-Christian philosophy of the secular liberal affluent West is singularly unsuited to an ending world – or to any other situation where things are getting worse rather than better. To make sense of imminent extinction, we might turn instead to non-Western philosophy – or to earlier figures in the Western tradition whose more stoical or realistic philosophy might be better able to take imminent extinction in its stride.

The ending world is especially destabilising for those philosophers who seek to combine a naturalist atheist metaphysical worldview with ambitious, optimistic ethical views, such as non-subjective accounts of well-being; the rejection of egoism, nihilism, or pessimism; and a commitment to liberal values and moderately demanding non-utilitarian ethics. It is no coincidence that Scheffler – whose philosophical worldview is optimistic secular liberalism – finds his own (more extreme) extinction scenarios so troubling. On the other hand, while stoics, hedonists, egoists, nihilists, utilitarians, and theists all need to adapt to the ending world, they need not be paralysed by it.

2.4 Why Make Human Extinction Inevitable?

I have argued that my slowly ending world is both an interesting thought experiment and a credible possible future. My stipulation that human extinction is *unavoidable* may seem to undermine both these claims – as it eliminates some of the most interesting ethical challenges surrounding human extinction (namely, those relating to the costs we should be prepared to pay to avoid extinction); and it is clearly unrealistic. In this section, I defend my stipulation of unavoidable extinction against both these objections. I argue that many interesting ethical issues remain, and that the stipulation is not implausible.

I begin by conceding that *avoidable* human extinction is also worth considering. Indeed, when I began thinking about human extinction, I did address the costs of *avoiding* extinction. I used a different thought experiment where we *can* escape imminent human extinction, but only at a very high present cost. In this Starship Choice scenario, when cosmic rays render the Earth uninhabitable, humanity can escape imminent extinction by sending a small group of pioneers on a long journey (lasting several generations) to a distant exo-planet where the human story might continue. We can *either* accept imminent extinction *or* escape to the stars (Mulgan 2020b).[8]

I used this disjunctive thought experiment to explore the contrast between contractualism and consequentialism. Launching generation starships is bad for most people who are currently alive; but it (hopefully) enables many more people to live in the further future. Indeed, we can construct imaginary cases where not launching starships would be better for everyone who ever lives, even though launching them would produce much greater total future welfare. Contractualists then *cannot* launch starships – no matter how great the potential payoff; while consequentialists *must* launch – no matter how low the probability of success or how great the present cost.[9] In my earlier work on human extinction, I then asked whether contractualists and consequentialists can moderate their positions and meet somewhere in the middle.

I still think this starship choice scenario is worth thinking about; and I hope to return to it in future work. However, I no longer believe this is the best place to begin our philosophical examination of human extinction. To understand the values at stake in extinction versus escape choices, we need to first think through the stay-at-home alternative. If humanity really did have only two centuries left, what might those centuries be like?

[8] The inspiration is the 'Generation Starship' genre of speculative fiction; for a history of this genre, see Caroti, *The Generation Starship in Science Fiction* (Caroti 2011).

[9] The starship futures case, thus, challenges Parfit's argument that (the best form of) rule-consequentialism delivers the same set of moral principles as (the best forms of) both Scanlonian and Kantian contractualism (Parfit 2011/17, 244–253).

Even a very small chance of escaping extinction is distracting. In the existential risk literature, total utilitarians argue that, given the potentially astronomical amount of future well-being at stake, even the smallest reduction in the probability of imminent human extinction justifies any (finite) present cost;[10] while the heroes of most fictional tales of human extinction, almost by definition, are those obtuse people who simply refuse to accept that extinction is unavoidable and then (absurdly) succeed in preventing it.[11] Human extinction presents itself as something we must avoid – and therefore the mere possibility of escape (however remote) is overwhelming.

This brings us to a deeper issue, which my stipulation of unavoidable extinction forces us to address head-on. The existing philosophical literature largely takes it for granted that human extinction is bad.[12] The existential threat literature is dominated by optimistic total utilitarians who assume that future human lives will (on balance) be worth living; while Scheffler's starting point is the intuitive repugnance of human extinction, which he then seeks to explain. By contrast, in my ending world, the removal of *any* possibility of escape forces us to address the prior question of whether human extinction really *is* a tragedy to be avoided at (almost) any cost. Perhaps we should instead devote our resources to the different challenge of ensuring that, when it does arrive, human extinction is not so bad after all. I have conceded that removing any possibility of escape does remove some of the most interesting and urgent ethical questions about extinction. However, every philosophical thought experiment sidelines some questions in order to highlight others; and, as we have just seen, my stipulation brings new important questions into sharper focus.

What about the charge of implausibility? I concede that any assumption of certainty about *when* humanity will become extinct is very artificial – as is any other presumption of certainty about the future. However, a specific scenario that is itself incredible can represent a broader range of possible futures that are (collectively) very credible. My ending world tale is not plausible. But future people might face unavoidable extinction – especially once we move from immediate extinction to imminent extinction. Indeed, while it may seem unlikely, something analogous to my scenario is more-or-less inevitable. Desperate trans-humanist fantasies notwithstanding, humanity will eventually become extinct sooner or later. Someone *will* inhabit an ending world.

10 See, for example, Beckstead (2013), *On the overwhelming importance of shaping the far future*.

11 Consider two examples: (1) In Neal Stephenson's novel *Seveneves*, the survival of humanity relies on a series of 'coincidences' that could most charitably be described as 'impossible'. (2) While P. D. James's *The Children of Men* provides the model for Scheffler's tale of (unavoidable) universal infertility, the novel's actual plot revolves around an unexpected (and unexplained) opportunity to avoid extinction.

12 One important recent exception is Crisp 2023.

As Mark Johnston points out in a review of Scheffler's book *Death and the Afterlife*, there is, therefore, something odd about arguing from the premise that it is undesirable to belong to the last human generation, to the conclusion that we ought to continue the human story (Johnston 2014). This is because extinction cannot be avoided; it can only be postponed. We cannot remove the burden of last-generation-hood. We can only avoid that burden for ourselves by passing it down the line to some unspecified future generation. Johnston likens this generational buck-passing to continuing a Ponzi scheme.

In a world where humanity enjoys an indefinite future, it is easy to forget the inevitability of extinction, because the last generation is lost in the mists of (future) time. In my ending world, where present people can only pass the burden a few generations down the line – where the last human generation would be (at most) our near descendants – the Ponzi challenge cannot be ignored.

One of the great challenges of future ethics is to dissolve Johnston's Ponzi challenge – to find ways to ensure that the last humans are not worse-off than their predecessors. We must somehow transform the moral landscape – enabling the last human generation to find meaning in their truncated present in ways that our generation could not.

3 Philosophical Pessimism at Humanity's End

In the rest of this paper, I explore three topics in more detail – corresponding to some of the main themes of my recent book (Mulgan 2024). In the book, I present transcripts of imaginary philosophical debates within the ending world. I imagine philosophers living at the start of my slowly ending world, who absorb the discovery that humanity has only two centuries to live, and then try to make philosophical sense of their unprecedented situation. I have chosen this dialogue format to avoid prescribing one specific future philosophy. My goal in the book, as in this paper, is primarily to persuade the reader that the ending world is worth exploring, rather than to defend any particular claims about where that exploration should lead.

The book contains three main debates, and a number of individual lectures, dealing with pessimism, procreative ethics, multi-generational optimism, virtual endings, and religious explanation. In this paper, I focus on the following three topics: philosophical pessimism, procreative freedom, and multi-generationalism. The book as a whole offers a sustained defence of the position I dub 'multi-generationalism'. I defend this view both as the best approach in an ending world, and as an underappreciated option today.

Pessimism is a perennial philosophical worry. Is life worth living? Can human lives be meaningful? Is a connection to something beyond this life – such as the human future – essential for a meaningful, worthwhile human life?[13]

Philosophical pessimists argue that life is either meaningless or not worth living. To explore pessimism in the ending world, we must distinguish three types of pessimism. Perennial pessimists argue that human life is meaningless or not worth living, even if humanity faces an indefinite future. By contrast, post-cataclysm pessimists argue instead that, while life would not (necessarily) be meaningless or terrible if humanity did face an indefinite future, the loss of that indefinite human future is sufficient to make life meaningless or not worth living. Finally, last-generation pessimists argue that, whatever is true for earlier generations, life will become meaningless or not worth living in the last generation.

One interesting philosophical question is the relationship between post-cataclysm pessimism and last-generation pessimism. Can they be separated in practice? In particular, can earlier generations enjoy meaningful lives if they know that life will soon become meaningless? Or does last-generation pessimism lead, inevitably, to pessimism throughout the ending world? If so, this connection would have implications for us today. Once we recognise the fact that humanity must end eventually, a slippery slope from post-cataclysm pessimism to last-generation pessimism would threaten to lead, inevitably, to present-day pessimism, even without imminent extinction.

The most plausible ending-world-specific arguments for pessimism focus on meaningfulness rather than well-being. We can imagine scenarios where life is very pleasant at humanity's end – where a small population live in blissful ignorance. But can life be *meaningful* at the end? Therefore, following Scheffler, I focus on future-dependent *meaning*. Scheffler argues that even our most present-focused projects pre-suppose an ongoing background of traditions, values, or relationships that extend into the future. Last generation pessimists insist that the loss of *all* future-dependent meaning makes life meaningless at humanity's end. Post-cataclysm pessimists extend this critique, arguing that future-dependent meaning is lost even earlier, because our current (pre-cataclysm) values require an indefinite human future.

What is the philosophical case for post-cataclysm pessimism? Why should we think that future-dependent meaning matters? Post-cataclysm pessimists might be inspired by a wide variety of previous philosophical traditions, including Scheffler's own work on the relationship between values and traditions; Jonathan Lear's work on radical hope (Lear 2008) – which links present

[13] My discussion of pessimism owes most to Beiser 2016; Benatar 2017; and Van der Lugt 2021.

meaning to future moral transformation; nineteenth-century German pessimism, especially now largely forgotten figures such as Eduard von Hartmann, who argued that, in a world of suffering, meaning can only be found in future cultural progress (Beiser 2016); and Mark Johnston's argument (2010) that good people literally 'live on' in future generations. More generally, ending pessimists argue that all secular replacements for a personal afterlife – all hopes to 'live on in the ongoing rush of humanity', as J. S. Mill put it – collapse in the face of imminent extinction.

In my book, I contrast post-cataclysm pessimism with four main opponents: perennial pessimists, theists, presentists, and multi-generationalists. Perennial pessimists argue that life has always been meaningless. Imminent extinction doesn't change anything – it only makes the absurdity of human existence harder to avoid.

Optimists reply, instead, that life is not necessarily meaningless, even in the last generation. We can divide optimist philosophies, very roughly, into three camps: theist, presentist, and multi-generational. Theist optimists concede that life would be meaningless without an indefinite human future if God did not exist. (Most theists, of course, will insist that the human future is not a satisfactory substitute for God – and, therefore, that life would be meaningless without God, even if humanity continued forever.) However, appropriate connections to eternal divine reality can provide sufficient meaning even to the last humans.

Our two remaining optimist views are resolutely secular. Presentists find sufficient meaning in present pleasures and achievements, or in care and compassion for the suffering of others. Two exemplars of the presentist approach are Scheffler's original commentators, Harry Frankfurt and Susan Wolf, who both extend our extinction-immune, present-directed reasons beyond what Scheffler would admit. Frankfurt (2013) argues that the value of immediate pleasure is independent of future-directed traditions; while Wolf (2013) highlights the important role of compassion as a source of meaning.

The final secular optimist position, multi-generationalism, takes a middle road. On the one hand, multi-generationalists agree with Scheffler that for us meaning, well-being, and making sense of our projects and traditions all require future generations – future descendants who will continue those projects and traditions. Multi-generationalists therefore agree with last generation pessimists that, if we were the last generation, then our lives would be meaningless. Meaning *is* lost in Scheffler's doomsday and infertility scenarios. On the other hand, multi-generationalists reject post-cataclysm pessimism. They insist that the loss of future-dependent meaning is a contingent feature of the way we have been raised or acculturated, rather than an essential feature of the human condition. People living at the start of the ending world could raise new generations for whom meaning, well-being, and value were not dependent on the existence of any (further) future people.

4 Procreative Ethics at Humanity's End

My ending world differs from Scheffler's immediate extinction scenarios because the first generation is not the last – because present people create future people. But is this permissible? In particular, is it permissible to create a last generation who cannot have children of their own?

The question of procreative permissibility is especially pressing for multi-generationalists. While presentists seek solace in the present and pessimists argue that no solace can be found, multi-generationalists base present meaning on collaborations with future people. Multi-generational projects are therefore permissible only if procreation is permissible.

There is a close connection between philosophical pessimism and anti-natalism – the view that no one should have children. Pessimism clearly supports anti-natalism. If life is not worth living, then it is (prima facie) wrong to create new people. Therefore, procreative liberals must first defeat post-cataclysm pessimism. However, this is not sufficient. Anti-natalism does not stand or fall with pessimism. Most procreative ethical theories set a higher threshold for permissible procreation than the requirement that one's future child's life is (barely) worth living. Anti-natalists might argue that, even if pessimism is false, life at humanity's end is too bad – or too uncertain – to permit procreation. The first generation in my slowly ending world must then eschew procreation, and shoulder the burden of membership of the last generation for themselves.

Anti-natalism is a minority view in contemporary philosophical procreative ethics (e.g., Benatar 2006). The default position is procreative liberty. People should be morally free to decide whether, when, how often, with whom, and in what ways they will have children. A central question in ending world procreative ethics is whether procreative liberty can survive. In an ending world, procreative freedom is challenged both (1) by post-cataclysm anti-natalists who insist that, even if procreation was permissible when humans faced an indefinite future, it is now forbidden; and (2) by post-cataclysm pro-natalists who argue that, when the fate of their future children is so uncertain, people will only create a new generation if they feel *obliged* to do so.

In my book, I focus on four contemporary procreative ethical theories, chosen to illustrate the breadth of procreative ethics: Elizabeth Harman's harm-based approach (2004); Melinda Roberts's person-affecting consequentialism (2002); Rivka Weinberg's contractualist principles of procreative justice (2015); and my own earlier collective consequentialist future ethics (Mulgan 2006). In each case, I ask whether the case for procreative liberty survives into the ending world.

One distinctive ending-world-specific challenge for procreative ethics is whether procreation is permissible if your child will be unable, permissibly, to have children of their own. Many justifications for procreative liberty cite the importance to potential parents of the parent–child relationship, the project of raising a child, or the decision whether to include these procreative goods in one's life in the first place. *Ex hypothesi*, people in the penultimate generation cannot create children who can enjoy these goods themselves. The procreative liberal now faces a dilemma. The more we emphasise the value of procreative projects to potential parents, the more we highlight the disvalue of life in the last generation.

Different procreative ethical theories offer different thresholds for permissible procreation. However, there are common themes. In particular, whatever our account of procreative ethics, procreative freedom is most likely to be justified in the ending world if we can both remove the harm of lost future-dependent meaning altogether, and also ensure that the last generation are no worse-off than previous generations. This strengthens the case for multi-generationalism, which offers the last generation the opportunity to join with earlier generations in bringing the human story to a satisfactory conclusion.

5 Exploring Multi-generational Optimism

Multi-generational secular optimism argues that, in a slowly ending world, present people can only make their own lives sufficiently meaningful by launching projects that extend over several generations. Suitable multi-generational projects might include: creating a just human society within a single generation – perhaps by correcting historical injustices; promoting ecological flourishing – or at least minimising non-human suffering; completing some vital human cultural achievement; creating a fitting memorial to humanity; or bringing our various traditions to a close.

Multi-generationalism faces many challenges. Could human traditions really be reimagined, within a few centuries, around the new ideal of a suitable ending? If so, what *is* a suitable ending for humanity? We are familiar with the idea that an individual human life – and perhaps an individual society, tradition, or culture – can have a 'good ending'. Can we imagine a good ending for humanity as a whole? And what can we learn from actual cases where some specific tradition, culture, religion, or way of life has faced extinction?

To meet these challenges, multi-generationalists draw on existing philosophical resources. I conclude this paper by briefly citing some examples.

Multi-generationalism needs radical moral transformation, where future people re-imagine existing traditions and values in new ways. Key to this transformation is moral imaginativeness. We must think creatively about what our future values should be, and not just ask how we can realise values we already have. Drawing on recent work on moral progress – especially on Allen Buchanan and Russell Powell's evolutionary account (2018) and my own previous work (Mulgan 2017, 2018b) – multi-generationalists argue that moral progress, moral imaginativeness, and moral transformation are all credible possibilities, given our knowledge of human nature, and of past moral transformations.

One particular inspiration for multi-generational optimism is Jonathan Lear's *Radical Hope* (2008) – a philosophical reflection on the life of the Crow leader Plenty Coups, who lead his people into a future where their whole way of life no longer made sense. Plenty Coups sought not merely a variation on a familiar theme (such as a new way of being courageous in battle), but something entirely new: a way to be courageous in a world without war. This challenge required moral imaginativeness, because traditional Crow ethics had no vocabulary or concepts to deal with this unprecedented and unforeseen challenge, and it was not obvious how to proceed.

Lear presents Plenty Coups' story as one of radical *multi-generational* hope. Plenty Coups looked to a future where his successors would flourish – even though he could not even imagine the standard against which that future flourishing might be judged. Multi-generationalism argues that the prospect of future intelligibility is sufficient for present meaning. Plenty Coups' hope that his descendants would find new meaning was sufficient to motivate him to continue – and to find meaning in – a life that no longer made sense to him.

Finally, multi-generational utopianism is inspired, somewhat ironically, by the difficulty of imagining a coherent inter-generational utopia. (To cite just one example: consider how many egalitarian visions fail to deal coherently with inheritance.) Perhaps utopia is only possible in a single generation with no future. If a perfectly just society can only last a single generation, and if human beings will never voluntarily opt for immediate extinction, then the true utopia can only exist at humanity's end – and the best way for earlier generations to find meaning is to pave the way for this perfect future. Our multi-generational utopian project is, then, not to create an impossible inter-generational utopia, but rather to lay the foundations for the future realisation of a vision of justice that can only come to fruition at humanity's end.

Those are some of the lessons that I think we might learn from imagining life in the ending world. Whatever readers may think of my use of it, I hope that I have, at least, convinced them that the thought experiment itself is worth thinking about.

Bibliography

Beckstead, Nicholas. 2013. *On the Overwhelming Importance of Shaping the Far Future*. PhD thesis, Rutgers, New Brunswick, NJ.

Beiser, Frederick. C. 2016. *Weltschmerz: Pessimism in German Philosophy, 1860–1900*. Oxford: Oxford University Press.

Benatar, David. 2006. *Better Never to Have Been*. Oxford: Oxford University Press.

2017. *The Human Predicament: A Candid Guide to Life's Biggest Questions*. Oxford: Oxford University Press.

Bostrom, Nick. 2013. "Existential Risk as a Global Priority." *Global Policy* 4: 15–31.

Bostrom, Nick and Milan Cirkovic, (eds.). 2008. *Global Catastrophic Risks*. Oxford: Oxford University Press.

Buchanan, Allen and Russell Powell. 2018. *The Evolution of Moral Progress: A Biocultural Theory*. Oxford: Oxford University Press.

Caroti, Simone. 2011. *The Generation Starship in Science Fiction: A Critical History 1934–2001*. Jefferson, NC: McFarland & Co.

Crisp, Roger. 2023. "Pessimism about the Future." *Midwest Studies in Philosophy* 46: 373–385.

Darwall, Stephen. 2009. *The Second-Person Standpoint*. Cambridge, MA: Harvard University Press.

Frankfurt, Harry. 2013. "How the Afterlife Matters." In *Death and the Afterlife*, edited by Samuel Scheffler, 131–142. Oxford: Oxford University Press.

Harman, Elizabeth. 2004. "Can We Harm and Benefit in Creating?" *Philosophical Perspectives* 18: 89–113.

Johnston, Mark. 2010. *Surviving Death*. Princeton, NJ: Princeton University Press.

2014. "Is Life a Ponzi Scheme?" *Boston Review*, 2 January 2014. www.bostonreview.net/articles/mark-johnston-samuel-scheffler-death-afterlife-humanity-ponzi-scheme/

Lear, Jonathan. 2008. *Radical Hope: Ethics in the Face of Cultural Devastation*. Cambridge, MA: Harvard University Press.

Mulgan, Tim. 2006. *Future People*. Oxford: Oxford University Press.

2011. *Ethics for a Broken World: Reimagining Philosophy after Catastrophe*. Montreal and Ithaca: McGill-Queen's University Press.

2014. "Ethics for Possible Futures." *Proceedings of the Aristotelian Society* 114: 57–73.

2015. "Utilitarianism for a Broken World." *Utilitas* 27: 92–114.

2017. "How Should Utilitarians Think about the Future?" *Canadian Journal of Philosophy* 47: 290–312.

2018a. "Answering to Future People." *The Journal of Applied Philosophy* 35: 532–548.

2018b. "Moral Imaginativeness, Moral Creativity and Possible Futures." In *Creativity and Philosophy*, edited by Berys N. Gaut and Matthew Kieran, 350–368. New York, NY: Routledge.

2019. "Corporate Agency and Possible Futures." *Journal of Business Ethics* 154: 901–916.

2020a. *Utilitarianism*. Cambridge: Cambridge University Press.

2020b. "What Exactly Is Wrong with Human Extinction?" In *Proceedings of the International Society for Utilitarian Studies*, edited by Christoph Schmidt-Petri and Michael Schefczyk, 267–283. Karlsruhe: KIT Scientific Publishing.

2024. *Philosophy for an Ending World*. Oxford: Oxford University Press.

Nozick, Robert. 1974. *Anarchy, State, and Utopia*. New York, NY: Basic Books.

Ord, Toby. 2020. *The Precipice: Existential Risk and the Future of Humanity*. Oxford: Oxford University Press.

Parfit, Derek. 1984. *Reasons and Persons*. Oxford: Oxford University Press.

2011/2017. *On What Matters*. Oxford: Oxford University Press.

Roberts, Melinda A. 2002. "A New Way of Doing the Best We Can: Person-based Consequentialism and the Equality Problem." *Ethics* 112: 315–350.

Scheffler, Samuel. 2013. *Death and the Afterlife*. Oxford: Oxford University Press.

2018. *Why Worry about Future Generations?* Oxford: Oxford University Press.

Schuster, Joshua and Derek Woods. 2021. *Calamity Theory: Three Critiques of Existential Risk*. Minneapolis, MN: University of Minnesota Press.

Van der Lugt, Mara. 2021. *Dark Matters: Pessimism and the Problem of Suffering*. Princeton, NJ: Princeton University Press.

Weinberg, Rivka. 2015. *The Risk of a Lifetime: How, When, and Why Procreation May Be Permissible*. Oxford: Oxford University Press.

Wolf, Susan. 2013. "The Significance of Doomsday." In *Death and the Afterlife*, edited by Samuel Scheffler, 113–130. Oxford: Oxford University Press.

Index

For EU product safety concerns, contact us at Calle de José Abascal, 56–1°, 28003 Madrid, Spain or eugpsr@cambridge.org.

www.ingramcontent.com/pod-product-compliance
Lightning Source LLC
LaVergne TN
LVHW020325220926
848484LV00001BB/108

* 9 7 8 1 0 0 9 3 4 3 7 4 9 *